W9-AVH-951

I

Langenscheidt

**Merriam-
Webster**
Guide to
Punctuation & Style

Merriam-Webster's
Guide to
Punctuation
and
Style

Second Edition

Merriam-Webster, Incorporated
Springfield, Massachusetts

ISBN: 0-87779-921-0

Printed and bound in the United States of America

12345QP/B04030201

Contents

5 Numbers 133

6 Quotations 159

7 Notes and Bibliographies 173

8 Copyediting and Proofreading 225

Appendixes

Index 343

Preface

Merriam-Webster's Guide to Punctuation and Style, Second Edition, is designed to be a practical handbook on the conventions of contemporary American English—in particular, the conventions of punctuation, capitalization, italicization, abbreviation, quotation, and documentation of sources.

Just as the Merriam-Webster dictionaries strive to mirror the language as it is actually used, this book strives to reflect the practices actually employed in published writing. It is based on a continuous study of the ways Americans use their language, and it draws on Merriam-Webster's extensive citation files of 15 million examples of English words used in context, gathered from a broad selection of books, newspapers, magazines, and other publications.

Firmly based on real-life source material, this book attempts to reflect both the consensus and the variety evident in mainstream American published writing. When a statement about style must be qualified, the word *usually, generally,* or *normally* indicates that a significant minority of writers and editors follow another practice. *Sometimes* is used when describing an alternative, minority practice. *Often* or *frequently* indicates that a convention is commonly but not universally followed; it does not necessarily identify a majority practice.

Whenever a practice raises questions that require an explanation, a brief note is provided. Conventions restricted to journalism or specialized fields are labeled as such.

This edition represents a thoroughgoing revision of the original work. A new chapter on the treatment of quotations has been added. The chapter on documentation has been expanded and updated, and a new chapter describes the special tasks of the copy editor and the proofreader. The chapter on composition and grammar has been replaced by an appendix glossary of grammatical terms. The chapter on problems in word usage has similarly been updated as an appendix and includes a new list of easily confused words.

The first edition of this book was adapted by Jocelyn White Franklin and Mark A. Stevens from *Merriam-Webster's Standard American Style Manual* and was thus based on work done by the latter's writers and editors. The present edition was adapted by Jocelyn White Franklin from *Merriam-Webster's Manual for Writers and Editors,* the retitled and thoroughly revised second edition of the *Style Manual.*

1 Punctuation

Punctuation marks are used to help clarify the structure and meaning of sentences. They separate groups of words for meaning and emphasis; they convey an idea of the variations in pitch, volume, pauses, and intonation of the spoken language; and they help avoid ambiguity. The choice of what punctuation to use, if any, will often be clear and unambiguous. In other cases, a sentence may allow for several punctuation patterns. In cases like these, varying notions of correctness have developed, and two writers might, with equal correctness, punctuate the same sentence quite differently, relying on their individual judgment and taste.

Apostrophe

The apostrophe is used to form most possessives and contractions as well as some plurals and inflections.

1. The apostrophe is used to indicate the possessive of nouns and indefinite pronouns. (For details, see the section beginning on page 94.)

   the girl's shoe
   the boys' fathers
   Simmons's role
   children's laughter
   anyone's guess
   the Browns' house
   Arkansas's capital

2. Apostrophes are sometimes used to form plurals of letters, numerals, abbreviations, symbols, and words referred to as words. (For details, see the section beginning on page 86.)

   cross your *t*'s
   three 8's *or* three 8s
   two L.H.D.'s *or* two L.H.D.s
   used &'s instead of *and*'s

3. Apostrophes mark omissions in contractions made of two or more words and in contractions of single words.

   wasn't
   they're
   she'd rather not
   Jake's had it
   ass'n
   dep't

4. The apostrophe is used to indicate that letters have been intentionally omitted from a word in order to imitate informal speech.

"Singin' in the Rain," the popular song and movie

"Snap 'em up" was his response.

Sometimes such words are so consistently spelled with an apostrophe that the spelling becomes an accepted variant.

rock 'n' roll [*for* rock and roll]
ma'am [*for* madam]
sou'wester [*for* southwester]

5. Apostrophes mark the omission of digits in numerals.

class of '98
fashion in the '90s

If the apostrophe is used when writing the plurals of numerals, either the apostrophe that stands for the missing figures is omitted or the word is spelled out.

90's *or* nineties *but not* '90's

6. In informal writing, apostrophes are used to produce forms of verbs that are made of individually pronounced letters. An apostrophe or a hyphen is also sometimes used to add an -*er* ending to an abbreviation; if no confusion would result, the apostrophe is usually omitted.

OK'd the budget
X'ing out the mistakes
4-H'er
49er

Brackets

Outside of mathematics and chemistry texts, brackets are primarily used for insertions into carefully handled quoted matter. They are rarely seen in general writing but are common in historical and scholarly contexts.

1. Brackets enclose editorial comments, corrections, and clarifications inserted into quoted matter.

> Surely that should have peaked [sic] the curiosity of a serious researcher.

> Here they much favour the tiorba [theorbo], the arclute [archlute], and the cittarone [chitarrone], while we at home must content ourselves with the lute alone.

> In Blaine's words, "All the vocal aristocracy showed up—Nat [Cole], Billy [Eckstine], Ella [Fitzgerald], Mabel Mercer—'cause nobody wanted to miss that date."

2. Brackets enclose insertions that take the place of words or phrases.

> And on the next page: "Their assumption is plainly that [Durocher] would be the agent in any such negotiation."

3. Brackets enclose insertions that supply missing letters.

> A postscript to a December 17 letter to Waugh notes, "If D[eutsch] won't take the manuscript, perhaps someone at Faber will."

4. Brackets enclose insertions that alter the form of a word used in an original text.

> He dryly observes (p. 78) that the Gravely investors had bought stocks because "they want[ed] to see themselves getting richer."

5. Brackets are used to indicate that capitalization has been altered. This is generally optional; it is standard practice only where meticulous handling of original source material is crucial (particularly legal and scholarly contexts).

> As Chief Justice Warren held for the Court, "[T]he Attorney General may bring an injunctive action . . ."
> *or in general contexts*
> "The Attorney General may bring . . ."

Brackets also enclose editorial notes when text has been italicized for emphasis.

> But tucked away on page 11 we find this fascinating note: "In addition, we anticipate that *siting these new plants in marginal neighborhoods will decrease the risk of organized community opposition*" [italics added].

6. Brackets function as parentheses within parentheses, especially where two sets of parentheses could be confusing.

> Posner's recent essays (including the earlier *Law and Literature* [1988]) bear this out.

7. In mathematical copy, brackets are used with parentheses to indicate units contained within larger units. They are also used with various meanings in chemical names and formulas.

> $x + 5[(x + y)(2x - y)]$
> $Ag[Pt(NO_2)_4]$

With Other Punctuation

8. Punctuation that marks the end of a phrase, clause, item in a series, or sentence follows any bracketed material appended to that passage.

> The report stated, "if we fail to find additional sources of supply [of oil and gas], our long-term growth will be limited."

When brackets enclose a complete sentence, closing punctuation is placed within the brackets.

> [Since this article was written, new archival evidence of document falsification has come to light.]

Colon

The colon is usually a mark of introduction, indicating that what follows it—generally a clause, a phrase, or a list—has been pointed to or described in what precedes it. (For the use of capitals following a colon, see paragraphs 7–8 on page 56.)

With Phrases and Clauses

1. A colon introduces a clause or phrase that explains, illustrates, amplifies, or restates what has gone before.

   An umbrella is a foolish extravagance: if you don't leave it in the first restaurant, a gust of wind will destroy it on the way home.

   Dawn was breaking: the distant peaks were already glowing with the sun's first rays.

2. A colon introduces an amplifying word, phrase, or clause that acts as an appositive. (For details on appositives, see the section on page 14.)

   That year Handley's old obsession was replaced with a new one: jazz.

   The issue comes down to this: Will we offer a reduced curriculum, or will we simply cancel the program?

3. A colon introduces a list or series, often following a phrase such as *the following* or *as follows*.

   She has trial experience on three judicial levels: county, state, and federal.

   Anyone planning to participate should be prepared to do the following: hike five miles with a backpack, sleep on the ground without a tent, and paddle a canoe through rough water.

   It is occasionally used like a dash to introduce a summary statement following a series.

Baseball, soccer, skiing, track: he excelled in every sport he took up.

4. Although the colon usually follows a full independent clause, it also often interrupts a sentence before the clause is complete.

The nine proposed program topics are: offshore supply, vessel traffic, ferry services, ship repair, . . .

Information on each participant includes: name, date of birth, mailing address, . . .

For example: 58 percent of union members voted, but only 44 percent of blue-collar workers as a whole.

The association will:

Act with trust, integrity, and professionalism.

Operate in an open and effective manner.

Take the initiative in seeking diversity.

With Quotations

5. A colon usually introduces lengthy quoted material that is set off from the rest of a text by indentation but not by quotation marks.

The *Rumpole* series has been nicely encapsulated as follows:

Rumpled, disreputable, curmudgeonly barrister Horace Rumpole often wins cases despite the disdain of his more aristocratic colleagues. Fond of cheap wine ("Château Thames Embankment") and Keats's poetry, he refers to his wife as "She Who Must Be Obeyed" (an allusion to the title character of H. Rider Haggard's *She*).

6. A colon is often used before a quotation in running text, especially when (1) the quotation is lengthy, (2) the quotation is a formal statement or is being given special emphasis, or (3) a full independent clause precedes the colon.

Said Murdoch: "The key to the success of this project is good planning. We need to know precisely what steps we will need to take, what kind of staff we will require, what the project will cost, and when we can expect completion."

The inscription reads: "Here lies one whose name was writ in water."

This was his verbatim response: "At this time Mr. Wilentz is still in the company's employ, and no change in his status is anticipated imminently."

Other Uses

7. A colon separates elements in bibliographic publication data and page references, in biblical citations, and in formulas used to express time and ratios. No space precedes or follows a colon between numerals.

> Stendhal, *Love* (New York: Penguin, 1975)
> *Paleobiology* 3:121
> John 4:10
> 8:30 a.m.
> a winning time of 3:43:02
> a ratio of 3:5

8. A colon separates titles and subtitles.

> *Southwest Stories: Tales from the Desert*

9. A colon follows the salutation in formal correspondence.

> Dear Judge Wright:
> Dear Laurence:
> Dear Product Manager:
> Ladies and Gentlemen:

10. A colon follows headings in memorandums, government correspondence, and general business letters.

> TO:
> SUBJECT:

VIA:
REFERENCE:

11. An unspaced colon separates the writer's and typ-
ist's initials in the identification lines of business
letters.

WAL:jml

A colon also separates copy abbreviations from the
initials of copy recipients. (The abbreviation *cc*
stands for *carbon* or *courtesy copy; bcc* stands for *blind
carbon or courtesy copy.*) A space follows a colon used
with the fuller name of a recipient.

cc:RSP
   JES
bcc:MWK
bcc: Mr. Jones

With Other Punctuation

12. A colon is placed outside quotation marks and
parentheses that punctuate the larger sentence.

> The problem becomes most acute in "Black Rose and
> Destroying Angel": plot simply ceases to exist.
> Wilson and Hölldobler remark on the same phenom-
> enon in *The Ants* (1990):

Comma

The comma is the most frequently used punctuation
mark in English and the one that provides the most difficulties to writers. Its most common uses are to separate items in a series and to set off or distinguish grammatical elements within sentences.

Between Main Clauses

1. A comma separates main clauses joined by a coordinating conjunction, such as *and, but, or, nor,* or *so.*

> She knew very little about the new system, and he volunteered nothing.
>
> The trial lasted for nine months, but the jury took only four hours to reach its verdict.
>
> We will not respond to any more questions on that topic this afternoon, nor will we respond to similar questions in the future.
>
> All the first-floor windows were barred, so he had clambered up onto the fire escape.

2. When one or both of the clauses are short or closely related in meaning, the comma is often omitted.

> They said good-bye and everyone hugged.

If commas set off another phrase that modifies the whole sentence, the comma between main clauses is often omitted.

> Six thousand years ago, the top of the volcano blew off in a series of powerful eruptions and the sides collapsed into the middle.

3. Commas are sometimes used to separate short and obviously parallel main clauses that are not joined by conjunctions.

> One day you're a successful corporate lawyer, the next day you're out of work.

Use of a comma to join clauses that are neither short nor obviously parallel, called *comma fault* or *comma splice,* is avoided. Clauses not joined by conjunctions are normally separated by semicolons. For details, see paragraph 1 on page 49.

4. If a sentence is composed of three or more clauses that are short and free of commas, the clauses are occasionally all separated by commas even if the last two are not joined by a conjunction. If the clauses are long or punctuated, they are separated with semicolons; the last two clauses are sometimes

separated by a comma if they are joined by a conjunction. (For more details, see paragraph 5 on page 50.)

> Small fish fed among the marsh weed, ducks paddled along the surface, an occasional muskrat ate greens along the bank.
>
> The kids were tired and whiny; Napoleon, usually so calm, was edgy; Tabitha seemed to be going into heat, and even the guinea pigs were agitated.

With Compound Predicates

5. Commas are not normally used to separate the parts of a compound predicate.

> The firefighter tried to enter the burning building but was turned back by the thick smoke.

However, they are often used if the predicate is long and complicated, if one part is being stressed, or if the absence of a comma could cause a momentary misreading.

> The board helps to develop the financing and marketing strategies for new corporate divisions, and issues periodic reports on expenditures, revenues, and personnel appointments.
>
> This is an unworkable plan, and has been from the start.
>
> I try to explain to him what I want him to do, and get nowhere.

With Subordinate Clauses and Phrases

6. Adverbial clauses and phrases that begin a sentence are usually set off with commas.

> Having made that decision, we turned our attention to other matters.
>
> In order to receive a high school diploma, a student must earn 16 credits from public or private secondary schools.

In addition, staff members respond to queries, take new orders, and initiate billing.

If the sentence can be easily read without a comma, the comma may be omitted. The phrase will usually be short—four words or less—but even after a longer phrase the comma is often omitted.

As cars age, they depreciate. *or* As cars age they depreciate.

In January the firm will introduce a new line of investigative services.

On the map the town appeared as a small dot in the midst of vast emptiness.

If nobody comes forward by Friday I will have to take further steps.

7. Adverbial clauses and phrases that introduce a main clause other than the first main clause are usually set off with commas. If the clause or phrase follows a conjunction, one comma often precedes the conjunction and one follows the clause or phrase. Alternatively, one comma precedes the conjunction and two more enclose the clause or phrase, or a single comma precedes the conjunction. Short phrases, and phrases in short sentences, tend not to be enclosed in commas.

They have redecorated the entire store, but[,] to the delight of their customers, it retains much of its original flavor.

We haven't left Springfield yet, but when we get to Boston we'll call you.

8. A comma is not used after an introductory phrase if the phrase immediately precedes the main verb.

From the next room came a loud expletive.

9. A subordinate clause or phrase that modifies a noun is not set off by commas if it is *restrictive* (or

essential)—that is, if its removal would alter the noun's meaning.

> The man who wrote this obviously had no firsthand knowledge of the situation.
> They entered through the first door that wasn't locked.

If the meaning would not be altered by its removal, the clause or phrase is considered *nonrestrictive* (or *nonessential*) and usually is set off by commas.

> The new approach, which was based on team teaching, was well received.
> Wechsler, who has done solid reporting from other battlefronts, is simply out of his depth here.
> They tried the first door, which led nowhere.

10. Commas set off an adverbial clause or phrase that falls between the subject and the verb.

> The Clapsaddle sisters, to keep up appearances, rode to the park every Sunday in their rented carriage.

11. Commas set off modifying phrases that do not immediately precede the word or phrase they modify.

> Scarbo, intent as usual on his next meal, was snuffling around the butcher's bins.
> The negotiators, tired and discouraged, headed back to the hotel.
> We could see the importance, both long-term and short-term, of her proposal.

12. An absolute phrase (a participial phrase with its own subject that is grammatically independent of the rest of the sentence) is set off with commas.

> Our business being concluded, we adjourned for refreshments.
> We headed southward, the wind freshening behind us, to meet the rest of the fleet in the morning.
> I'm afraid of his reaction, his temper being what it is.

With Appositives

13. Commas set off a word, phrase, or clause that is in apposition to (that is, equivalent to) a preceding or following noun and that is nonrestrictive.

> It sat nursing its front paw, the injured one.
>
> Aleister Crowley, Britain's most infamous satanist, is the subject of a remarkable new biography.
>
> A cherished landmark in the city, the Hotel Sandburg has managed once again to escape the wrecking ball.
>
> The committee cochairs were a lawyer, John Larson, and an educator, Mary Conway.

14. Restrictive appositives are not set off by commas.

> He next had a walk-on role in the movie *The Firm*.
>
> Longfellow's poem *Evangeline* was a favorite of my grandmother's.
>
> The committee cochairs were the lawyer John Larson and the educator Mary Conway.
>
> Lord Castlereagh was that strange anomaly[,] a Labor-voting peer.

With Introductory and Interrupting Elements

15. Commas set off transitional words and phrases.

> Indeed, close coordination will be essential.
>
> Defeat may be inevitable; however, disgrace is not.
>
> The second report, on the other hand, shows a strong bias.

When such words and phrases fall in the middle of a clause, commas are sometimes unnecessary.

> They thus have no chips left to bargain with.
>
> The materials had indeed arrived.
>
> She would in fact see them that afternoon.

16. Commas set off parenthetical elements, such as authorial asides.

> All of us, to tell the truth, were completely amazed.
> It was, I should add, not the first time I'd seen him in this condition.

17. Commas are often used to set off words or phrases that introduce examples or explanations, such as *namely, for example,* and *that is.*

> He expects to visit three countries, namely, France, Spain, and Germany.
> I would like to develop a good, workable plan, that is, one that would outline our goals and set a timetable for accomplishing them.

Such introductory words and phrases may also often be preceded by a dash, parenthesis, or semicolon. Regardless of the punctuation that precedes the word or phrase, a comma usually follows it.

> Sports develop two valuable traits—namely, self-control and the ability to make quick decisions.
> In writing to the manufacturer, be as specific as possible (i.e., list the missing or defective parts, describe the malfunction, and identify the store where the unit was purchased).
> Most had traveled great distances to participate; for example, three had come from Australia, one from Japan, and two from China.

18. Commas set off words in direct address.

> This is our third and final notice, Mr. Sutton.
> The facts, my fellow Americans, are very different.

19. Commas set off mild interjections or exclamations.

> Ah, the mosaics in Ravenna are matchless.
> Uh-oh, His Eminence seems to be on the warpath this morning.

With Contrasting Expressions

20. A comma is sometimes used to set off contrasting expressions within a sentence.

> This project will take six months, not six weeks.

21. When two or more contrasting modifiers or prepositions, one of which is introduced by a conjunction or adverb, apply to a noun that follows immediately, the second is set off by two commas or a single comma, or not set off at all.

> A solid, if overly wordy, assessment
>> *or* a solid, if overly wordy assessment
>> *or* a solid if overly wordy assessment
>
> This street takes you away from, not toward, the capitol.
>> *or* This street takes you away from, not toward the capitol.
>
> grounds for a civil, and maybe a criminal, case
>> *or* grounds for a civil, and maybe a criminal case
>> *or* grounds for a civil and maybe a criminal case

Dashes or parentheses are often used instead of commas in such sentences.

> grounds for a civil (and maybe a criminal) case

22. A comma does not usually separate elements that are contrasted through the use of a pair of correlative conjunctions such as *either . . . or, neither . . . nor,* and *not only . . . but also.*

> Neither my brother nor I noticed the error.
> He was given the post not only because of his diplomatic connections but also because of his great tact and charm.

When correlative conjunctions join main clauses, a comma usually separates the clauses unless they are short.

Not only did she have to see three salesmen and a visiting reporter, but she also had to prepare for next day's meeting.

Either you do it my way or we don't do it at all.

23. Long parallel contrasting and comparing clauses are separated by commas; short parallel phrases are not.

The more that comes to light about him, the less savory he seems.

The less said the better.

With Items in a Series

24. Words, phrases, and clauses joined in a series are separated by commas.

Men, women, and children crowded aboard the train.

Her job required her to pack quickly, to travel often, and to have no personal life.

He responded patiently while reporters shouted questions, flashbulbs popped, and the crowd pushed closer.

When the last two items in a series are joined by a conjunction, the final comma is often omitted, especially where this would not result in ambiguity. In individual publications, the final comma is usually consistently used, consistently omitted, or used only where a given sentence would otherwise be ambiguous or hard to read. It is consistently used in most nonfiction books; elsewhere it tends to be used or generally omitted equally often.

We are looking for a house with a big yard, a view of the harbor[,] and beach and docking privileges.

25. A comma is not generally used to separate items in a series all of which are joined with conjunctions.

I don't understand what this policy covers or doesn't cover or only partially covers.

They left behind the fogs and the wood storks and the lonesome soughing of the wind.

26. When the elements in a series are long or complex or consist of clauses that themselves contain commas, the elements are usually separated by semicolons, not commas. See paragraph 7 on page 51.

With Coordinate Modifiers

27. A comma is generally used to separate two or more adjectives, adverbs, or phrases that modify the same word or phrase.

She spoke in a calm, reflective manner.
They set to their work again grimly, intently.

The comma is often omitted when the adjectives are short.

one long thin strand
a small white stone
little nervous giggles
skinny young waiters
in this harsh new light

The comma is generally omitted where it is ambiguous whether the last modifier and the noun—or two of the modifiers—constitute a unit.

the story's stark dramatic power
a pink stucco nightclub

In some writing, especially works of fiction, commas may be omitted from most series of coordinate modifiers as a matter of style.

28. A comma is not used between two adjectives when the first modifies the combination of the second plus the noun it modifies.

    the last good man
    a good used car
    his protruding lower lip
    the only fresh water
    the only freshwater lake
    their black pickup truck

A comma is also not used to separate an adverb from the adjective or adverb that it modifies.

    this formidably difficult task

In Quotations

29. A comma usually separates a direct quotation from a phrase identifying its source or speaker. If the quotation is a question or an exclamation and the identifying phrase follows the quotation, the comma is replaced by a question mark or an exclamation point.

    She answered, "I'm afraid it's all we've got."
    "The comedy is over," he muttered.
    "How about another round?" Elaine piped up.
    "I suspect," said Mrs. Horowitz, "we haven't seen the last of her."
    "You can sink the lousy thing for all I care!" Trumbull shouted back.
    "And yet . . . [,]" she mused.
    "We can't get the door op—" Captain Hunt is heard shouting before the tape goes dead.

In some cases, a colon can replace a comma preceding a quotation; see paragraph 6 on page 7.

30. When short or fragmentary quotations are used in a sentence that is not primarily dialogue, they are usually not set off by commas.

    He glad-handed his way through the small crowd with a "Looking good, Joe" or "How's the wife" for every beaming face.

Just because he said he was "about to leave this minute" doesn't mean he actually left.

Sentences that fall within sentences and do not constitute actual dialogue are not usually set off with commas. These may be mottoes or maxims, unspoken or imaginary dialogue, or sentences referred to as sentences; and they may or may not be enclosed in quotation marks. Where quotation marks are not used, a comma is often inserted to mark the beginning of the shorter sentence clearly. (For the use of quotation marks with such sentences, see paragraph 6 on page 45.)

"The computer is down" was the response she dreaded.

He spoke with a candor that seemed to insist, This actually happened to me and in just this way.

The first rule is, When in doubt, spell it out.

When the shorter sentence functions as an appositive (the equivalent to an adjacent noun), it is set off with commas when nonrestrictive and not when restrictive.

We had the association's motto, "We make waves," printed on our T-shirts.

He was fond of the slogan "Every man a king, but no man wears a crown."

31. A comma introduces a directly stated question, regardless of whether it is enclosed in quotation marks or if its first word is capitalized. It also introduces a tag question.

I wondered, what is going on here?

The question is, How do we get out of this situation?

That's obvious, isn't it?

A comma is not used to set off indirect discourse or indirect questions introduced by a conjunction (such as *that* or *what*).

Margot replied quietly that she'd never been happier.
I wondered what was going on here.
The question is how do we get out of this situation.

32. The comma is usually omitted before quotations that are very short exclamations or representations of sounds.

He jumped up suddenly and cried "I've got it!"

Replacing Omitted Words

33. A comma may indicate the omission of a word or phrase in parallel constructions where the omitted word or phrase appears earlier in the sentence. In short sentences, the comma is usually omitted.

The larger towns were peopled primarily by shopkeepers, artisans, and traders; the small villages, by peasant farmers.
Seven voted for the proposal, three against.
He critiqued my presentation and I his.

34. A comma sometimes replaces the conjunction *that*.

The smoke was so thick, they were forced to crawl.
Chances are, there are still some tickets left.

With Addresses, Dates, and Numbers

35. Commas set off the elements of an address except for zip codes.

Write to Bureau of the Census, Washington, DC 20233.
In Needles, California, their luck ran out.

When a city name and state (province, country, etc.) name are used together to modify a noun that follows, the second comma may be omitted but is more often retained.

We visited their Enid, Oklahoma plant.

but more commonly
We visited their Enid, Oklahoma, plant.

36. Commas set off the year in a full date.

On July 26, 1992, the court issued its opinion.
Construction for the project began on April 30, 1995.

When only the month and year are given, the first comma is usually omitted.

In December 1903, the Wright brothers finally succeeded in keeping an airplane aloft for a few seconds.
October 1929 brought an end to all that.

37. A comma groups numerals into units of three to separate thousands, millions, and so on.

2,000 case histories
15,000 units
a population of 3,450,000
a fee of $12,500

Certain types of numbers do not contain commas, including decimal fractions, street addresses, and page numbers. (For more on the use of the comma with numbers, see paragraphs 1–3 on page 139.)

2.5544
12537 Wilshire Blvd.
page 1415

With Names, Degrees, and Titles

38. A comma separates a surname from a following professional, academic, honorary, or religious degree or title, or an abbreviation for a branch of the armed forces.

Amelia P. Artandi, M.D.
Robert Hynes Menard, Ph.D., L.H.D.
John L. Farber, Esq.

Sister Mary Catherine, S.C.
Admiral Herman Washington, USN

39. A comma is often used between a surname and the
abbreviations *Jr.* and *Sr.*

Douglas Fairbanks, Sr.   *or*   Douglas Fairbanks Sr.
Dr. Martin Luther King, Jr.
   or   Dr. Martin Luther King Jr.

40. A comma is often used to set off corporate identi-
fiers such as *Incorporated, Inc., Ltd., P.C.,* and *L.P.*
However, many company names omit this comma.

StarStage Productions, Incorporated
Hart International Inc.
Walsh, Brandon & Kaiser, P.C.
The sales manager from Doyle Southern, Inc., spoke
   at Tuesday's meeting.

Other Uses

41. A comma follows the salutation in informal correspondence and usually follows the complimentary
close in both informal and formal correspondence.

Dear Rachel,
Affectionately,
Very truly yours,

42. The comma is used to avoid ambiguity when the
juxtaposition of two words or expressions could
cause confusion.

Under Mr. Thomas, Jefferson High School has flour-
   ished.
He scanned the landscape that opened out before
   him, and guided the horse gently down.

43. When normal sentence order is inverted, a comma
often precedes the subject and verb. If the structure is clear without it, it is often omitted.

That we would succeed, no one doubted.
And a splendid occasion it was.

With Other Punctuation

44. Commas are used next to brackets, ellipsis points,
parentheses, and quotation marks. Commas are
not used next to colons, dashes, exclamation
points, question marks, or semicolons. If one of the
latter falls at the same point where a comma would
fall, the comma is dropped. (For more on the use
of commas with other punctuation, see the sections
for each individual mark.)

> "If they find new sources [of oil and gas], their earn-
> ings will obviously rebound. . . ."
> "This book takes its place among the most serious, . . .
> comprehensive, and enlightened treatments of its
> great subject."
> There are only six small files (at least in this format),
> which take up very little disk space.
> According to Hartmann, the people are "savage,"
> their dwellings are "squalid," and the landscape is "a
> pestilential swamp."

Dash

The dash can function like a comma, a colon, or a
parenthesis. Like commas and parentheses, dashes set
off parenthetical material such as examples, supple-
mental facts, and explanatory or descriptive phrases.
Like a colon, a dash introduces clauses that explain or
expand upon something that precedes them. Though
sometimes considered a less formal equivalent of the
colon and parenthesis, the dash may be found in all
kinds of writing, including the most formal, and the
choice of which mark to use is often a matter of personal preference.

The common dash (also called the *em dash,* since it is approximately the width of a capital M in typeset material) is usually represented by two hyphens in typed and keyboarded material. (Word-processing programs make it available as a special character.)

Spacing around the dash varies. Most newspapers insert a space before and after the dash; many popular magazines do the same; but most books and journals omit spacing.

The *en dash* and the *two-* and *three-em dashes* have more limited uses, which are explained in paragraphs 13–15 on pages 28–29.

Abrupt Change or Suspension

1. The dash marks an abrupt change or break in the structure of a sentence.

   > The students seemed happy enough with the new plan, but the alumni—there was the problem.

2. A dash is used to indicate interrupted speech or a speaker's confusion or hesitation.

   > "The next point I'd like to bring up—" the speaker started to say.
   > "Yes," he went on, "yes—that is—I guess I agree."

Parenthetical and Amplifying Elements

3. Dashes are used in place of commas or parentheses to emphasize or draw attention to parenthetical or amplifying material.

   > With three expert witnesses in agreement, the defense can be expected to modify its strategy—somewhat.
   > This amendment will finally prevent corporations—large and small—from buying influence through exorbitant campaign contributions.

When dashes are used to set off parenthetical elements, they often indicate that the material is more digressive than elements set off with commas but less digressive than elements set off by parentheses. For examples, see paragraph 16 on page 15 and paragraph 1 on page 35.

4. Dashes set off or introduce defining phrases and lists.

> The fund sought to acquire controlling positions—a minimum of 25% of outstanding voting securities—in other companies.
>
> Davis was a leading innovator in at least three styles—bebop, cool jazz, and jazz-rock fusion.

5. A dash is often used in place of a colon or semicolon to link clauses, especially when the clause that follows the dash explains, summarizes, or expands upon the preceding clause in a somewhat dramatic way.

> The results were in—it had been a triumphant success.

6. A dash or a pair of dashes often sets off illustrative or amplifying material introduced by such phrases as *for example, namely,* and *that is,* when the break in continuity is greater than that shown by a comma, or when the dash would clarify the sentence structure better than a comma. (For more details, see paragraph 17 on page 15.)

> After some discussion the motion was tabled—that is, it was removed indefinitely from the board's consideration.
>
> Lawyers should generally—in pleadings, for example—attempt to be as specific as possible.

7. A dash may introduce a summary statement that follows a series of words or phrases.

Crafts, food booths, children's activities, cider-making demonstrations—there was something for everyone.

Once into bankruptcy, the company would have to pay cash for its supplies, defer maintenance, and lay off workers—moves that could threaten its future.

8. A dash often precedes the name of an author or source at the end of a quoted passage—such as an epigraph, extract, or book or film blurb—that is not part of the main text. The attribution may appear immediately after the quotation or on the next line.

> "I return to her stories with more pleasure, and await them with more anticipation, than those of any of her contemporaries."—William Logan, *Chicago Tribune*

> Only the sign is for sale.
>
> —Søren Kierkegaard

With Other Punctuation

9. If a dash appears at a point where a comma could also appear, the comma is omitted.

> Our lawyer has read the transcript—all 1,200 pages of it—and he has decided that an appeal would not be useful.
>
> If we don't succeed—and the critics say we won't—then the whole project is in jeopardy.

In a series, dashes that would force a comma to be dropped are often replaced by parentheses.

> The holiday movie crowds were being entertained by street performers: break dancers, a juggler (who doubled as a sword swallower), a steel-drummer, even a three-card-monte dealer.

10. If the second of a pair of dashes would fall where a period should also appear, the dash is omitted.

Instead, he hired his mother—an odd choice by any standard.

Much less frequently, the second dash will be dropped in favor of a colon or semicolon.

Valley Health announced general improvements to its practice—two to start this week: evening office hours and a voice-mail message system.

His conduct has always been exemplary—near-perfect attendance, excellent productivity, a good attitude; nevertheless, his termination cannot be avoided.

11. When a pair of dashes sets off material ending with an exclamation point or a question mark, the mark is placed inside the dashes.

His hobby was getting on people's nerves—especially mine!—and he was extremely good at it.

There would be a "distinguished guest speaker"—was there ever any other kind?—and plenty of wine afterwards.

12. Dashes are used inside parentheses, and vice versa, to indicate parenthetical material within parenthetical material. The second dash is omitted if it would immediately precede the closing parenthesis; a closing parenthesis is never omitted.

We were looking for a narrator (or narrators—sometimes a script calls for more than one) who could handle a variety of assignments.

The wall of the Old City contains several gates—particularly Herod's Gate, the Golden Gate, and Zion Gate (or "David's Gate")—with rich histories.

En Dash and Long Dashes

13. The *en dash* generally appears only in typeset material; in typed or keyboarded material the simple hyphen is usually used instead. (Word-processing programs provide the en dash as a special character.) Newspapers similarly use the hyphen in place

of the en dash. The en dash is shorter than the em dash but longer than the hyphen. It is most frequently used between numbers, dates, or other notations to signify "(up) to and including."

pages 128–34
1995–97
September 24–October 5
8:30 a.m.–4:30 p.m.

The en dash replaces a hyphen in compound adjectives when at least one of the elements is a two-word compound. It replaces the word *to* between capitalized names, and is used to indicate linkages such as boundaries, treaties, and oppositions.

post–Cold War era
Boston–Washington train
New Jersey–Pennsylvania border
male–female differences *or* male-female differences

14. A *two-em dash* is used to indicate missing letters in a word and, less frequently, to indicate a missing word.

The nearly illegible letter is addressed to a Mr. P——
of Baltimore.

15. A *three-em dash* indicates that a word has been left out or that an unknown word or figure is to be supplied.

The study was carried out in ———, a fast-growing
Sunbelt city.

Ellipsis Points

Ellipsis points (also known as *ellipses, points of ellipsis,* and *suspension points*) are periods, usually in groups of three, that signal an omission from quoted material or indicate a pause or trailing off of speech. A space usually precedes and follows each ellipsis point. (In newspaper style, spaces are usually omitted.)

1. Ellipsis points indicate the omission of one or more words within a quoted sentence.

> We the People of the United States . . . do ordain and establish this Constitution for the United States of America.

2. Ellipsis points are usually not used to indicate the omission of words that precede the quoted portion. However, in some formal contexts, especially when the quotation is introduced by a colon, ellipsis points are used.

> He ends with a stirring call for national resolve that "government of the people, by the people, for the people shall not perish from the earth."
> Its final words define the war's purpose in democratic terms: ". . . that government of the people, by the people, for the people shall not perish from the earth."

Ellipsis points following quoted material are omitted when it forms an integral part of a larger sentence.

> She maintained that it was inconsistent with "government of the people, by the people, for the people."

3. Punctuation used in the original that falls on either side of the ellipsis points is often omitted; however, it may be retained, especially if this helps clarify the sentence structure.

> Now we are engaged in a great civil war, testing whether that nation . . . can long endure.
> We the People of the United States, in Order to . . . establish Justice, . . . and secure the Blessings of Liberty . . . , do ordain and establish this Constitution for the United States of America.

For details on punctuating omissions within block quotations, see Chapter 6, "Quotations."

4. If the last words of a quoted sentence are omitted and the original sentence ends with punctuation other than a period, the end punctuation often follows the ellipsis points, especially if it helps clarify the quotation.

> He always ends his harangues with some variation on the question, "What could you have been thinking when you . . . ?"

5. When ellipsis points are used to indicate that a quotation has been intentionally left unfinished, the terminal period is omitted. No space separates the last ellipsis point and the quotation mark.

> The paragraph beginning "Recent developments suggest . . ." should be deleted.

6. A line of ellipsis points indicates that one or more lines have been omitted from a poem. Its length usually matches the length of the line above. (For more details on quoting verse, see the section beginning on page 170.)

> When I heard the learned astronomer,
> . . . .
> How soon unaccountable I became tired and sick,
> Til rising and gliding out I wandered off by myself,
> In the mystical moist night-air, and from time to
>   time,
> Looked up in perfect silence at the stars.

7. Ellipsis points are used to indicate faltering speech, especially if the faltering involves a long pause or a sentence that trails off or is intentionally left unfinished. Generally no other terminal punctuation is used.

> The speaker seemed uncertain. "Well, that's true . . . but even so . . . I think we can do better."
> "Despite these uncertainties, we believe we can do it, but . . ."
> "I mean . . ." he said, "like . . . How?"

8. Ellipsis points are sometimes used informally as a stylistic device to catch a reader's attention, often replacing a dash or colon.

> They think that nothing can go wrong . . . but it does.

9. In newspaper and magazine columns consisting of social notes, local events listings, or short items of celebrity news, ellipsis points often take the place of paragraphing to separate the items. (Ellipsis points are also often used in informal personal correspondence in place of periods or paragraphing.)

> Congratulations to Debra Morricone, our up-and-coming singing star, for her full scholarship to the Juilliard School this fall! . . . And kudos to Paul Chartier for his winning All-State trumpet performance last Friday in Baltimore! . . . Look for wit and sparkling melody when the Lions mount their annual Gilbert & Sullivan show at Syms Auditorium. This year it's . . .

Exclamation Point

The exclamation point is used to mark a forceful comment or exclamation.

1. An exclamation point can punctuate a sentence, phrase, or interjection.

> There is no alternative!
> Without a trace!
> My God! It's monstrous!

2. The exclamation point may replace the question mark when an ironic, angry, or emphatic tone is more important than the actual question.

> Aren't you finished yet!
> Do you realize what you've done!
> Why me!

Occasionally it is used *with* the question mark to indicate a very forceful question.

> How much did you say?!
> You did what!?

3. The exclamation point falls within brackets, dashes, parentheses, and quotation marks when it punctuates only the enclosed material. It is placed outside them when it punctuates the entire sentence.

> All of this proves—at long last!—that we were right from the start.
> Somehow the dog got the gate open (for the third time!) and ran into the street.
> He sprang to his feet and shouted "Point of order!"
> At this rate the national anthem will soon be replaced by "You Are My Sunshine"!

4. If an exclamation point falls where a comma could also go, the comma is dropped.

> "Absolutely not!" he snapped.
> They wouldn't dare! she told herself over and over.

If the exclamation point is part of a title, it may be followed by a comma. If the title falls at the end of a sentence, no period follows it.

> *Hello Dolly!,* which opened in 1964, would become one of the ten longest-running shows in Broadway history.
> His favorite management book is still *Up the Organization!*

Hyphen

Hyphens have a variety of uses, the most significant of which is to join the elements of compound nouns and modifiers.

1. Hyphens are used to link elements in compound words. (For more on compound words, see the section beginning on page 98.)

   > secretary-treasurer
   > cost-effective
   > fund-raiser
   > spin-off

2. In some words, a hyphen separates a prefix, suffix, or medial element from the rest of the word. Consult a dictionary in doubtful cases. (For details on using a hyphen with a prefix or a suffix, see the section beginning on page 111.)

   > anti-inflation
   > umbrella-like
   > jack-o'-lantern

3. In typed and keyboarded material, a hyphen is generally used between numbers and dates with the meaning "(up) to and including." In typeset material it is replaced by an en dash. (For details on the en dash, see paragraph 13 on page 28.)

   > pages 128–34
   > the years 1995–97

4. A hyphen marks an end-of-line division of a word.

   > In 1975 smallpox, formerly a great scourge, was declared totally eradicated by the World Health Organization.

5. A hyphen divides letters or syllables to give the effect of stuttering, sobbing, or halting speech.

"S-s-sammy, it's my t-toy!"

6. Hyphens indicate a word spelled out letter by letter.

   l-i-a-i-s-o-n

7. Hyphens are sometimes used to produce inflected forms of verbs made of individually pronounced letters or to add an *-er* ending to an abbreviation. However, apostrophes are more commonly used for these purposes. (For details on these uses of the apostrophe, see paragraph 6 on page 3.)

   DH-ing for the White Sox
      or DH'ing for the White Sox
   a dedicated UFO-er *or* a dedicated UFO'er

Parentheses

Parentheses generally enclose material that is inserted into a main statement but is not intended to be an essential part of it. For some of the cases described below, commas or dashes are frequently used instead. (For examples, see paragraph 16 on page 15 and paragraph 3 on page 25.) Parentheses are particularly used when the inserted material is only incidental. Unlike commas and dashes, an opening parenthesis is always followed by a closing one. Because parentheses are almost always used in pairs, and their shapes indicate their relative functions, they often clarify a sentence's structure better than commas or dashes.

Parenthetical Elements

1. Parentheses enclose phrases and clauses that provide examples, explanations, or supplementary facts or numerical data.

   Nominations for principal officers (president, vice president, treasurer, and secretary) were heard and approved.

Four computers (all outdated models) will be replaced.

Although we liked the restaurant (their Italian food was the best), we seldom had time for the long trip into the city.

First-quarter sales figures were good (up 8%), but total revenues showed a slight decline (down 1%).

2. Parentheses sometimes enclose phrases and clauses introduced by expressions such as *namely, that is, e.g.,* and *i.e.,* particularly where parentheses would clarify the sentence's structure better than commas. (For more details, see paragraph 17 on page 15.)

In writing to the manufacturer, be as specific as possible (i.e., list the defective parts, describe the malfunction, and identify the store where the unit was purchased), but also as concise.

3. Parentheses enclose definitions or translations in the main part of a sentence.

The company announced plans to sell off its housewares (small-appliances) business.

The *grand monde* (literally, "great world") of prewar Parisian society consisted largely of titled aristocracy.

4. Parentheses enclose abbreviations that follow their spelled-out forms, or spelled-out forms that follow abbreviations.

She cited a study by the Food and Drug Administration (FDA).

They attended last year's convention of the ABA (American Booksellers Association).

5. Parentheses often enclose cross-references and bibliographic references.

Specialized services are also available (see list of stores at end of brochure).

The diagram (Fig. 3) illustrates the action of the
pump.

Subsequent studies (Braxton 1990; Roh and Wein-
glass 1993) have confirmed these findings.

6. Parentheses enclose numerals that confirm a
spelled-out number in a business or legal context.

Delivery will be made in thirty (30) days.

The fee is Four Thousand Dollars ($4,000), payable to
UNCO, Inc.

7. Parentheses enclose the name of a state that is inserted into a proper name for identification.

the Kalispell (Mont.) Regional Hospital

the *Sacramento* (Calif.) *Bee*

8. Parentheses may be used to enclose personal
asides.

Claims were made of its proven efficacy (some of us
were skeptical).

or

Claims were made of its proven efficacy. (Some of us
were skeptical.)

9. Parentheses are used to enclose quotations that illustrate or support a statement made in the main
text.

After he had a few brushes with the police, his stepfa-
ther had him sent to jail as an incorrigible ("It will
do him good").

Other Uses

10. Parentheses enclose unpunctuated numbers or letters indicating individual elements or items in a series within a sentence.

Sentences can be classified as (1) simple, (2) multiple
or compound, and (3) complex.

11. Parentheses indicate alternative terms.

    > Please sign and return the enclosed form(s).

12. Parentheses may be used to indicate losses in accounting.

	Operating Profits (in millions)
Cosmetics	26.2
Food products	47.7
Food services	54.3
Transportation	(17.7)
Sporting goods	(11.2)
Total	99.3

With Other Punctuation

13. When an independent sentence is enclosed in parentheses, its first word is capitalized and a period (or other closing punctuation) is placed inside the parentheses.

    > The discussion was held in the boardroom. (The results are still confidential.)

    A parenthetical expression that occurs within a sentence—even if it could stand alone as a separate sentence—does not end with a period but may end with an exclamation point, a question mark, or quotation marks.

    > Although several trade organizations opposed the legislation (there were at least three paid lobbyists working on Capitol Hill), the bill passed easily.
    > The conference was held in Portland (Me., not Ore.).
    > After waiting in line for an hour (why do we do these things?), we finally left.

    A parenthetical expression within a sentence does not require capitalization unless it is a quoted sentence.

He was totally confused ("What can we do?") and re-
fused to see anyone.

14. If a parenthetical expression within a sentence is
composed of two independent clauses, a semicolon
rather than a period usually separates them. Independent sentences enclosed together in parentheses employ normal sentence capitalization and
punctuation.

> We visited several showrooms, looked at the prices (it
> wasn't a pleasant experience; prices in this area have
> not gone down), and asked all the questions we
> could think of.
>
> We visited several showrooms and looked at the
> prices. (It wasn't a pleasant experience. Prices in this
> area have not gone down.)

Entire paragraphs are rarely enclosed in parentheses; instead, paragraphs of incidental material often appear as footnotes or endnotes.

15. No punctuation (other than a period after an abbreviation) is placed immediately before an opening parenthesis within a sentence; if punctuation is
required, it follows the final parenthesis.

> I'll get back to you tomorrow (Friday), when I have
> more details.
>
> Tickets cost $14 in advance ($12 for seniors); the
> price at the door is $18.
>
> The relevant figures are shown below (in millions of
> dollars):

16. Parentheses sometimes appear within parentheses
when no confusion would result; alternatively, the
inner parentheses are replaced with brackets.

> Checks must be drawn in U.S. dollars. (*Please note:*
> We cannot accept checks drawn on Canadian banks
> for amounts less than four U.S. dollars ($4.00).
> The same regulation applies to Canadian money
> orders.)

17. Dashes and parentheses may be used together to set off parenthetical material. (For details, see paragraph 12 on page 28.)

> The orchestra is spirited, and the cast—an expert and enthusiastic crew of Savoyards (some of them British imports)—comes through famously.

Period

Periods almost always serve to mark the end of a sentence or abbreviation.

1. A period ends a sentence or a sentence fragment that is neither a question nor an exclamation.

> From the Format menu, choose Style.
> Robert decided to bring champagne.
> Unlikely. In fact, inconceivable.

Only one period ends a sentence.

> The jellied gasoline was traced to the Trenton-based Quality Products, Inc.
> Miss Toklas states categorically that "This is the best way to cook frogs' legs."

2. A period punctuates some abbreviations. No space follows an internal period within an abbreviation. (For details on punctuating abbreviations, see the section beginning on page 117.)

Assn.	Dr.	etc.
Ph.D.	e.g.	p.m.

3. Periods are used with a person's initials, each followed by a space. (Newspaper style omits the space.) If the initials replace the name, they are unspaced and may also be written without periods.

> J. B. S. Haldane
> L.B.J. *or* LBJ

4. A period follows numerals and letters when they are used without parentheses in outlines and vertical lists.

> I. Objectives
>   A. Economy
>   1. Low initial cost
>   2. Low maintenance cost
>   B. Ease of operation
> Required skills are:
>   1. Shorthand
>   2. Typing
>   3. Transcription

5. A period is placed within quotation marks, even when it did not punctuate the original quoted material. (In British practice, the period goes outside the quotation marks whenever it does not belong to the original quoted material.)

> The founder was known to his employees as "the old man."
>
> "I said I wanted to fire him," Henry went on, "but she said, 'I don't think you have the contractual privilege to do that.'"

6. When brackets or parentheses enclose an independent sentence, the period is placed inside them. When brackets or parentheses enclose a sentence that is part of a larger sentence, the period for the enclosed sentence is omitted.

> Arturo finally arrived on the 23rd with the terrible news that Katrina had been detained by the police. [This later proved to be false; see letter 255.]
>
> I took a good look at her (she was standing quite close to me).

Question Mark

The question mark always indicates a question or doubt.

1. A question mark ends a direct question.

   > What went wrong?
   > "When do they arrive?" she asked.

   A question mark follows a period only when the period punctuates an abbreviation. No period follows a question mark.

   > Is he even an M.D.?
   > "Will you arrive by 10 p.m.?"
   > A local professor would be giving a paper with the title "Economic Stagnation or Equilibrium?"

2. Polite requests that are worded as questions usually take periods, because they are not really questions. Conversely, a sentence that is intended as a question but whose word order is that of a statement is punctuated with a question mark.

   > Could you please send the necessary forms.
   > They flew in yesterday?

3. The question mark ends a question that forms part of a sentence. An indirect question is not followed by a question mark.

   > What was her motive? you may be asking.
   > I naturally wondered, Will it really work?
   > I naturally wondered whether it would really work.
   > He asked when the report was due.

4. The question mark punctuates each element of a series of questions that share a single beginning and are neither numbered nor lettered. When the series is numbered or lettered, only one question mark is generally used.

   > Can you give us a reasonable forecast? Back up your predictions? Compare them with last year's earnings?
   > Can you (1) give us a reasonable forecast, (2) back up your predictions, and (3) compare them with last year's earnings?

5. The question mark indicates uncertainty about a fact or the accuracy of a transcription.

> Homer, Greek epic poet (9th–8th? cent. B.C.)
> He would have it that Farjeon[?] is the onlie man for us.

6. The question mark is placed inside brackets, dashes, parentheses, or quotation marks when it punctuates only the material enclosed by them and not the sentence as a whole. It is placed outside them when it punctuates the entire sentence.

> I took a vacation in 1992 (was it really that long ago?), but I haven't had time for one since.
> What did Andrew mean when he called the project "a fiasco from the start"?
> Williams then asks, "Do you realize the extent of the problem [the housing shortage]?"

Quotation Marks

The following paragraphs describe the use of quotation marks to enclose quoted matter in regular text, and for other, less frequent uses. For the use of quotation marks to enclose titles, see paragraph 70 on page 79.

Basic Uses

1. Quotation marks enclose direct quotations but not indirect quotations or paraphrases.

> Dr. Mee added, "We'd be grateful for anything you could do."
> "We just got the lab results," he crowed, "and the blood types match!"
> "I'm leaving," she whispered. "This meeting could go on forever."
> "Mom, we *tried* that already!" they whined in unison.
> "Ssshh!" she hissed.

She said she was leaving.

Algren once said something like, Don't ever play poker with anyone named Doc, and never eat at a diner called Mom's.

2. Quotation marks enclose fragments of quoted matter.

The agreement makes it clear that he "will be paid only upon receipt of an acceptable manuscript."

As late as 1754, documents refer to him as "yeoman" and "husbandman."

3. Quotation marks enclose words or phrases borrowed from others, and words of obvious informality introduced into formal writing. Words introduced as specialized terminology are sometimes enclosed in quotation marks but more often italicized.

Be sure to send a copy of your résumé—or as some folks would say, your "biodata summary."

They were afraid the patient had "stroked out"—had had a cerebrovascular accident.

New Hampshire's only "green" B&B

referred to as "closed" or "privately held" corporations

but more frequently

referred to as *closed* or *privately held* corporations

4. Quotation marks are sometimes used to enclose words referred to as words. Italics are also frequently used for this purpose.

changed every "he" to "she"

or

changed every *he* to *she*

5. Quotation marks may enclose representations of sounds, though these are also frequently italicized.

If it sounds like "quank, quank" [*or* like *quank, quank*], it may be the green treefrog.

6. Quotation marks often enclose short sentences that fall within longer sentences, especially when the shorter sentence is meant to suggest spoken dialogue. Mottoes and maxims, unspoken or imaginary dialogue, and sentences referred to as sentences may all be treated in this way.

> On the gate was the inscription "Arbeit macht frei" [or *Arbeit macht frei*]—"Work will make you free."
> The fact was, the poor kid didn't know "C'mere" from "Sic 'em."
> In effect, the voters were saying "You blew it, and you don't get another chance."
> Their reaction could only be described as "Kill the messenger."
> She never got used to their "That's the way it goes" attitude.
> *or*
> She never got used to their that's-the-way-it-goes attitude.

Quotation marks are often omitted in sentences of this kind when the structure is clear without them. (For the use of commas in such sentences, see paragraphs 29–30 on page 19.)

> The first rule is, When in doubt, spell it out.

7. Direct questions are enclosed in quotation marks when they represent quoted dialogue, but usually not otherwise.

> She asked, "What went wrong?"
> The question is, What went wrong?
> We couldn't help wondering, Where's the plan?
> *or*
> We couldn't help wondering, "Where's the plan?"

8. Quotation marks enclose translations of foreign or borrowed terms.

> This is followed by the Dies Irae ("Day of Wrath"), a climactic movement in many settings of the Requiem.

The term comes from the Latin *sesquipedalis,* meaning "a foot and a half long."

They also frequently enclose definitions.

Concupiscent simply means "lustful."
or
Concupiscent simply means lustful.

9. Quotation marks sometimes enclose letters referred to as letters.

The letter "m" is wider than the letter "i."
Put an "x" in the right spot.

However, such letters are more frequently italicized (or underlined), or left undifferentiated from the surrounding text where no confusion would result.

How many *e*'s are in her name?
a V-shaped blade
He was happy to get a B in the course.

With Longer Quotations

10. Quotation marks are not used with longer passages of prose or poetry that are indented as separate paragraphs, called *block quotations* or *extracts.* For a thorough discussion of quotations, see Chapter 6.

11. Quotation marks enclose lines of poetry run in with the text. A spaced slash separates the lines. (For details on poetry set as an extract, see the section beginning on page 170.)

When Gerard Manley Hopkins wrote that "Nothing is so beautiful as spring— / When weeds, in wheels, shoot long and lovely and lush," he probably had my yard in mind.

12. Quotation marks are not used with epigraphs. However, they are generally used with advertising

blurbs. (For details on epigraphs and blurbs, see the section beginning on page 167.)

> The whole of science is nothing more than a refinement of everyday thinking.
>
> —Albert Einstein

> "A brutal irony, a slam-bang humor and a style of writing as balefully direct as a death sentence."—*Time*

With Other Punctuation

13. When a period or comma follows text enclosed in quotation marks, it is placed within the quotation marks, even if the original language quoted was not followed by a period or comma.

> He smiled and said, "I'm happy for you."
>
> But perhaps Pound's most perfect poem was "The Return."
>
> The cameras were described as "waterproof," but "moisture-resistant" would have been a better description.

In British usage, the period or comma goes outside the quoted matter whenever the original text did not include the punctuation.

14. When a colon or semicolon follows text enclosed in quotation marks, the colon or semicolon is placed outside the quotation marks.

> But they all chimed in on "O Sole Mio": raw adolescents, stately matrons, decrepit old pensioners, their voices soaring in passion together.
>
> She spoke of her "little cottage in the country"; she might better have called it a mansion.

15. The dash, question mark, and exclamation point are placed inside quotation marks when they punctuate the quoted matter only, but outside the quotation marks when they punctuate the whole sentence.

"I can't see how—" he started to say.

He thought he knew where he was going—he re-membered her saying, "Take two lefts, then stay to the right"—but the streets didn't look familiar.

He asked, "When did they leave?"

What is the meaning of "the open door"?

She collapsed in her seat with a stunned "Good God!"

Save us from his "mercy"!

Single Quotation Marks

16. Single quotation marks replace double quotation marks when the quoted material occurs within quoted material.

> The witness said, "I distinctly heard him say, 'Don't be late,' and then I heard the door close."
>
> "We'd like to close tonight with that great Harold Arlen wee-hours standard, 'One for My Baby.'"
>
> This analysis is indebted to Del Banco's "Elizabeth Bishop's 'Insomnia': An Inverted View."

When both single and double quotation marks occur at the end of a sentence, the period falls within both sets of marks.

> The witness said, "I distinctly heard him say, 'Don't be late.'"

British usage often reverses American usage, enclosing quoted material in single quotation marks, and enclosing quotations within quotations in double quotation marks. In British usage, commas and periods following quoted material go inside only those quotation marks that enclose material that originally included the period or comma.

17. A quotation within a quotation within a quotation is usually enclosed in double quotation marks. (Such constructions are usually avoided by rewriting.)

As the *Post* reported it, "Van Houten's voice can be clearly heard saying, 'She said "You wouldn't dare" and I said "I just did."'"

or

The *Post* reported that Van Houten's voice was clearly heard saying, "She said 'You wouldn't dare' and I said 'I just did.'"

Semicolon

The semicolon may be used much like the comma, period, or colon, depending on the context. Like a comma, it may separate elements in a series. Like a period or colon, it frequently marks the end of a complete clause, and like a colon it signals that the remainder of the sentence is closely related to the first part. However, in each case the semicolon is normally used in a distinctive way. It serves as a higher-level comma; it connects clauses, as a period does not; and it does not imply any following exemplification, amplification, or description, as a colon generally does.

Between Clauses

1. A semicolon separates related independent clauses joined without a coordinating conjunction.

    Cream the shortening and sugar; add the eggs and beat well.

    The river rose and overflowed its banks; roads became flooded and impassable; freshly plowed fields disappeared from sight.

2. A semicolon often replaces a comma between two clauses joined by a coordinating conjunction if the sentence might otherwise be confusing—for example, because of particularly long clauses or the presence of other commas.

In a society that seeks to promote social goals, government will play a powerful role; and taxation, once simply a means of raising money, becomes, in addition, a way of furthering those goals.

3. A semicolon joins two clauses when the second includes a conjunctive adverb such as *accordingly, however, indeed,* or *thus,* or a phrase that acts like a conjunctive adverb such as *in that case, as a result,* or *on the other hand.*

Most people are covered by insurance of some kind; indeed, many don't even see their medical bills.
It won't be easy to sort out the facts; a decision must be made, however.
The case could take years to work its way through the courts; as a result, many plaintiffs will accept settlements.

When *so* and *yet* are treated as conjunctive adverbs, they are often preceded by a semicolon and followed by a comma. When treated as coordinating conjunctions, as they usually are, they are generally only preceded by a comma.

The new recruits were bright, diligent, and even enthusiastic; yet[,] the same problems persisted.
His grades improved sharply, yet the high honor roll still eluded him.

4. A semicolon may join two statements when the second clause is elliptical, omitting essential words that are supplied by the first. In short sentences, a comma often replaces the semicolon.

The conference sessions, designed to allow for full discussions, were much too long; the breaks between them, much too short.
The aged Scotch was haunting, the Asiago piquant.

5. When a series of clauses are separated by semicolons and a coordinating conjunction precedes

the final clause, the final semicolon is sometimes replaced with a comma.

> The bars had all closed hours ago; a couple of coffee shops were open but deserted[, *or* ,] and only a few lighted upper-story windows gave evidence of other victims of insomnia.

6. A semicolon is often used before introductory expressions such as *for example, that is,* and *namely,* in place of a colon, comma, dash, or parenthesis. (For more details, see paragraph 17 on page 15.)

> On one point only did everyone agree; namely, too much money had been spent already.
>
> We were fairly successful on that project; that is, we made our deadlines and met our budget.

In a Series

7. A semicolon is used in place of a comma to separate phrases or items in a series when the phrases or items themselves contain commas. A comma may replace the semicolon before a conjunction that precedes the last item in a series.

> The assets in question include $22 million in land, buildings, and equipment; $34 million in cash, investments, and accounts receivable; and $8 million in inventory.
>
> The votes against were: Precinct 1, 418; Precinct 2, 332; Precinct 3, 256.
>
> The debate about the nature of syntactic variation continues to this day (Labov 1991; Dines 1991, 1993; Romaine 1995).
>
> The Pissarro exhibition will travel to Washington, D.C.; Manchester, N.H.; Portland, Ore.; and Oakland, Calif.

When the items in a series are long or are sentences themselves, they are usually separated by semicolons even if they lack internal commas.

Among the committee's recommendations were the following: more hospital beds in urban areas where there are waiting lines for elective surgery; smaller staff size in half-empty rural hospitals; and review procedures for all major purchases.

With Other Punctuation

8. A semicolon that punctuates the larger sentence is placed outside quotation marks and parentheses.

> I heard the senator on yesterday's "All Things Considered"; his views on Medicare are encouraging.
> She found him urbane and entertaining (if somewhat overbearing); he found her charmingly ingenuous.

Slash

The slash (also known as the *virgule, diagonal, solidus, oblique,* and *slant*) is most commonly used in place of a short word or a hyphen or en dash, or to separate numbers or text elements. There is generally no space on either side of the slash.

1. A slash represents the words *per* or *to* when used between units of measure or the terms of a ratio.

> 40,000 tons/year
> 29 mi/gal
> price/earnings ratio   *or*   price–earnings ratio
> cost/benefit analysis   *or*   cost–benefit analysis
> a 50/50 split   *or*   a 50-50 split
> 20/20 vision

2. A slash separates alternatives, usually representing the words *or* or *and/or.*

> alumni/ae
> his/her
> the *affect/effect* problem   *or*   the *affect-effect* problem

3. A slash replaces the word *and* in some compound terms.

> air/sea cruise   *or*   air-sea cruise
> the May/June issue   *or*   the May-June Issue
> 1996/97   *or*   1996–97
> travel/study trip   *or*   travel-study trip

4. A slash is sometimes used to replace certain prepositions such as *at, versus,* and *for.*

> U.C./Berkeley   *or*   U.C.–Berkeley
> parent/child issues   *or*   parent–child issues
> Vice President/Editorial
>   *or*   Vice President, Editorial

5. A slash punctuates a few abbreviations.

> w/o [*for* without]
> c/o [*for* care of]
> I/O [*for* input/output]
> d/b/a [*for* doing business as]
> w/w [*for* wall-to-wall]
> o/a [*for* on or about]

6. The slash separates the elements in a numerical date, and numerators and denominators in fractions.

> 11/29/95
> 2 3/16 inches wide   *or* $2\frac{3}{16}$ inches wide
>
> a 7/8-mile course   *or*   a $\frac{7}{8}$-mile course

7. The slash separates lines of poetry that are run in with the text around them. A space is usually inserted before and after the slash.

> Alexander Pope once observed: "'Tis with our judgments as our watches, none / Go just alike, yet each believes his own."

2 Capitals and Italics

Words and phrases are capitalized or italicized (underlining takes the place of italics in typed or handwritten text) to indicate that they have a special significance in particular contexts. (Quotation marks sometimes perform the same functions; see paragraphs 69–71 on page 79 and the section on quotation marks beginning on page 43.)

Beginnings

1. The first word of a sentence or sentence fragment is capitalized.

   They make a desert and call it peace.
   So many men, so many opinions.
   O times! O customs!

2. The first word of a sentence contained within parentheses is capitalized. However, a parenthetical sentence occurring inside another sentence is not capitalized unless it is a complete quoted sentence.

   No one answered the telephone. (They were probably on vacation.)
   The road remains almost impassable (the locals don't seem to care), and the journey is only for the intrepid.

After waiting in line for an hour (what else could we do?), we finally left.

In the primary election Evans placed third ("My campaign started late")

3. The first word of a direct quotation is capitalized. However, if the quotation is interrupted in mid-sentence, the second part does not begin with a capital.

> The department manager explained, "We have no budget for new computers."
>
> "We have no budget for new computers," explained the department manager, "but we may next year."

4. When a quotation, whether a sentence fragment or a complete sentence, is syntactically dependent on the sentence in which it occurs, the quotation does not begin with a capital.

> The brochure promised a tour of "the most exotic ancient sites."
>
> His first response was that "there is absolutely no truth to the reports."

5. The first word of a sentence within a sentence that is not a direct quotation is usually capitalized. Examples include mottoes and rules, unspoken or imaginary dialogue, sentences referred to as sentences, and direct questions. (For the use of commas and quotation marks with such sentences, see paragraphs 30–31 on pages 19–21 and paragraphs 6–7 on page 45.)

> You know the saying "Fools rush in where angels fear to tread."
>
> The first rule is, When in doubt, spell it out.
>
> One ballot proposition sought to enforce the sentencing rule of "Three strikes and you're out."
>
> My question is, When can we go?

6. The first word of a line of poetry is traditionally capitalized. However, in the poetry of this century

line beginnings are often lowercased. The poem's
original capitalization is always reproduced.

> Death is the mother of beauty, mystical,
> Within whose burning bosom we devise
> Our earthly mothers waiting, sleeplessly.
> —Wallace Stevens

> If tributes cannot
> be implicit,
> give me diatribes and the fragrance of iodine,
> the cork oak acorn grown in Spain . . .
> —Marianne Moore

7. The first word following a colon is lowercased
when it begins a list and usually lowercased when it
begins a complete sentence. However, when the
sentence introduced is lengthy and distinctly separate from the preceding clause, it is often capitalized.

> In the early morning they broadcast an urgent call
> for three necessities: bandages, antibiotics, and
> blood.
> The advantage of this system is clear: it's inexpensive.
> The situation is critical: This company cannot hope to
> recoup the fourth-quarter losses that were sustained
> in five operating divisions.

8. If a colon introduces a series of sentences, the first
word of each sentence is capitalized.

> Consider the steps we have taken: A subcommittee
> has been formed to evaluate past performance. New
> sources of revenue are being explored. Several can-
> didates have been interviewed for the new post of
> executive director.

9. The first words of items that form complete sentences in run-in lists are usually capitalized, as are
the first words of items in vertical lists. However,
numbered phrases within a sentence are lower-

cased. For details, see the section beginning on page 149.

10. The first word in an outline heading is capitalized.

   I. Editorial tasks
   II. Production responsibilities
      A. Cost estimates
      B. Bids

11. In minutes and legislation, the introductory words *Whereas* and *Resolved* are capitalized (and *Resolved* is also italicized). The word immediately following is also capitalized.

   Whereas, Substantial benefits . . .
   Resolved, That . . .

12. The first word and certain other words of the salutation of a letter and the first word of a complimentary close are capitalized.

   Dear Sir or Madam:
   Ladies and Gentlemen:
   To whom it may concern:
   Sincerely yours,
   Very truly yours,

13. The first word and each subsequent major word following a SUBJECT or TO heading in a memorandum are capitalized.

   SUBJECT: Pension Plans
   TO: All Department Heads and Editors

Proper Nouns and Adjectives

The following paragraphs describe the ways in which a broad range of proper nouns and adjectives are styled.

Capitals are always employed, sometimes in conjunction with italics or quotation marks.

Abbreviations

1. Abbreviated forms of proper nouns and adjectives are capitalized, just as the spelled-out forms would be. (For details on capitalizing abbreviations, see the section beginning on page 119.)

> Jan. [*for* January]
> NATO [*for* North Atlantic Treaty Organization]

Abstractions and Personifications

2. Abstract concepts and qualities are sometimes capitalized when the concept or quality is being personified. If the term is simply used in conjunction with other words that allude to human characteristics or qualities, it is not capitalized.

> as Autumn paints each leaf in fiery colors
> the statue of Justice with her scales
> hoping that fate would lend a hand

Academic Degrees

3. The names of academic degrees are capitalized when they follow a person's name. The names of specific degrees used without a person's name are usually lowercased. More general names for degrees are lowercased.

> Lawton I. Byrne, Doctor of Laws
> earned his associate in science degree
>   *or* earned his Associate in Science degree
> completed course work for his doctorate
> working for a master's degree

Abbreviations for academic degrees are always capitalized. (For details, see paragraphs 11–12 on page 125.)

Susan L. Wycliff, M.S.W.
received her Ph.D. in clinical psychology

Animals and Plants

4. The common names of animals and plants are not capitalized unless they contain a proper noun, in which case the proper noun is usually capitalized and any name element preceding (but not following) it is often capitalized. When in doubt, consult a dictionary. (For scientific names, see the section on pages 75–77.)

the springer spaniel	Queen Anne's lace
Holstein cows	black-eyed Susan
California condor	mayflower
a Great Dane	jack-in-the-pulpit

Awards and Prizes

5. Names of awards and prizes are capitalized. Words and phrases that are not actually part of the award's name are lowercased.

Academy Award
Emmy
Rhodes Scholarship
Rhodes scholar
Pulitzer Prize–winning novelist
Nobel Prize winner
Nobel Prize in medicine
   but
Nobel Peace Prize

Derivatives of Proper Names

6. Derivatives of proper names are capitalized when used in their primary sense. If the derived term has taken on a specialized meaning, it is often lowercased. Consult a dictionary when in doubt.

Roman sculpture
Viennese culture
Victorian prudery
a Britishism
Hodgkin's disease
chinaware
pasteurized milk
french fries
    but
American cheese
Dutch door

Geographical and Topographical References

7. Terms that identify divisions of the earth's surface and distinct areas, regions, places, or districts are capitalized, as are derivative nouns and adjectives.

the Pacific Rim	Burgundy
the Great Lakes	Burgundians
Arnhem Land	the Highlands
the Golan Heights	Highland attitudes

8. Popular names of localities are capitalized.

Little Italy	the Sunbelt
the Left Bank	the Big Easy

9. Compass points are capitalized when they refer to a geographical region or form part of a place-name or street name. They are lowercased when they refer to a simple direction.

the Southwest	North Pole
West Coast	north of the Rio Grande
North Atlantic	born in the East
East Pleasant Street	driving east on I-90

10. Nouns and adjectives that are derived from compass points and that designate or refer to a specific geographical region are usually capitalized.

Southern hospitality
Easterners
Southwestern recipes
Northern Europeans

11. Words designating global, national, regional, and local political divisions are capitalized when they are essential elements of specific names. They are usually lowercased when they precede a proper name or are not part of a specific name.

> the Roman Empire
> British Commonwealth nations
> New York State
> the state of New York
> the Third Precinct
> voters in three precincts

In legal documents, such words are often capitalized regardless of position.

> the State of New York

12. Generic geographical terms (such as *lake, mountain, river,* or *valley*) are capitalized if they are part of a proper name.

Lake Tanganyika	Cape of Good Hope
Great Salt Lake	Massachusetts Bay
Atlas Mountains	Cayman Islands
Mount Everest	Yosemite Valley

When a place-name is subsequently referred to by its generic term, the term is lowercased.

> They went water-skiing on Lake Michigan that afternoon; the lake was calm and the weather beautiful.

When *the* precedes the generic term, the term is lowercased.

> the river Nile

13. Generic geographical terms preceding two or more names are usually capitalized.

Lakes Huron and Erie
Mounts McKinley, Whitney, and Shasta

14. Generic geographical terms that are not used as part of a single proper name are not capitalized. These include plural terms that follow two or more proper names, and terms that are used descriptively or alone.

the Indian and South Pacific oceans
the Mississippi and Missouri rivers
the Pacific coast of Mexico
Caribbean islands
the river delta

15. The names of streets, monuments, parks, landmarks, well-known buildings, and other public places are capitalized. However, common terms that are part of these names (such as *street, park,* or *bridge*) are lowercased when they occur after multiple names or are used alone.

State Street	Golden Gate Bridge
the Lincoln Memorial	Empire State Building
Statue of Liberty	Beverly Hills Hotel
the Pyramids	back to the hotel
Grant Park	Main and Oak streets

Well-known shortened forms of place-names are capitalized.

the Hill [*for* Capitol Hill]
the Channel [*for* English Channel]
the Street [*for* Wall Street]

Governmental, Judicial, and Political Bodies

16. Full names of legislative, deliberative, executive, and administrative bodies are capitalized, as are easily recognizable short forms of these names.

However, nonspecific noun and adjective references to them are usually lowercased.

> United States Congress
> Congress
> the House
> the Fed
> congressional hearings
> a federal agency

When words such as *department, committee,* or *agency* are used in place of a full name, they are most often capitalized when the department or agency is referring to itself, but otherwise usually lowercased.

> This Department welcomes constructive criticism . . .
> The department claimed to welcome such criticism . . .

When such a word is used in the plural to describe more than one specific body, it is usually capitalized when it precedes the names and lowercased when it follows them.

> involving the Departments of State and Justice
> a briefing from the State and Justice departments

17. Full names of high courts are capitalized. Short forms of such names are often capitalized in legal documents but lowercased otherwise.

   > . . . in the U.S. Court of Appeals for the Ninth Circuit
   > International Court of Justice
   > The court of appeals [*or* Court of Appeals] held . . .
   > the Virginia Supreme Court
   > a federal district court
   > the state supreme court

However, both the full and short names of the U.S. Supreme Court are capitalized.

> the Supreme Court of the United States

> the Supreme Court
> the Court

18. Names of city and county courts are usually lower-cased.

> the Springfield municipal court
> small-claims court
> the county court
> juvenile court

19. The noun *court,* when it applies to a specific judge or presiding officer, is capitalized in legal documents.

> It is the opinion of this Court that . . .
> The Court found that . . .

20. The terms *federal* and *national* are capitalized only when they are essential elements of a name or title. (*Federal* is also capitalized when it refers to a historical architectural style, to members of the original Federalist party, or to adherents of the Union in the Civil War.)

> Federal Election Commission
> a federal commission
> Federalist principles
> National Security Council
> national security

21. The word *administration* is sometimes capitalized when it refers to the administration of a specific U.S. president, but is more commonly lowercased. Otherwise, it is lowercased except when it is a part of the official name of a government agency.

> the Reagan administration
>   *or* the Reagan Administration
> the administration *or* the Administration
> from one administration to the next
> the Social Security Administration

22. Names of political organizations and their adherents are capitalized, but the word *party* is often lowercased.

> the Democratic National Committee
> the Republican platform
> the Christian Coalition
> most Republicans
> the Democratic party *or* the Democratic Party
> party politics

Names of less-distinct political groupings are usually lowercased, as are their derivative forms.

> the right wing
> the liberals
> the conservative agenda
> *but often*
> the Left
> the Right

23. Terms describing political and economic philosophies are usually lowercased; if derived from proper names, they are usually capitalized. Consult a dictionary for doubtful cases.

> authoritarianism   nationalism
> democracy   social Darwinist
> fascism *or* Fascism   Marxist

Historical Periods and Events

24. The names of some historical and cultural periods and movements are capitalized. When in doubt, consult a dictionary or encyclopedia.

> Bronze Age   Third Reich
> Middle Ages   the atomic age
> Prohibition   Victorian era
> the Renaissance   age of Pericles
> New Deal   the baby boom
> Fifth Republic

25. Century and decade designations are normally lowercased.

> the nineteenth century
> the twenties
> the turn of the century
> a 12th-century manuscript
> > *but*
> Gay Nineties
> Roaring Twenties

26. The names of conferences, councils, expositions, and specific sporting, cultural, and historical events are capitalized.

> Fourth World Conference on Women
> Council of Trent
> New York World's Fair
> Super Bowl
> Cannes Film Festival
> Miss America Contest
> San Francisco Earthquake
> Johnstown Flood

27. Full names of specific treaties, laws, and acts are capitalized.

> Treaty of Versailles
> the Nineteenth Amendment
> the Bill of Rights
> Clean Air Act of 1990
> > *but*
> gun-control laws
> an equal-rights amendment

28. The words *war, revolution,* and *battle* are capitalized when they are part of a full name. Official names of actions are capitalized. Descriptive terms such as *assault* and *siege* are usually lowercased even when used in conjunction with a place-name.

War of the Roses
World War II
the French Revolution
Battle of Gettysburg
Operation Desert Storm
between the two world wars
the American and French revolutions
the siege of Leningrad
Washington's winter campaign

Hyphenated Compounds

29. The second (third, etc.) element of a hyphenated
compound is generally capitalized only if it is itself
a proper noun or adjective. (For hyphenated titles,
see paragraph 65 on page 78.)

Arab-Israeli negotiations
or Arab–Israeli negotiations
East-West trade agreements
or East–West trade agreements
French-speaking peoples
Forty-second street
twentieth-century architecture

30. When joined to a proper noun or adjective, common prefixes (such as *pre-* or *anti-*) are usually lowercased, but geographical and ethnic combining
forms (such as *Anglo-* or *Sino-*) are capitalized. (For
details, see paragraphs 45 and 52 on pages 112 and
114.)

anti-Soviet forces
Sino-Japanese relations

Legal Material

31. The names of the plaintiff and defendant in legal
case titles are italicized. The *v.* (for *versus*) may be

roman or italic. Cases that do not involve two opposing parties are also italicized. When the party
involved rather than the case itself is being discussed, the reference is not italicized. In running
text, a case name involving two opposing parties
may be shortened.

> *Jones* v. *Massachusetts*
> *Smith et al. v. Jones*
> *In re Jones*
> She covered the Jones trial for the newspaper.
> The judge based his ruling on a precedent set in the
> *Jones* decision.

Medical Terms

32. Proper names that are elements in terms designating diseases, symptoms, syndromes, and tests
are capitalized. Common nouns are lowercased;
however, abbreviations of such nouns are all-
capitalized.

> Alzheimer's disease black lung disease
> Tourette's syndrome mumps
> Schick test   AIDS

33. Scientific names of disease-causing organisms follow the rules discussed in paragraph 58 on pages
75–76. The names of diseases or conditions derived
from scientific names of organisms are lowercased
and not italicized.

> a neurotoxin produced by *Clostridium botulinum*
> nearly died of botulism

34. Generic names of drugs are lowercased; trade
names should be capitalized.

> retinoic acid
> Retin-A

Military Terms

35. The full titles of branches of the U.S. armed forces are capitalized, as are standard short forms.

> U.S. Marine Corps the Marines
> the Marine Corps the Corps

Those of other countries are capitalized when the precise title is used; otherwise they are usually lowercased. The plurals of *army, navy, air force,* and *coast guard* are lowercased.

> Royal Air Force
> the Guatemalan army
> the tiny armies of both countries

The modifiers *army, navy, marine, coast guard,* and *air force* are usually lowercased; *naval* is lowercased unless it is part of an official name. The noun *marine* is usually lowercased.

> an army helicopter the first naval engagement
> a career navy man the Naval Reserves
> the marine barracks a former marine

Full or shortened names of specific units of a branch are usually capitalized.

> U.S. Army Corps of Engineers
> the Third Army
> the Eighty-second [*or* 82nd] Airborne
> the U.S. Special Forces, or Green Berets
> . . . of the First Battalion. The battalion commander ordered . . .

36. Military ranks are capitalized when they precede the names of their holders, or replace the name in direct address. Otherwise they are lowercased.

> Major General Smedley Butler

Please be seated, Admiral.
The major arrived precisely on time.

37. The names of decorations, citations, and medals are capitalized.

Medal of Honor
Purple Heart

Numerical Designations

38. A noun introducing a reference number is usually capitalized. The abbreviation *No.* is usually omitted.

Order 704	Form 2E
Flight 409	Policy 118-4-Y

39. Nouns used with numbers or letters to refer to major reference entities or actual captions in books or periodicals are usually capitalized. Nouns that designate minor reference entities and do not appear in captions are lowercased.

Book II	Figure D.4
Volume 5	page 101
Chapter 2	line 8
Table 3	paragraph 6.1
Example 16.2	question 21

Organizations

40. Names of organizations, corporations, and institutions, and terms derived from those names to designate their members, are capitalized.

the League of Women Voters
General Motors Corporation
the Smithsonian Institution
the University of the South
the Rotary Club
all Rotarians

Common nouns used descriptively or occurring after the names of two or more organizations are lowercased.

> enrolled at the university
> Yale and Harvard universities
> *but*
> the Universities of Utah and Nevada

41. Words such as *agency, department, division, group,* or *office* that designate corporate and organizational units are capitalized only when used as part of a specific proper name. (For governmental units, see paragraph 16 on pages 62–63.)

> head of the Sales Division of K2 Outfitters
> a memo to the sales divisions of both companies

42. Nicknames for organizations are capitalized.

> the Big Six accounting firms
> referred to IBM as Big Blue
> trading on the Big Board

People

43. The names and initials of persons are capitalized. If a name is hyphenated, both elements are capitalized. Particles forming the initial elements of surnames (such as *de, della, der, du, l', la, le, ten, ter, van,* and *von*) may or may not be capitalized, depending on the practice of the family or individual. However, the particle is always capitalized at the beginning of a sentence. The prefixes *Mac, Mc,* and *O'* are always capitalized.

> Cecil Day-Lewis
> Agnes de Mille
> Cecil B. DeMille
> Walter de la Mare
> Mark deW. Howe

Martin Van Buren
. . . of van Gogh's life. Van Gogh's technique is . . .

44. A nickname or epithet that either is added to or replaces the name of a person or thing is capitalized.

Babe Ruth	the Sun King
Stonewall Jackson	Deep Throat
Billy the Kid	Big Mama Thornton

A nickname or epithet placed between a person's first and last name is enclosed in quotation marks or parentheses or both. If it precedes the first name, it is sometimes enclosed in quotation marks but more often not.

Charlie "Bird" [*or* ("Bird") *or* (Bird)] Parker
Mother Maybelle Carter

45. Words of family relationship preceding or used in place of a person's name are capitalized; otherwise, they are lowercased.

Uncle Fred	her uncle's book
Mother's birthday	my mother's legacy

46. Words designating languages, nationalities, peoples, races, religious groups, and tribes are capitalized. Designations based on color are usually lowercased.

Spanish	Muslims
Spaniards	Assiniboin
Chinese	both blacks and whites
Asians	white, black, and Hispanic jurors

47. Corporate, professional, and governmental titles are capitalized when they immediately precede a person's name, unless the name is being used as an appositive.

President John Tyler

Professor Wendy Doniger of the University of Chicago

Senator William Fulbright of Arkansas

Arkansas's late former senator, William Fulbright

48. When corporate or governmental titles are used as part of a descriptive phrase to identify a person rather than as part of the name itself, the title is lowercased.

Marcia Ramirez, president of Logex Corp.

the president of Logex Corp., Marcia Ramirez

but

Logex Corp.'s prospects for the coming year were outlined by President Marcia Ramirez.

49. High governmental titles may be capitalized when used in place of individuals' names. In minutes and official records of proceedings, corporate or organizational titles are capitalized when used in place of individuals' names.

The Secretary of State objected.

The Judge will respond to questions in her chambers.

The Treasurer then stated his misgivings about the project.

but

The report reached the senator's desk yesterday.

The judge's rulings were widely criticized.

The co-op's treasurer, it turned out, had twice been convicted of embezzlement.

50. The word *president* may be capitalized whenever it refers to the U.S. presidency, but more commonly is capitalized only when it refers to a specific U.S. president.

It is the duty of the president [*or* President] to submit a budget to Congress.

The President's budget, due out on Wednesday, is being eagerly awaited.

51. Titles are capitalized when they are used in direct address.

> Is it very contagious, Doctor?
> You may call your next witness, Counselor.

Religious Terms

52. Words designating the supreme being are capitalized. Plural forms such as *gods, goddesses,* and *deities* are not.

Allah	the Almighty
Brahma	the Trinity
Jehovah	in the eyes of God
Yahweh	the angry gods

53. Personal pronouns referring to the supreme being are often capitalized, especially in religious writing. Relative pronouns (such as *who, whom,* and *whose*) usually are not.

> God gave His [*or* his] Son
> Allah, whose Prophet, Muhammad . . .

54. Traditional designations of apostles, prophets, and saints are capitalized.

the Madonna	the Twelve
the Prophet	St. John of the Cross
Moses the Lawgiver	John the Baptist

55. Names of religions, denominations, creeds and confessions, and religious orders are capitalized, as are adjectives and nouns derived from these names.

Judaism	Eastern Orthodox
Church of England	Islamic
Apostles' Creed	Jesuit teachers
Society of Jesus	a Buddhist

Full names of specific places of worship are capitalized, but terms such as *church, synagogue,* and *mosque* are lowercased when used alone. The word *church* is sometimes capitalized when it refers to the worldwide Catholic Church.

> Hunt Memorial Church
> the local Baptist church
> Beth Israel Synagogue
> services at the synagogue

56. Names of the Bible and other sacred works, their books and parts, and versions or editions of them are capitalized but not italicized. Adjectives derived from the names of sacred books are capitalized, except for the words *biblical* and *scriptural.*

> | | |
> |---|---|
> | Bible | biblical |
> | the Scriptures | Talmud |
> | Revised Standard Version | Talmudic |
> | Old Testament | Koran *or* Qur'an |
> | Book of Revelation | Koranic *or* Qur'anic |

57. The names of prayers and well-known passages of the Bible are capitalized.

> | | |
> |---|---|
> | the Ave Maria | Ten Commandments |
> | Lord's Prayer | Sermon on the Mount |
> | the Our Father | the Beatitudes |

Scientific Terms

58. Genus names in biological binomial nomenclature are capitalized; species names are lowercased, even when derived from a proper name. Both names are italicized.

> Both the wolf and the domestic dog are included in the genus *Canis.*
> The California condor (*Gymnogyps californianus*) is facing extinction.

The names of races, varieties, or subspecies are lowercased and italicized.

Hyla versicolor chrysoscelis
Otis asio naevius

59. The New Latin names of classes, families, and all groups above the genus level in zoology and botany are capitalized but not italicized. Their derivative nouns and adjectives are lowercased.

Gastropoda	gastropod
Thallophyta	thallophytic

60. The names, both scientific and informal, of planets and their satellites, stars, constellations, and other specific celestial objects are capitalized. However, except in technical writing, the words *sun, earth,* and *moon* are usually lowercased unless they occur with other astronomical names. A generic term that follows the name of a celestial object is usually lowercased.

Jupiter	Mars, Venus, and Earth
the North Star	life on earth
Andromeda	a voyage to the moon
Ursa Major	Halley's comet
the Little Dipper	

Names of meteorological phenomena are lowercased.

aurora australis
northern lights
parhelic circle

61. Terms that identify geological eons, eras, periods, systems, epochs, and strata are capitalized. The generic terms that follow them are lowercased.

Mesozoic era
Upper Cretaceous epoch
Quaternary period

in the Middle Ordovician
the Age of Reptiles

62 Proper names that are elements of the names of
scientific laws, theorems, and principles are capitalized, but the common nouns *law, theorem, theory,*
and the like are lowercased. In the names of popular or fanciful theories or observations, such words
are usually capitalized as well.

Mendel's law
the Pythagorean theorem
Occam's razor
Einstein's theory of relativity
Murphy's Law
the Peter Principle

63. The names of computer services and databases are
capitalized. Some names of computer languages
are written with an initial capital letter, some with
all letters capitalized, and some commonly both
ways. When in doubt, consult a dictionary.

America Online
World Wide Web
CompuServe
Microsoft Word
Pascal   *or*   PASCAL
BASIC
Internet   *or*   internet

Time Periods and Dates

64. The names of the days of the week, months of the
year, and holidays and holy days are capitalized.
Names of the seasons are lowercased.

Tuesday	Ramadan
June	Holy Week
Yom Kippur	last winter's storm
Veterans Day	

Titles of Works

65. Words in titles of books, magazines, newspapers, plays, movies, long poems, and works of art such as paintings and sculpture are capitalized except for internal articles, coordinating conjunctions, prepositions, and the *to* of infinitives. Prepositions of four or more letters are often capitalized. The entire title is italicized. For sacred works, see paragraph 56 on page 75.

> *Far from* [or *From*] *the Madding Crowd*
> Wolfe's *Of Time and the River*
> *Publishers Weekly*
> *USA Today*
> the original play *A Streetcar Named Desire*
> *All about* [or *About*] *Eve*, with Bette Davis
> Monet's *Water-Lily Pool,* in the Louvre
> Rodin's *Thinker*

The elements of hyphenated compounds in titles are usually capitalized, but articles, coordinating conjunctions, and prepositions are lowercased.

> *Knock-offs and Ready-to-Wear: The Low End of Fashion*
> *Politics in Early Seventeenth-Century England*

66. The first word following a colon in a title is capitalized.

> *Jane Austen: A Literary Life*

67. An initial article that is part of a title is capitalized and italicized. It is often omitted if it would be awkward in context.

> *The Oxford English Dictionary*
> the 20-volume *Oxford English Dictionary*

68. In the titles of newspapers, the city or local name is usually italicized, but the preceding *the* is usually not italicized or capitalized. (In newspaper writing, any *the* is generally capitalized, see example in paragraph 69 below.)

> reported in the *New York Times*
> last Thursday's *Atlanta Constitution*

09. Many periodicals, especially newspapers, do not use italics for titles, but instead either simply capitalize the important words of the title or, more commonly, capitalize the words and enclose the title in quotation marks.

> the NB. column in The Times Literary Supplement
> The Nobel committee singled out Walcott's book-length epic "Omeros."

70. The titles of articles in periodicals, short poems, short stories, essays, lectures, dissertations, chapters of books, episodes of radio and television programs, and novellas published in a collection are capitalized and enclosed in quotation marks. The capitalization of articles, conjunctions, and prepositions follows the rules explained in paragraph 65 above.

> an article on Rwanda, "After the Genocide," in the *New Yorker*
> Robert Frost's "Death of the Hired Man"
> O'Connor's story "Good Country People"
> "The Literature of Exhaustion," John Barth's seminal essay
> last Friday's lecture, "Labor's Task: A View for the Nineties"
> *The Jungle Book*'s ninth chapter is the well-known "Rikki-tikki-tavi."
> *M*A*S*H*'s final episode, "Goodbye, Farewell and Amen"

71. The titles of long musical compositions are generally capitalized and italicized; the titles of songs and other short compositions are capitalized and enclosed in quotation marks, as are the popular names of longer works. The titles of compositions identified primarily by their musical forms (such as

quartet, sonata, or *mass*) are capitalized only, as are movements identified by their tempo markings.

Mozart's *The Magic Flute*
Frank Loesser's *Guys and Dolls*
"The Lady Is a Tramp"
Beethoven's "Für Elise"
the Piano Sonata in C-sharp minor, Op. 27, No. 2, or "Moonlight" Sonata
Symphony No. 104 in D major
Brahms's Violin Concerto in D
the Adagietto movement from Mahler's Fifth Symphony

72. Common titles of book sections (such as *preface, introduction,* or *index*) are usually capitalized when they refer to a section of the same book in which the reference is made. Otherwise, they are usually lowercased. (For numbered sections of books, see paragraph 39 on page 70.)

See the Appendix for further information.
In the introduction to her book, the author explains her goals.

Trademarks

73. Registered trademarks, service marks, collective marks, and brand names are capitalized. They do not normally require any further acknowledgment of their special status.

Frisbee	Jacuzzi	Levi's
Coke	Kleenex	Vaseline
College Board	Velcro	Dumpster
Realtor	Xerox	Scotch tape
Walkman	Band-Aid	Teflon

Transportation

74. The names of individual ships, submarines, airplanes, satellites, and space vehicles are capitalized

and italicized. The designations *U.S.S., S.S., M.V.,* and *H.M.S.* are not italicized.

> *Challenger*
> *Enola Gay*
> H.M.S. *Bounty*

The names of train lines, types of aircraft, and space programs are not italicized.

> Metroliner
> Boeing 727
> Pathfinder Program

Other Styling Conventions

1. Foreign words and phrases that have not been fully adopted into English are italicized. In general, any word that appears in the main section of *Merriam-Webster's Collegiate Dictionary* does not need to be italicized.

   > These accomplishments will serve as a monument, *aere perennius,* to the group's skill and dedication.
   > "The cooking here is *wunderbar!*"
   > The prix fixe lunch was $20.
   > The committee meets on an ad hoc basis.

   A complete foreign-language sentence (such as a motto) can also be italicized. However, long sentences are usually treated as quotations; that is, they are set in roman type and enclosed in quotation marks. (For details, see paragraph 6 on page 45.)

   > The inscription *Honi soit qui mal y pense* encircles the seal.

2. In nonfiction writing, unfamiliar words or words that have a specialized meaning are set in italics on

their first appearance, especially when accompanied by a short definition. Once these words have been introduced and defined, they are not italicized in subsequent references.

> *Vitiligo* is a condition in which skin pigment cells stop making pigment. Vitiligo usually affects . . .
> Another method is the *direct-to-consumer* transaction, in which the publisher markets directly to the individual by mail or door-to-door.

3. Italics are often used to indicate words referred to as words. However, if the word was actually spoken, it is usually enclosed in quotation marks instead.

> Purists still insist that *data* is a plural noun.
> *Only* can also be an adverb, as in "I *only* tried to help."
> We heard his warning, but we weren't sure what "repercussions" meant in that context.

4. Italics are often used for letters referred to as letters, particularly when they are shown in lowercase.

> You should dot your *i*'s and cross your *t*'s.

If the letter is being used to refer to its sound and not its printed form, slashes or brackets are used instead of italics in technical contexts.

> The pure /p/ sound is rarely heard in the mountain dialect.

A letter used to indicate a shape is capitalized but not italicized. Such letters are often set in sans-serif type.

> an A-frame house
> the I beam
> Churchill's famous V sign
> forming a giant X

5. Italics are often used to show numerals referred to as numerals. However, if there is no chance of confusion, they are usually not italicized.

The first *2* and the last *1* are barely legible.
Anyone whose ticket number ends in 4 or 6 will win a door prize.

6. Italics are used to emphasize or draw attention to words in a sentence.

Students must notify the dean's office *in writing* of any added or dropped courses.
It was not *the* model for the project, but merely *a* model.

7. Italics are used to indicate a word created to suggest a sound.

Its call is a harsh, drawn-out *kreee-awww*.

8. Individual letters are sometimes italicized when used for lists within sentences or for identifying elements in an illustration.

providing information about *(a)* typing, *(b)* transcribing, *(c)* formatting, and *(d)* graphics
located at point *A* on the diagram

9. Commas, colons, and semicolons that follow italicized words are usually italicized.

the Rabbit tetralogy *(Rabbit Run, Rabbit Redux, Rabbit Is Rich,* and *Rabbit at Rest); Bech: A Book; S;* and others

However, question marks, exclamation points, quotation marks, and apostrophes are not italicized unless they are part of an italicized title.

Did you see the latest issue of *Newsweek*?
Despite the greater success of *Oklahoma!* and *South Pacific,* Rodgers was fondest of *Carousel.*
"Over Christmas vacation he finished *War and Peace.*"
Students always mistake the old script *s*'s for *f*'s.

Parentheses and brackets may be italicized if most of the words they enclose are also italicized, or if both the first and last words are italicized.

(see also Limited Partnership)
[German, *Dasein*]
(and is replaced throughout by *&)*

10. Full capitalization is occasionally used for emphasis
    or to indicate that a speaker is talking very loudly.
    It is avoided in formal writing, where italics are far
    more often used for emphasis.

    > Term papers received after Friday, May 18, WILL BE
    > RETURNED UNREAD.
    > Scalpers mingled in the noisy crowd yelling "SIXTY
    > DOLLARS!"

11. The text of signs, labels, and inscriptions may be re-
    produced in various ways.

    > a poster reading SPECIAL THRILLS COMING
    > SOON
    > a gate bearing the infamous motto "Arbeit macht
    > frei"
    > a Do Not Disturb sign
    > a barn with an old CHEW MAIL POUCH ad on the side
    > the stop sign

12. *Small capitals,* identical to large capitals but usually
    about the height of a lowercase *x,* are commonly
    used for era designations and computer com-
    mands. They may also be used for cross-references,
    for headings in constitutions and bylaws, and for
    speakers in a dramatic dialogue.

    > The dwellings date from A.D. 200 or earlier.
    > Press ALT+CTRL+PLUS SIGN on the numeric keyboard.
    > (See LETTERS AS LETTERS, page 162.)
    > SECTION IV. The authority for parliamentary proce-
    > dure in meetings of the Board . . .
    > LADY WISHFORT. O dear, has my Nephew made his
    > Addresses to Millamant? I order'd him.
    > FOIBLE. Sir Wilfull is set in to drinking, Madam, in the
    > Parlour.

13. *Underlining* indicates italics in typed material. It is almost never seen in typeset text.

14. *Boldface* type has traditionally been used primarily for headings and captions. It is sometimes also used in place of italics for terminology introduced in the text, especially for terms that are accompanied by definitions; for cross-references; for headwords in listings such as glossaries, gazetteers, and bibliographies; and for page references in indexes that locate a specific kind of material, such as illustrations, tables, or the main discussions of a given topic. (In mathematical texts, arrays, tensors, vectors, and matrix notation are standardly set bold as well.)

> **Application Forms and Tests** Many offices require applicants to fill out an employment form. Bring a copy . . .
> **Figure 4.2: The Electromagnetic Spectrum**
> The two axes intersect at a point called the **origin**.
> See **Medical Records**, page 123.
>
> **antecedent:** the noun to which a pronoun refers
> **appositive:** a word, phrase, or clause that is equivalent to a preceding noun
>
> Records, medical, **123–37**, 178, 243
> Referrals, **38–40**, 139

Punctuation that follows boldface type is set bold when it is part of a heading or heading-like text; otherwise it is generally set roman.

> **Table 9:** Metric Conversion
> **Warning:** This and similar medications . . .
> Excellent fourth-quarter earnings were reported by the pharmaceutical giants **Abbott Laboratories**, **Glaxo Wellcome**, and **Merck**.

3 Plurals, Possessives, and Compounds

This chapter describes the ways in which plurals, possessives, and compounds are most commonly formed.

In regard to plurals and compounds, consulting a dictionary will solve many of the problems discussed in this chapter. A good college dictionary, such as *Merriam-Webster's Collegiate Dictionary,* will provide plural forms for any common word, as well as a large number of permanent compounds. Any dictionary much smaller than the *Collegiate* will often be more frustrating in what it fails to show than helpful in what it shows.

Plurals

The basic rules for writing plurals of English words, stated in paragraph 1, apply in the vast majority of cases. The succeeding paragraphs treat the categories of words whose plurals are most apt to raise questions.

Most good dictionaries give thorough coverage to irregular and variant plurals, and many of the rules provided here are reflected in the dictionary entries.

The symbol → is used here to link the singular and plural forms.

1. The plurals of most English words are formed by adding -*s* to the singular. If the noun ends in -*s*, -*x*, -*z*, -*ch*, or -*sh*, so that an extra syllable must be added in order to pronounce the plural, -*es* is added. If the noun ends in a -*y* preceded by a consonant, the -*y* is changed to -*i* and -*es* is added.

> voter → voters
> anticlimax → anticlimaxes
> blitz → blitzes
> blowtorch → blowtorches
> calabash → calabashes
> allegory → allegories

Abbreviations

2. The plurals of abbreviations are commonly formed by adding -*s* or -*'s;* however, there are some significant exceptions. (For details, see paragraphs 1–5 on pages 120–21.)

> yr. → yrs.   M.B.A. → M.B.A.'s
> TV → TVs   p. → pp.

Animals

3. The names of many fishes, birds, and mammals have both a plural formed with a suffix and one that is identical with the singular. Some have only one or the other.

> bass → bass   *or*   basses
> partridge → partridge   *or*   partridges
> sable → sables   *or*   sable
> lion → lions
> sheep → sheep

Many of the animals that have both plural forms are ones that are hunted, fished, or trapped; those who hunt, fish for, and trap them are most likely to use the unchanged form. The -*s* form is often used to emphasize diversity of kinds.

> caught three bass
> *but*
> basses of the Atlantic Ocean
> a place where antelope feed
> *but*
> antelopes of Africa and southwest Asia

Compounds and Phrases

4. Most compounds made up of two nouns—whether they appear as one word, two words, or a hyphenated word—form their plurals by pluralizing the final element only.

> courthouse → courthouses
> judge advocate → judge advocates
> player-manager → player-managers

5. The plural form of a compound consisting of an *-er* noun and an adverb is made by pluralizing the noun element only.

> runner-up → runners-up
> onlooker → onlookers
> diner-out → diners-out
> passerby → passersby

6. Nouns made up of words that are not nouns form their plurals on the last element.

> show-off → show-offs
> pushover → pushovers
> tie-in → tie-ins
> lineup → lineups

7. Plurals of compounds that consist of two nouns separated by a preposition are normally formed by pluralizing the first noun.

> sister-in-law → sisters-in-law
> attorney-at-law → attorneys-at-law

power of attorney → powers of attorney
chief of staff → chiefs of staff
grant-in-aid → grants-in-aid

8. Compounds that consist of two nouns separated by a preposition and a modifier form their plurals in various ways.

snake in the grass → snakes in the grass
justice of the peace → justices of the peace
jack-in-the-box → jack-in-the-boxes
                    or jacks-in-the-box
will-o'-the wisp → will-o'-the-wisps

9. Compounds consisting of a noun followed by an adjective are usually pluralized by adding -s to the noun. If the adjective tends to be understood as a noun, the compound may have more than one plural form.

attorney general → attorneys general
                    or attorney generals
sergeant major → sergeants major
                    or sergeant majors
poet laureate → poets laureate or poet laureates
heir apparent → heirs apparent
knight-errant → knights-errant

Foreign Words and Phrases

10. Many nouns of foreign origin retain the foreign plural. However, most also have a regular English plural.

alumnus → alumni
genus → genera
crisis → crises
criterion → criteria
appendix → appendixes or appendices
concerto → concerti or concertos
symposium → symposia or symposiums

11. Phrases of foreign origin may have a foreign plural, an English plural, or both.

> pièce de résistance → pièces de résistance
> hors d'oeuvre → hors d'oeuvres
> beau monde → beau mondes *or* beaux mondes

Irregular Plurals

12. A few English nouns form their plurals by changing one or more of their vowels, or by adding *-en* or *-ren*.

foot → feet	woman → women
goose → geese	tooth → teeth
louse → lice	ox → oxen
man → men	child → children
mouse → mice	

13. Some nouns do not change form in the plural. (See also paragraph 3 above.)

series → series	corps → corps
politics → politics	species → species

14. Some nouns ending in *-f, -fe,* and *-ff* have plurals that end in *-ves.* Some of these also have regularly formed plurals.

> elf → elves
> loaf → loaves
> scarf → scarves *or* scarfs
> wife → wives
> staff → staffs *or* staves

Italic Elements

15. Italicized words, phrases, abbreviations, and letters are usually pluralized by adding *-s* or *-'s* in roman type. (See also paragraphs 16, 21, and 26 below.)

three *Fortune*s missing from the stack
a couple of *Gravity's Rainbow*s in stock
used too many *etc.*'s in the report
a row of *x*'s

Letters

16. The plurals of letters are usually formed by adding
-'s, although capital letters are often pluralized by
adding -s alone.

p's and q's
V's of migrating geese   *or*   Vs of migrating geese
dot your *i*'s
straight As   *or*   straight A's

Numbers

17. Numerals are pluralized by adding -s or, less commonly, -'s.

two par 5s   *or*   two par 5's
1990s   *or*   1990's
in the 80s   *or*   in the 80's   *or*   in the '80s
the mid-$20,000s   *or*   the mid-$20,000's

18. Written-out numbers are pluralized by adding -s.

all the fours and eights
scored three tens

Proper Nouns

19. The plurals of proper nouns are usually formed
with -s or -es.

Clarence → Clarences
Jones → Joneses
Fernandez → Fernandezes

20. Plurals of proper nouns ending in -y usually retain
the -y and add -s.

Sunday → Sundays
Timothy → Timothys
Camry → Camrys

Words ending in -*y* that were originally proper nouns are usually pluralized by changing -*y* to -*i* and adding -*es*, but a few retain the -*y*.

bobby → bobbies
johnny → johnnies
Tommy → Tommies
Bloody Mary → Bloody Marys

Quoted Elements

21. The plural of words in quotation marks are formed by adding -*s* or -*'s* within the quotation marks, or -*s* outside the quotation marks. (See also paragraph 26 below.)

too many "probably's" [*or* "probablys"] in the statement
one "you" among millions of "you"s
a record number of "I can't recall"s

Symbols

22. When symbols are referred to as physical characters, the plural is formed by adding either -*s* or -*'s*.

printed three *s
used &'s instead of *and*'s
his π's are hard to read

Words Ending in *-ay*, *-ey*, and *-oy*

23. Words that end in -*ay*, -*ey*, or -*oy*, unlike other words ending in -*y*, are pluralized by simply adding -*s*.

castaways
donkeys
envoys

Words Ending in *-ful*

24. Any noun ending in *-ful* can be pluralized by adding *-s*, but most also have an alternative plural with *-s* preceding the suffix.

> handful → handfuls
> teaspoonful → teaspoonfuls
> armful → armfuls *or* armsful
> bucketful → bucketfuls *or* bucketsful

Words Ending in *-o*

25. Most words ending in *-o* are normally pluralized by adding *-s*. However, some words ending in *-o* preceded by a consonant take *-es* plurals.

> solo → solos
> photo → photos
> tomato → tomatoes
> potato → potatoes
> hobo → hoboes
> hero → heroes
> cargo → cargoes *or* cargos
> proviso → provisos *or* provisoes
> halo → haloes *or* halos
> echo → echoes
> motto → mottoes

Words Used as Words

26. Words referred to as words and italicized usually form their plurals by adding *-'s* in roman type. (See also paragraph 21 above.)

> five *and*'s in one sentence
> all those *wherefore*'s and *howsoever*'s

When a word referred to as a word has become part of a fixed phrase, the plural is usually formed by adding *-s* without the apostrophe.

oohs and aahs
dos and don'ts   *or*   do's and don'ts

Possessives

Common Nouns

1. The possessive of singular and plural common nouns that do not end in an *s* or *z* sound is formed by adding -*'s* to the end of the word.

   the child's skates
   women's voices
   the cat's dish
   this patois's range
   people's opinions
   the criteria's common theme

2. The possessive of singular nouns ending in an *s* or *z* sound is usually formed by adding -*'s*. A less common alternative is to add -*'s* only when it is easily pronounced; if it would create a word that is difficult to pronounce, only an apostrophe is added.

   the witness's testimony
   the disease's course
   the race's sponsors
   the prize's recipient
   rickets's symptoms   *or*   rickets' symptoms

   A multisyllabic singular noun that ends in an *s* or *z* sound drops the -*s* if it is followed by a word beginning with an *s* or *z* sound.

   for appearance' sake
   for goodness' sake

3. The possessive of plural nouns ending in an *s* or *z* sound is formed by adding only an apostrophe.

However, the possessive of one-syllable irregular plurals is usually formed by adding -'s.

dogs' leashes   buyers' guarantees
birds' migrations   lice's lifespans

Proper Names

4. The possessives of proper names are generally formed in the same way as those of common nouns. The possessive of singular proper names is formed by adding -'s.

> Jane's rules of behavior
> three books of Carla's
> Tom White's presentation
> Paris's cafes

The possessive of plural proper names, and of some singular proper names ending in an *s* or *z* sound, is made by adding just an apostrophe.

> the Stevenses' reception
> the Browns' driveway
> Massachusetts' capital
> New Orleans' annual festival
> the United States' trade deficit
> Protosystems' president

5. The possessive of singular proper names ending in an *s* or *z* sound may be formed by adding either -'s or just an apostrophe. Adding -'s to all such names, without regard for the pronunciation of the resulting word, is more common than adding just the apostrophe. (For exceptions see paragraph 6 below.)

> Jones's car   *or*   Jones' car
> Bliss's statue   *or*   Bliss' statue
> Dickens's novels   *or*   Dickens' novels

6. The possessive form of classical and biblical names of two or more syllables ending in -s or -es is usually made by adding just an apostrophe. If the name has only one syllable, the possessive form is made by adding -'s.

Socrates' students   Elias' prophecy
Claudius' reign   Zeus's warnings
Ramses' kingdom   Cis's sons

The possessives of the names *Jesus* and *Moses* are always formed with just an apostrophe.

Jesus' disciples
Moses' law

7. The possessive of names ending in a silent -s, -z, or -x are usually formed with -'s.

Des Moines's recreation department
Josquin des Prez's music
Delacroix's painting

8. When the possessive ending is added to an italicized name, it is not italicized.

East of Eden's main characters
the *Spirit of St. Louis*'s historic flight
Brief Encounter's memorable ending

Pronouns

9. The possessive of indefinite pronouns is formed by adding -'s.

anyone's rights
everybody's money
someone's coat
somebody's wedding
one's own
either's preference

Some indefinite pronouns usually require an *of* phrase to indicate possession.

> the rights of each
> the inclination of many
> the satisfaction of all

10. Possessive pronouns do not include apostrophes.

> mine   hers
> ours   his
> yours   theirs
> its

Miscellaneous Styling Conventions

11. No apostrophe is generally used today with plural nouns that are more descriptive than possessive.

> weapons systems
> managers meeting
> singles bar
> steelworkers union
> awards banquet

12. The possessive form of a phrase is made by adding an apostrophe or -'s to the last word in the phrase.

> his father-in-law's assistance
> board of directors' meeting
> from the student of politics' point of view
> after a moment or so's thought

Constructions such as these are often rephrased.

> from the point of view of the student of politics
> after thinking for a moment or so

13. The possessive form of words in quotation marks can be formed in two ways, with -'s placed either inside the quotation marks or outside them.

> the "Marseillaise"'s [*or* "Marseillaise's"] stirring melody

Since both arrangements look awkward, this construction is usually avoided.

> the stirring melody of the "Marseillaise"

14. Possessives of abbreviations are formed like those of nouns that are spelled out. The singular possessive is formed by adding -'s; the plural possessive, by adding an apostrophe only.

> the IRS's ruling
> AT&T's long-distance service
> IBM Corp.'s annual report
> Eli Lilly & Co.'s chairman
> the HMOs' lobbyists

15. The possessive of nouns composed of numerals is formed in the same way as for other nouns. The possessive of singular nouns is formed by adding -'s; the possessive of plural nouns is formed by adding an apostrophe only.

> 1996's commencement speaker
> the 1920s' greatest jazz musicians

16. Individual possession is indicated by adding -'s to each noun in a sequence. Joint possession may be indicated in the same way, but is most commonly indicated by adding an apostrophe or -'s to the last noun in the sequence.

> Joan's and Emily's friends
> Jim's, Ed's, and Susan's reports
> her mother and father's anniversary
> Peter and Jan's trip *or* Peter's and Jan's trip

Compounds

A compound is a word or word group that consists of two or more parts that work together as a unit to express a specific concept. Compounds can be formed by combining two or more words (as in *double-check*, *cost-effective*, *farmhouse*, *graphic equalizer*, *park bench*, *around-the-clock*, or *son of a gun*), by combining prefixes or suffixes with words (as in *ex-president*, *shoeless*, *presorted*, or *uninterruptedly*), or by combining two or more word elements (as in *macrophage* or *photochromism*). Compounds are written in one of three ways: solid (as in cottonmouth), hyphenated (*screenwriter-director*), or open (*health care*). Because of the variety of standard practice, the choice among these styles for a given compound represents one of the most common and vexing of all style issues that writers encounter.

A good dictionary will list many *permanent compounds*, compounds so commonly used that they have become permanent parts of the language. It will not list *temporary compounds*, those created to meet a writer's need at a particular moment. Most compounds whose meanings are self-evident from the meanings of their component words will not be listed, even if they are permanent and quite widely used. Writers thus cannot rely wholly on dictionaries to guide them in writing compounds.

One approach is to hyphenate all compounds not in the dictionary, since hyphenation immediately identifies them as compounds. But hyphenating all such compounds runs counter to some well-established American practice and can therefore call too much attention to the compound and momentarily distract the reader. Another approach (which applies only to compounds whose elements are complete words) is to leave open any compound not in the dictionary. Though this is widely done, it can result in the reader's failing to recognize a compound for what it is. A third approach is to pattern the compound after other similar ones. Though this approach is likely to be more complicated, it can make the compound look more familiar and thus less distracting or confusing. The paragraphs that follow are intended to help you use this approach.

As a general rule, writing meant for readers in specialized fields usually does not hyphenate compounds, especially technical terminology.

Compound Nouns

Compound nouns are combinations of words that function in a sentence as nouns. They may consist of two or more nouns, a noun and a modifier, or two or more elements that are not nouns.

Short compounds consisting of two nouns often begin as open compounds but tend to close up as they become familiar.

1. **noun + noun** Compounds composed of two nouns that are short and commonly used, of which the first is accented, are usually written solid.

farmhouse	paycheck
hairbrush	football
lifeboat	workplace

2. When a noun + noun compound is short and common but pronounced with nearly equal stress on both nouns, it is more likely to be open.

fuel oil	health care
park bench	desk lamp

3. Noun + noun compounds that consist of longer nouns and are self-evident or temporary are usually written open.

   costume designer
   computer terminal
   billiard table

4. When a noun + noun compound describes a double title or double function, the compound is hyphenated.

   hunter-gatherer
   secretary-treasurer
   bar-restaurant

Sometimes a slash is used in place of the hyphen.

> bar/restaurant

5. Compounds formed from a noun or adjective followed by *man, woman, person,* or *people* and denoting an occupation are normally solid.

anchorman	spokesperson
congresswoman	salespeople

6. Compounds that are units of measurement are hyphenated.

foot-pound	column-inch
kilowatt-hour	light-year

7. **adjective + noun** Most adjective + noun compounds are written open.

municipal court	minor league
genetic code	nuclear medicine
hazardous waste	basic training

8. Adjective + noun compounds consisting of two short words are often written solid when the first word is accented. However, some are usually written open, and a few are hyphenated.

notebook	dry cleaner
bluebird	steel mill
shortcut	two-step

9. **participle + noun** Most participle + noun compounds are written open.

landing craft	barbed wire
frying pan	preferred stock
sounding board	informed consent

10. **noun's + noun** Compounds consisting of a possessive noun followed by another noun are usually written open; a few are hyphenated. Compounds

of this type that have become solid have lost the apostrophe.

fool's gold	cat's-paw
hornet's nest	bull's-eye
seller's market	foolscap
Queen Anne's lace	menswear

11. **noun + verb + -er or -ing** Compounds in which the first noun is the object of the verb are most often written open but sometimes hyphenated. Permanent compounds like these are sometimes written solid.

problem solver	fund-raiser
deal making	gene-splicing
air conditioner	lifesaving

12. **object + verb** Noun compounds consisting of a verb preceded by a noun that is its object are written in various ways.

fish fry	bodyguard
eye-opener	roadblock

13. **verb + object** A few, mostly older compounds are formed from a verb followed by a noun that is its object; they are written solid.

cutthroat	carryall
breakwater	pickpocket

14. **noun + adjective** Compounds composed of a noun followed by an adjective are written open or hyphenated.

sum total	president-elect
consul general	secretary-general

15. **particle + noun** Compounds consisting of a particle (usually a preposition or adverb) and a noun

are usually written solid, especially when they are short and the first syllable is accented.

downturn	undertone
outfield	upswing
input	afterthought
outpatient	onrush

A few particle + noun compounds, especially when composed of longer elements or having equal stress on both elements, are hyphenated or open.

on-ramp	off year
cross-reference	cross fire

16. **verb + particle; verb + adverb** These compounds may be hyphenated or solid. Compounds with particles such as *to, in,* and *on* are often hyphenated. Compounds with particles such as *up, off,* and *out* are hyphenated or solid with about equal frequency. Those with longer particles or adverbs are usually solid.

lean-to	spin-off
trade-in	payoff
add-on	time-out
start-up	turnout
backup	hideaway

17. **verb + -er + particle; verb + -ing + particle** Except for *passerby,* these compounds are hyphenated.

runner-up	carrying-on
diners-out	talking-to
listener-in	falling-out

18. **letter + noun** Compounds formed from a single letter (or sometimes a combination of them) followed by a noun are either open or hyphenated.

T square	T-shirt
B vitamin	f-stop

V neck	H-bomb
Rh factor	A-frame
D major	E-mail *or* e-mail

19. **Compounds of three or four elements** Compounds of three or four words may be either hyphenated or open. Those incorporating prepositional phrases are more often open; others are usually hyphenated.

editor in chief	right-of-way
power of attorney	jack-of-all-trades
flash in the pan	give-and-take
base on balls	rough-and-tumble

20. **Reduplication compounds** Compounds that are formed by reduplication and so consist of two similar-sounding elements are hyphenated if each element has more than one syllable. If each element has only one syllable, the compound is often written solid. Very short words and newly coined words are more often hyphenated.

namby-pamby	singsong
razzle-dazzle	sci-fi
crisscross	hip-hop

Compound Adjectives

Compound adjectives are combinations of words that work together to modify a noun—that is, they work as *unit modifiers*. As unit modifiers they can be distinguished from other strings of adjectives that may also precede a noun.

For instance, in "a low, level tract of land" the two adjectives each modify the noun separately; the tract is both low and level. These are *coordinate* (i.e., equal) *modifiers*. In "a low monthly fee" the first adjective modifies the noun plus the second adjective; the phrase denotes a monthly fee that is low. It could not be revised to "a monthly and low fee" without altering or confusing its meaning. Thus, these are *noncoordinate modifiers*. However, "low-level radiation" does not mean radiation that is low and level or level radiation that is low, but rather radiation that is at a low level. Both words work as a unit to modify the noun.

Unit modifiers are usually hyphenated, in order to help readers grasp the relationship of the words and to avoid confusion. The hyphen in "a call for more-specialized controls" removes any ambiguity as to which word *more* modifies. By contrast, the lack of a hyphen in a phrase like "graphic arts exhibition" may give it an undesirable ambiguity.

21. **Before the noun (attributive position)** Most two-word compound adjectives are hyphenated when placed before the noun.

> the fresh-cut grass
> its longer-lasting effects
> her lace-trimmed dress
> a made-up excuse
> his best-selling novel
> projected health-care costs

22. Compounds whose first word is an adverb ending in -*ly* are usually left open.

> a privately chartered boat
> politically correct opinions
> its weirdly skewed perspective
> a tumultuously cascading torrent

23. Compounds formed of an adverb not ending in -*ly* followed by a participle (or sometimes an adjective) are usually hyphenated when placed before a noun.

> the well-worded statement
> more-stringent measures
> his less-exciting prospects
> their still-awaited assignments
> her once-famous uncle

24. The combination of *very* + adjective is not a unit modifier. (See also paragraph 33 below.)

    a very happy baby

25. When a compound adjective is formed by using a compound noun to modify another noun, it is usually hyphenated.

    a hazardous-waste site
    the basic-training period
    a minor-league pitcher
    a roll-call vote
    their problem-solving abilities

    Some familiar open compound nouns are frequently left open when used as adjectives.

    a high school diploma   *or*   a high-school diploma
    a real estate license   *or*   a real-estate license
    an income tax refund   *or*   an income-tax refund

26. A proper name used as a modifier is not hyphenated. A word that modifies the proper name is attached by a hyphen (or an en dash in typeset material).

    the Civil War era
    a New England tradition
    a *New York Times* article
    the Supreme Court decision
    the splendid *Gone with the Wind* premiere
    a Los Angeles–based company
    a Pulitzer Prize–winning author
    pre–Bull Run skirmishes

27. Compound adjectives composed of foreign words are not hyphenated when placed before a noun unless they are hyphenated in the foreign language itself.

    per diem expenses
    an ad hoc committee
    her *faux-naïf* style

a comme il faut arrangement
the a cappella chorus
a ci-devant professor

28. Compounds that are quoted, capitalized, or italicized are not hyphenated.

a "Springtime in Paris" theme
the book's "I'm OK, you're OK" tone
his AMERICA FIRST sign
the *No smoking* notice

29. Chemical names and most medical names used as modifiers are not hyphenated.

a sodium hypochlorite bleach
the amino acid sequence
a new Parkinson's disease medication

30. Compound adjectives of three or more words are hyphenated when they precede the noun.

step-by-step instructions
state-of-the-art equipment
a wait-and-see attitude
a longer-than-expected list
turn-of-the-century medicine

31. **Following the noun** When a compound adjective follows the noun it modifies, it usually ceases to be a unit modifier and is therefore no longer hyphenated.

instructions that guide you step by step
a list that was longer than expected

However, a compound that follows the noun it modifies often keeps its hyphen if it continues to function as a unit modifier, especially if its first element is a noun.

hikers who were ill-advised to cross the glacier
an actor too high-strung to relax
industries that could be called low-tech

metals that are corrosion-resistant
tends to be accident-prone

32. Permanent compound adjectives are usually written as they appear in the dictionary even when they follow the noun they modify.

for reasons that are well-known
a plan we regarded as half-baked
The problems are mind-boggling.

However, compound adjectives of three or more words are normally not hyphenated when they follow the noun they modify, since they usually cease to function as adjectives.

These remarks are off the record.
medical practice of the turn of the century

When compounds of three or more words appear as hyphenated adjectives in dictionaries, the hyphens are retained as long as the phrase is being used as a unit modifier.

The candidate's position was middle-of-the-road.

33. When an adverb modifies another adverb that is the first element of a compound modifier, the compound may lose its hyphen. If the first adverb modifies the whole compound, however, the hyphen is retained.

a very well developed idea
but
a delightfully well-written book
a most ill-timed event

34. Adjective compounds that are color names in which each element can function as a noun are almost always hyphenated.

red-orange fabric
The fabric was red-orange.

Color names in which the first element can only be an adjective are often unhyphenated before a noun and usually unhyphenated after

a bright red tie
the pale yellow-green chair
reddish orange fabric   *or*   reddish-orange fabric
The fabric was reddish orange.

35. Compound modifiers that include a number followed by a noun (except for the noun *percent*) are hyphenated when they precede the noun they modify, but usually not when they follow it. (For details on measurement, see paragraph 42 on page 156.)

the four-color press
a 12-foot-high fence
a fence 12 feet high
a 300-square-mile area
an area of 300 square miles
  but
a 10 percent raise

If a currency symbol precedes the number, the hyphen is omitted.

an $8.5 million deficit

36. An adjective composed of a number followed by a noun in the possessive is not hyphenated.

a nine days' wonder
a two weeks' wait
  but
a two-week wait

Compound Adverbs

37. Adverb compounds consisting of preposition + noun are almost always written solid. However, there are a few important exceptions.

> downstairs
> uphill
> offshore
> overnight
> *but*
> in-house
> off-key
> on-line

38. Compound adverbs of more than two words are usually written open, and they usually follow the words they modify.

> here and there
> more or less
> head and shoulders
> hand in hand
> every which way
> once and for all
> *but*
> a more-or-less certain result

A few three-word adverbs are usually hyphenated, but many are written open even if the corresponding adjective is hyphenated.

> placed back-to-back
> met face-to-face
> *but*
> a word-for-word quotation
> quoted word for word
> software bought off the shelf

Compound Verbs

39. Two-word verbs consisting of a verb followed by an adverb or a preposition are written open.

> follow up   take on
> roll back   run across
> strike out   set back

40. A compound composed of a particle followed by a verb is written solid.

overlook	undercut
outfit	download

41. A verb derived from an open or hyphenated compound noun is hyphenated.

double-space	water-ski
rubber-stamp	field-test

42. A verb derived from a solid noun is written solid.

mastermind	brainstorm
highlight	sideline

Compounds Formed with Word Elements

Many new and temporary compounds are formed by adding word elements to existing words or by combining word elements. There are three basic kinds of word elements: prefixes (such as *anti-, non-, pre-, post-, re-, super-*), suffixes (such as *-er, -fold, -ism, -ist, -less, -ness*), and combining forms (such as *mini-, macro-, pseudo-, -graphy, -logy*). Prefixes and suffixes are usually attached to existing words; combining forms are usually combined to form new words.

43. **prefix + word** Except as specified in the paragraphs below, compounds formed from a prefix and a word are usually written solid.

anticrime	subzero
nonaligned	superheroine
premedical	transnational
reorchestration	postdoctoral

44. If the prefix ends with a vowel and the word it is attached to begins with the same vowel, the compound is usually hyphenated.

anti-incumbent	semi-independent
de-escalate	intra-arterial
co-organizer	pre-engineered

However, there are many exceptions.

> reelect
> preestablished
> cooperate

45. If the base word or compound to which a prefix is added is capitalized, the resulting compound is almost always hyphenated.

> pre-Victorian
> anti-Western
> post-Darwinian
> non-English-speaking
> > *but*
> transatlantic
> transalpine

If the prefix and the base word together form a new proper name, the compound may be solid with the prefix capitalized.

> Postimpressionists
> Precambrian
> > *but*
> Pre-Raphaelite

46. Compounds made with *ex-*, in its "former" sense, and *self-* are hyphenated.

> ex-mayor   self-control
> ex-husband   self-sustaining

Compounds formed from *vice-* are usually hyphenated. Some permanent compounds are open.

> vice-chair   vice president
> vice-consul   vice admiral

A temporary compound with *quasi(-)* or *pseudo(-)* may be written open (if *quasi* or *pseudo* is being treated as a modifier) or hyphenated (if it is being treated as a combining form).

quasi intellectual   *or*   quasi-intellectual
pseudo liberal   *or*   pseudo-liberal

47. If a prefix is added to a hyphenated compound, it
    may be either followed by a hyphen or closed up
    solid to the next element. Permanent compounds
    of this kind should be checked in a dictionary.

    unair-conditioned
    ultra-up-to-date
    non-self-governing
    unself-confident

48. If a prefix is added to an open compound, the hy-
    phen is often replaced by an en dash in typeset ma-
    terial.

    ex–campaign treasurer
    post–World War I era

49. A compound that would be identical with another
    word if written solid is usually hyphenated to pre-
    vent misreading.

    a re-creation of the setting
    shopped at the co-op
    multi-ply fabric

50. Compounds that might otherwise be solid are
    often hyphenated in order to clarify their forma-
    tion, meaning, or pronunciation.

tri-city	non-news
de-iced	anti-fur
re-oil	pro-choice

51. When prefixes are attached to numerals, the com-
    pounds are hyphenated.

    pre-1995 models
    post-1945 economy
    non-19th-century architecture

52. Compounds created from proper ethnic or national combining forms are hyphenated when the second element is an independent word, but solid when it is a combining form.

Anglo-Saxon	Anglophile
Judeo-Christian	Francophone
Sino-Japanese	Sinophobe

53. Prefixes that are repeated in the same compound are separated by a hyphen.

    re-refried
    post-postmodern

54. Compounds consisting of different prefixes or adjectives with the same base word which are joined by *and* or *or* are shortened by pruning the first compound back to a hyphenated prefix.

    pre- and postoperative care
    anti- or pro-Revolutionary sympathies
    over- and underachievers
    early- and mid-20th-century painters
    4-, 6-, and 8-foot lengths

55. **word + suffix** Except as noted in the paragraphs below, compounds formed by adding a suffix to a word are written solid.

Fourierism	characterless
benightedness	custodianship
yellowish	easternmost

56. Compounds made with a suffix or a terminal combining form are often hyphenated if the base word is more than two syllables long, if it ends with the same letter the suffix begins with, or if it is a proper name.

industry-wide	jewel-like
recession-proof	Hollywood-ish
American-ness	Europe-wide

57. Compounds made from a number + -odd are hyphenated. A number + -fold is written solid if the number is spelled out but hyphenated if it is in numerals.

> fifty-odd   tenfold
> 50-odd   10-fold

58. Most compounds formed from an open or hyphenated compound + a suffix do not separate the suffix with a hyphen. But combining forms that also exist as independent words, such as -like, -wide, -worthy, and -proof, are attached by a hyphen.

> self-righteousness
> middle-of-the-roadism
> bobby-soxer
> a Red Cross-like approach
> a New York-wide policy

Open compounds often become hyphenated when a suffix is added unless they are proper nouns.

> flat-taxer
> Ivy Leaguer
> World Federalist

59. **combining forms** New terms in technical fields created with one or more combining forms are normally written solid.

> cyberworld
> macrographic

4 Abbreviations

Abbreviations may be used to save space and time, to avoid repetition of long words and phrases, or simply to conform to conventional usage.

The contemporary styling of abbreviations is inconsistent and arbitrary, and no set of rules can hope to cover all the possible variations, exceptions, and peculiarities encountered in print. The form abbreviations take—capitalized vs. lowercased, punctuated vs. unpunctuated—often depends on a writer's preference or a publisher's or organization's policy. However, the following paragraphs provide a number of useful guidelines to contemporary practice. In doubtful cases, a good general dictionary or a dictionary of abbreviations will usually show standard forms for common abbreviations.

The present discussion deals largely with general, nontechnical writing. In scientific writing, abbreviations are almost never punctuated.

An abbreviation is not divided at the end of a line.

Abbreviations are almost never italicized. An abbreviation consisting of single initial letters, whether punctuated or not, never standardly has spacing between the letters. (Initials of personal names, however, normally are separated by spaces.)

The first reference to any frequently abbreviated term or name that could be confusing or unfamiliar is commonly spelled out, often followed immediately by its abbreviation in parentheses. Later references employ the abbreviation alone.

Punctuation

1. A period follows most abbreviations that are formed by omitting all but the first few letters of a word.

> cont. [*for* continued]
> enc. [*for* enclosure]
> Oct. [*for* October]
> univ. [*for* university]

Former abbreviations that are now considered words do not need a period.

> lab   photo
> gym   ad

2. A period follows most abbreviations that are formed by omitting letters from the middle of a word.

> govt. [*for* government]
> atty. [*for* attorney]
> bros. [*for* brothers]
> Dr. [*for* Doctor]

Some abbreviations, usually called *contractions,* replace the omitted letters with an apostrophe. Such contractions do not end with a period. (In American usage, very few contractions other than two-word contractions involving verbs are in standard use.)

> ass'n   *or*   assn. [*for* association]
> dep't   *or*   dept. [*for* department]
> nat'l   *or*   natl. [*for* national]
> can't [*for* cannot]

3. Periods are usually omitted from abbreviations made up of single initial letters. However, for some of these abbreviations, especially uncapitalized ones, the periods are usually retained. No space follows an internal period.

> GOP [*for* Grand Old Party]
> PR [*for* public relations]
> CEO   *or*   C.E.O. [*for* chief executive officer]
> a.m. [*for* ante meridiem]

4. A few abbreviations are punctuated with one or more slashes in place of periods. (For details on the slash, see the section beginning on page 52.)

> c/o [*for* care of]
> d/b/a   *or*   d.b.a. [*for* doing business as]
> w/o [*for* without]
> w/w [*for* wall-to-wall]

5. Terms in which a suffix is added to a numeral are not genuine abbreviations and do not require a period. (For details on ordinal numbers, see the section on page 137.)

> 1st   3d
> 2nd   8vo

6. Isolated letters of the alphabet used to designate a shape or position in a sequence are not abbreviations and are not punctuated.

> T square
> A1
> F minor

7. When a punctuated abbreviation ends a sentence, its period becomes the terminal period.

> For years she claimed she was "the oldest living fossil at Briggs & Co."

Capitalization

1. Abbreviations are capitalized if the words they represent are proper nouns or adjectives.

    F [*for* Fahrenheit]
    IMF [*for* International Monetary Fund]
    Jan. [*for* January]
    Amer. [*for* American]
    LWV [*for* League of Women Voters]

2. Abbreviations are usually all-capitalized when they represent initial letters of lowercased words. However, some common abbreviations formed in this way are often lowercased.

    IQ [*for* intelligence quotient]
    U.S. [*for* United States]
    COLA [*for* cost-of-living allowance]
    FYI [*for* for your information]
    f.o.b. *or* FOB [*for* free on board]
    c/o [*for* care of]

3. Most abbreviations formed from single initial letters that are pronounced as words, rather than as a series of letters, are capitalized. Those that are not proper nouns and have been assimilated into the language as words in their own right are most often lowercased.

    OSHA   snafu
    NATO   laser
    CARE   sonar
    NAFTA   scuba

4. Abbreviations that are ordinarily capitalized are commonly used to begin sentences, but abbreviations that are ordinarily uncapitalized are not.

    Dr. Smith strongly disagrees.

OSHA regulations require these new measures.
Page 22 [*not* P. 22] was missing.

Plurals, Possessives, and Compounds

1. Punctuated abbreviations of single words are pluralized by adding *-s* before the period.

   yrs. [*for* years]
   hwys. [*for* highways]
   figs. [*for* figures]

2. Punctuated abbreviations that stand for phrases or compounds are usually pluralized by adding *-'s* after the last period.

   M.D.'s   *or*   M.D.s
   Ph.D.'s   *or*   Ph.D.s
   LL.B.'s   *or*   LL.B.s
   v.p.'s

3. All-capitalized, unpunctuated abbreviations are usually pluralized by adding a lowercase *-s*.

   IRAs   CPAs
   PCs   SATs

4. The plural form of a few lowercase one-letter abbreviations is made by repeating the letter.

   ll. [*for* lines]
   pp. [*for* pages]
   nn. [*for* notes]
   vv. [*for* verses]
   ff.   *or*   ff [*for* and the following ones *or* folios]

5. The plural form of abbreviations of units of measurement (including one-letter abbreviations) is

the same as the singular form. (For more on units of measurement, see the section on pages 156–57.)

> 10 cc *or* cc. [*for* cubic centimeters]
> 90 m *or* m. [*for* meters]
> 15 mm *or* mm. [*for* millimeters]
> 24 h. [*for* hours]
> 10 min. [*for* minutes]
> 45 mi. [*for* miles]

However, in informal nontechnical text several such abbreviations are pluralized like other single-word abbreviations.

> lbs.   qts.
> gals.   hrs.

6. Possessives of abbreviations are formed like those of spelled-out nouns: the singular possessive is formed by adding -'s, the plural possessive simply by adding an apostrophe.

> the CEO's speech
> Apex Co.'s profits
> the PACs' influence
> Brown Bros.' ads

7. Compounds that consist of an abbreviation added to another word are formed in the same way as compounds that consist of spelled-out nouns.

> an FDA-approved drug
> an R&D-driven company
> the Eau Claire, Wisc.–based publisher

Compounds formed by adding a prefix or suffix to an abbreviation are usually hyphenated.

> pre-CD recordings
> non-IRA deductions
> a CIA-like operation
> a PCB-free product

Specific Styling Conventions

A and *An*

1. The choice of the article *a* or *an* before abbreviations depends on the sound, rather than the actual letter, with which the abbreviation begins. If it begins with a consonant sound, *a* is normally used; if with a vowel sound, *an* is used.

> a CD-ROM version
> a YAF member
> a U.S. Senator
> an FDA-approved drug
> an M.D. degree
> an ABA convention

A.D. and B.C.

2. The abbreviations A.D. and B.C. and other abbreviated era designations usually appear in books and journals as small capitals; in newspapers and in typed or keyboarded material, they usually appear as full capitals. The abbreviation B.C. follows the date; A.D. usually precedes the date, though in many publications A.D. follows the date as well. In references to whole centuries, A.D. follows the century. (For more on era designations, see paragraph 12 on page 146.)

> A.D. 185   *but also*   185 A.D.
> 41 B.C.
> the fourth century A.D.

Agencies, Associations, Organizations, and Companies

3. The names of agencies, associations, and organizations are usually abbreviated after being spelled

out on their first occurrence in a text. If a company is easily recognizable from its initials, the abbreviation is likewise usually employed after the first mention. The abbreviations are usually all-capitalized and unpunctuated. (In contexts where the abbreviation will be recognized, it often replaces the full name throughout.)

> Next, the president of the Pioneer Valley Transit Authority presented the annual PVTA award.
> . . . at the American Bar Association (ABA) meeting in June. The ABA's new offices . . .
> International Business Machines released its first-quarter earnings figures today. An IBM spokesperson . . .

4. The words *Company, Corporation, Incorporated,* and *Limited* in company names are commonly abbreviated even at their first appearance, except in quite formal writing.

> Procter & Gamble Company
> *or* Procter & Gamble Co.
> Brandywine Corporation *or* Brandywine Corp.

Ampersand

5. The ampersand (&), representing the word *and,* is often used in the names of companies.

> H&R Block
> Standard & Poor's
> Ogilvy & Mather

It is not used in the names of federal agencies.

> U.S. Fish and Wildlife Service
> Office of Management and Budget

Even when a spelled-out *and* appears in a company's official name, it is often replaced by an ampersand in writing referring to the company, whether for the sake of consistency or because of the writer's inability to verify the official styling.

6. When an ampersand is used in an abbreviation, there is usually no space on either side of the ampersand.

> The Barkers welcome all guests to their B&B at 54 West Street.
> The S&P 500 showed gains in technology stocks.
> The Texas A&M Aggies prevailed again on Sunday.

7. When an ampersand is used between the last two elements in a series, the comma is omitted.

> Jones, Kuhn & Malloy, Attorneys at Law

Books of the Bible

8. Books of the Bible are spelled out in running text but generally abbreviated in references to chapter and verse.

> The minister based his first Advent sermon on Matthew.
> Ye cannot serve God and mammon.—Matt. 6:24

Compass Points

9. Compass points are normally abbreviated when they follow street names; these abbreviations may be punctuated and are usually preceded by a comma.

> 1600 Pennsylvania Avenue[,] NW [N.W.]

When a compass point precedes the word *Street*, *Avenue*, etc., or when it follows the word but forms an integral part of the street name, it is usually spelled out.

> 230 West 43rd Street
> 50 Park Avenue South

Dates

10. The names of days and months are spelled out in running text

> at the Monday editorial meeting
> the December issue of *Scientific American*
> a meeting held on August 1, 1998

The names of months usually are not abbreviated in datelines of business letters, but they are often abbreviated in government and military correspondence.

business dateline: November 1, 1999
   military dateline: 1 Nov 99

Degrees and Professional Ratings

11. Abbreviations of academic degrees are usually punctuated; abbreviations of professional ratings are slightly more commonly unpunctuated.

> Ph.D.
> B.Sc.
> M.B.A.
> PLS   *or*   P.L.S. [*for* Professional Legal Secretary]
> CMA   *or*   C.M.A. [*for* Certified Medical Assistant]
> FACP   *or*   F.A.C.P. [*for* Fellow of the American College of Physicians]

12. Only the first letter of each element in abbreviations of degrees and professional ratings is generally capitalized.

> D.Ch.E. [*for* Doctor of Chemical Engineering]
> Litt.D. [*for* Doctor of Letters]
> D.Th. [*for* Doctor of Theology]
>   *but*
> LL.B. [*for* Bachelor of Laws]
> LL.M. [*for* Master of Laws]
> LL.D. [*for* Doctor of Laws]

Geographical Names

13. When abbreviations of state names are used in running text immediately following the name of a city or county, the traditional state abbreviations are often used.

> Ellen White of 49 Lyman St., Saginaw, Mich., has been chosen . . .
> the Dade County, Fla., public schools
> *but*
> Grand Rapids, in western Michigan, . . .

Official postal service abbreviations for states are used in mailing addresses.

> 6 Bay Rd.
> Gibson Island, MD 21056

14. Terms such as *Street, Road,* and *Boulevard* are often written as punctuated abbreviations in running text when they form part of a proper name.

> an accident on Windward Road [*or* Rd.]
> our office at 1234 Cross Blvd. [*or* Boulevard]

15. Names of countries are usually spelled in full in running text.

> South Africa's president urged the United States to impose meaningful sanctions.

Abbreviations for country names (in tables, for example), are usually punctuated. When formed from the single initial letters of two or more individual words, they are sometimes unpunctuated.

> Mex.   Scot.
> Can.   U.K. *or* UK
> Ger.   U.S. *or* US

16. *United States* is normally abbreviated when used as an adjective or attributive. When used as a noun, it is generally spelled out.

the U.S. Department of Justice
U.S. foreign policy
The United States has declined to participate.

17. *Saint* is usually abbreviated when it is part of a geographical or topographical name. *Mount, Point,* and *Fort* may be either spelled out or abbreviated. (For the abbreviation of *Saint* with personal names, see paragraph 25 below.)

St. Paul, Minnesota   *or*   Saint Paul, Minnesota
St. Thomas, U.S.V.I.   *or*   Saint Thomas
Mount Vernon   *or*   Mt. Vernon
Point Reyes   *or*   Pt. Reyes
Fort Worth   *or*   Ft. Worth
Mt. Kilimanjaro   *or*   Mount Kilimanjaro

Latin Words and Phrases

18. Several Latin words and phrases are almost always abbreviated. They are punctuated, lowercased, and usually not italicized.

etc.	ibid.
i.e.	op. cit.
e.g.	q.v.
cf.	c. *or* ca.
viz.	fl.
et al.	et seq.

Versus is usually abbreviated *v.* in legal writing, *vs.* otherwise.

Da Costa v. *United States*
good vs. evil
   or   good versus evil

Latitude and *Longitude*

19. The words *latitude* and *longitude* are abbreviated in tables and in technical contexts but often written out in running text.

in a table: lat. 10°20′N *or* lat. 10-20N

in text: from 10°20′ north latitude to 10°30′ south
latitude

or from lat. 10°20′N to lat. 10°30′S

Military Ranks and Units

20. Official abbreviations for military ranks follow specific unpunctuated styles for each branch of the
armed forces. Nonmilitary writing usually employs
a punctuated and less concise style.

in the military:	BG Carter R. Stokes, USA
	LCDR Dawn Wills-Craig, USN
	Col S. J. Smith, USMC
	LTJG Carlos Ramos, USCG
	Sgt Bernard P. Brodkey, USAF
outside the military:	Brig. Gen. Carter R. Stokes
	Lt. Comdr. Dawn Wills-Craig
	Col. S. J. Smith
	Lt. (j.g.) Carlos Ramos
	Sgt. Bernard P. Brodkey

21. Outside the military, military ranks are usually
given in full when used with a surname only but abbreviated when used with a full name.

Major Mosby
Maj. John S. Mosby

Number

22. The word *number,* when followed by a numeral, is
usually abbreviated to *No.* or *no.*

The No. 1 priority is to promote profitability.
We recommend no. 6 thread.
Policy No. 123-5-X
Publ. Nos. 12 and 13

Personal Names

23. When initials are used with a surname, they are spaced and punctuated. Unspaced initials of a few famous persons, which may or may not be punctuated, are sometimes used in place of their full names.

> E. M. Forster
> C. P. E. Bach
> JFK *or* J.F.K.

24. The abbreviations *Jr.* and *Sr.* may or may not be preceded by a comma.

> Martin Luther King Jr. *or* Martin Luther King, Jr.

Saint

25. The word *Saint* is often abbreviated when used before the name of a saint. When it forms part of a surname or an institution's name, it follows the style used by the person or institution. (For the styling of *Saint* in geographical names, see paragraph 17 on page 127.)

> St. [*or* Saint] Teresa of Avila
> Augustus Saint-Gaudens
> Ruth St. Denis
> St. Martin's Press
> St. John's College

Scientific Terms

26. In binomial nomenclature, a genus name may be abbreviated to its initial letter after the first reference. The abbreviation is always capitalized, punctuated, and italicized.

> . . . its better-known relative *Atropa belladonna* (deadly nightshade).
> Only *A. belladonna* is commonly found in . . .

27. Abbreviations for the names of chemical compounds and the symbols for chemical elements and formulas are unpunctuated.

MSG	O
PCB	NaCl
Pb	FeS

28. Abbreviations in computer terms are usually unpunctuated.

PC	Esc
RAM	Alt
CD-ROM	Ctrl
I/O	ASCII
DOS	EBCDIC

Time

29. When time is expressed in figures, the abbreviations *a.m. (ante meridiem)* and *p.m. (post meridiem)* are most often written as punctuated lowercase letters, sometimes as punctuated small capital letters. In newspapers, they usually appear in full-size capitals. (For more on *a.m.* and *p.m.*, see paragraph 39 on page 155.)

> 8:30 a.m. *or* 8:30 A.M. *or* 8:30 A.M.
> 10:00 p.m. *or* 10:00 P.M. *or* 10:00 P.M.

Time-zone designations are usually capitalized and unpunctuated.

> 9:22 a.m. EST [*for* eastern standard time]
> 4:45 p.m. CDT [*for* central daylight time]

Titles and Degrees

30. The courtesy titles *Mr., Ms., Mrs.,* and *Messrs.* occur only as abbreviations today. The professional titles *Doctor, Professor, Representative,* and *Senator* are often abbreviated.

Ms. Lee A. Downs
Messrs. Lake, Mason, and Nambeth
Doctor Howe *or* Dr. Howe

31. Despite some traditional objections, the honorific titles *Honorable* and *Reverend* are often abbreviated, with and without *the* preceding the titles.

the Honorable Samuel I. O'Leary
or [the] Hon. Samuel I. O'Leary
the Reverend Samuel I. O'Leary
or [the] Rev. Samuel I. O'Leary

32. When an abbreviation for an academic degree, professional certification, or association membership follows a name, no courtesy or professional title precedes it.

Dr. Jesse Smith *or* Jesse Smith, M.D.
but not Dr. Jesse Smith, M.D.
Katherine Fox Derwinski, CLU
Carol W. Manning, M.D., FACPS
Michael B. Jones II, J.D.
Peter D. Cohn, Jr., CPA

33. The abbreviation *Esq.* (for *Esquire*) often follows attorneys' names in correspondence and in formal listings, and less often follows the names of certain other professionals, including architects, consuls, clerks of court, and justices of the peace. It is not used if a degree or professional rating follows the name, or if a courtesy title or honorific (*Mr., Ms., Hon., Dr.,* etc.) precedes the name.

Carolyn B. West, Esq.
not Ms. Carolyn B. West, Esq.
and not Carolyn B. West, J.D., Esq.

Units of Measurement

34. A unit of measurement that follows a figure is often abbreviated, especially in technical writing. The fig

ure and abbreviation are separated by a space. If the numeral is written out, the unit should also be written out.

> 15 cu. ft. *but* fifteen cubic feet
> What is its capacity in cubic feet?

35. Abbreviations for metric units are usually unpunctuated; those for traditional units are usually punctuated in nonscientific writing. (For more on units of measurement, see the section on pages 156–57.)

14 ml	8 ft.
12 km	4 sec.
50 m	20 min.

5 Numbers

The treatment of numbers presents special difficulties because there are so many conventions to follow, some of which may conflict in a particular passage. The major issue is whether to spell out numbers or to express them in figures, and usage varies considerably on this point.

Numbers as Words or Figures

At one style extreme—usually limited to proclamations, legal documents, and some other types of very formal writing—all numbers (sometimes even including dates) are written out. At the other extreme, some types of technical writing may contain no written-out numbers. Figures are generally easier to read than spelled-out numbers; however, the spelled-out forms are helpful in certain circumstances, and are often felt to be less jarring than figures in nontechnical writing.

Basic Conventions

1. Two alternative basic conventions are in common use. The first and more widely used system requires that numbers up through nine be spelled out, and that figures be used for exact numbers greater than nine. (In a variation of this system, the number ten is spelled out.) Round numbers that consist of a

whole number between one and nine followed by *hundred, thousand, million,* etc., may either be spelled out or expressed in figures.

> The museum includes four rooms of early American tools and implements, 345 pieces in all.
>
> He spoke for almost three hours, inspiring his audience of 19,000 devoted followers.
>
> They sold more than 700 [*or* seven hundred] TVs during the 10-day sale.
>
> She'd told him so a thousand times.

2. The second system requires that numbers from one through ninety-nine be spelled out, and that figures be used for all exact numbers above ninety-nine. (In a variation of this system, the number one hundred is spelled out.) Numbers that consist of a whole number between one and ninety-nine followed by *hundred, thousand, million,* etc., are also spelled out.

> Audubon's engraver spent nearly twelve years completing these four volumes, which comprise 435 hand-colored plates.
>
> In the course of four hours, she signed twenty-five hundred copies of her book.

3. Written-out numbers only use hyphens following words ending in *-ty.* The word *and* before such words is usually omitted.

> twenty-two
> five hundred ninety-seven
> two thousand one hundred forty-nine

Sentence Beginnings

4. Numbers that begin a sentence are written out. An exception is occasionally made for dates. Spelled-out numbers that are lengthy and awkward are usually avoided by restructuring the sentence.

Sixty-two new bills will be brought before the committee.

  or   There will be 62 new bills brought before the committee.

Nineteen ninety-five was our best earnings year so far.

  or occasionally   1995 was our best earnings year so far.

One hundred fifty-seven illustrations, including 86 color plates, are contained in the book.

  or   The book contains 157 illustrations, including 86 color plates.

Adjacent Numbers and Numbers In Series

5. Two separate figures are generally not written adjacent to one another in running text unless they form a series. Instead, either the sentence is rephrased or one of the figures is spelled out—usually the figure with the shorter written form.

    sixteen ½-inch dowels
    worked five 9-hour days in a row
    won twenty 100-point games
    lost 15 fifty-point matches
    By 1997, thirty schools . . .

6. Numbers paired at the beginning of a sentence are usually written alike. If the first word of the sentence is a spelled-out number, the second number is also spelled out. However, each number may instead be styled independently, even if that results in an inconsistent pairing.

    Sixty to seventy-five copies will be required.
    or   Sixty to 75 copies will be required.

7. Numbers that form a pair or a series within a sentence or a paragraph are often treated identically even when they would otherwise be styled differ-

ently. The style of the largest number usually determines that of the others. If one number is a mixed or simple fraction, figures are used for all the numbers in the series.

> She wrote one composition for English and translated twelve [or 12] pages for French that night.
> His total record sales came to a meager 8 [or eight] million; Bing Crosby's, he mused, may have surpassed 250 million.
> The three jobs took 5, 12, and 4½ hours, respectively.

Round Numbers

8. Approximate or round numbers, particularly those that can be expressed in one or two words, are often spelled out in general writing. In technical and scientific writing, they are expressed as numerals.

> seven hundred people   *or*   700 people
> five thousand years   *or*   5,000 years
> four hundred thousand volumes
>   *or*   400,000 volumes
>   *but not*   400 thousand volumes
>   *but in technical writing*
> 200 species of fish
> 50,000 people per year
> 300,000 years

9. Round (and round-appearing) numbers of one million and above are often expressed as figures followed by the word *million, billion,* and so forth. The figure may include a one- or two-digit decimal fraction; more exact numbers are written entirely in figures.

> the last 600 million years
> about 4.6 billion years old
> 1.2 million metric tons of grain
> $7.25 million
> $3,456,000,000

Ordinal Numbers

10. Ordinal numbers generally follow the styling rules for cardinal numbers. In technical writing, ordinal numbers are usually written as figure-plus-suffix combinations. Certain ordinal numbers—for example, those for percentiles and latitudes—are usually set as figures even in nontechnical contexts.

> entered the seventh grade
> wrote the 9th [*or* ninth] and 12th [*or* twelfth] chapters
> in the 21st [*or* twenty-first] century
> the 7th percentile
> the 38th parallel

11. In figure-plus-suffix combinations where the figure ends in 2 or 3, either a one- or a two-letter suffix may be used. A period does not follow the suffix.

> 2d   *or*   2nd
> 33d   *or*   33rd
> 102d   *or*   102nd

Roman Numerals

12. Roman numerals are traditionally used to differentiate rulers and popes with identical names.

> King George III
> Henri IV
> Innocent X

13. When Roman numerals are used to differentiate related males with the same name, they are used only with the full name. Ordinals are sometimes used instead of Roman numerals. The possessive is formed in the usual way. (For the use of *Jr.* and *Sr.*, see paragraph 24 on page 129.)

> James R. Watson II
> James R. Watson 2nd *or* 2d
> James R. Watson II's [*or* 2nd's *or* 2d's] alumni gift

14. Lowercase Roman numerals are generally used to number book pages that precede the regular Arabic sequence (often including a table of contents, acknowledgments, foreword, or other material).

> on page iv of the preface
> See Introduction, pp. ix–xiii.

15. Roman numerals are used in outlines; see paragraph 23 on page 151.

16. Roman numerals are found as part of a few established scientific and technical terms. Chords in the study of music harmony are designated by capital and lowercase Roman numerals (often followed by small Arabic numbers). Most technical terms that include numbers, however, express them in Arabic form.

> blood-clotting factor VII
> cranial nerves II and IX
> cancer stage III
> Population II stars
> type I error
> vii_6 chord
>   *but*
> adenosine 3′,5′-monophosphate
> cesium 137
> HIV-2

17. Miscellaneous uses of Roman numerals include the Articles, and often the Amendments, of the Constitution. Roman numerals are still sometimes used for references to the acts and scenes of plays and occasionally for volume numbers in bibliographic references.

> Article IX
> Act III, Scene ii   *or*   Act 3, Scene 2
> (III, ii)   *or*   (3, 2)
> Vol. XXIII, No. 4   *but usually*   Vol. 23, No. 4

Punctuation

These paragraphs provide general rules for the use of commas, hyphens, and en dashes with compound and large numbers. For specific categories of numbers, such as dates, money, and decimal fractions, see Specific Styling Conventions, beginning on page 143.

Commas in Large Numbers

1. In general writing, figures of four digits may be written with or without a comma; including the comma is more common. If the numerals form part of a tabulation, commas are necessary so that four-digit numerals can align with numerals of five or more digits.

    2,000 cases   *or less commonly*   2000 cases

2. Whole numbers of five digits or more (but not decimal fractions) use a comma to separate three-digit groups, counting from the right.

    a fee of $12,500
    15,000 units
    a population of 1,500,000

3. Certain types of numbers of four digits or more do not contain commas. These include decimal fractions and the numbers of policies and contracts, checks, street addresses, rooms and suites, telephones, pages, military hours, and years.

    2.5544   Room 1206
    Policy 33442   page 145
    check 34567   1650 hours
    12537 Wilshire Blvd. in 1929

4. In technical writing, the comma is frequently replaced by a thin space in numerals of five or more digits. Digits to the right of the decimal point are

also separated in this way, counting from the decimal point.

28 666 203
209.775 42

Hyphens

5. Hyphens are used with written-out numbers between 21 and 99.

   forty-one years old
   his forty-first birthday
   Four hundred twenty-two visitors were counted.

6. A hyphen is used in a written-out fraction employed as a modifier. A nonmodifying fraction consisting of two words only is usually left open, although it may also be hyphenated. (For details on fractions, see the section beginning on page 148.)

   a one-half share
   three fifths of her paycheck
   or   three-fifths of her paycheck
   but
   four five-hundredths

7. Numbers that form the first part of a modifier expressing measurement are followed by a hyphen. (For units of measurement, see the section on pages 156–57.)

   a 5-foot board
   a 28-mile trip
   an eight-pound baby
   but
   a $6 million profit

8. Serial numbers, Social Security numbers, telephone numbers, and extended zip codes often contain hyphens that make lengthy numerals more readable or separate coded information.

020-42-1691
413-734-3134   *or*   (413) 734-3134
01102-2812

9. Numbers are almost never divided at the end of a line. If division is unavoidable, the break occurs only after a comma.

Inclusive Numbers

10 Inclusive numbers—those that express a range—are usually separated either by the word *to* or by a hyphen or en dash, meaning "(up) to and including."

spanning the years 1915 to 1941
the fiscal year 1994–95
the decade 1920–1929
pages 40 to 98
pp. 40–98

Inclusive numbers separated by a hyphen or en dash are not used after the words *from* or *between*.

from page 385 to page 419   *not*   from page 385–419
from 9:30 to 5:30   *not*   from 9:30–5:30
between 1997 and 2000   *not*   between 1997–2000
between 80 and 90 percent
    not   between 80–90 percent

11. Inclusive page numbers and dates may be either written in full or elided (i.e., shortened) to save space or for ease of reading.

pages 523–526   *or*   pages 523–26
1955–1969   *or*   1955–69

However, inclusive dates that appear in titles and other headings are almost never elided. Dates that appear with era designations are also not elided.

> *England and the French Revolution 1789–1797*
> 1900–1901   *not*   1900–01   *and not*   1900–1
> 872–863 B.C.   *not*   872–63 B.C.

12. The most common style for the elision of inclusive numbers is based on the following rules: Never elide inclusive numbers that have only two digits.

> 24–28   *not*   24–8
> 86–87   *not*   86–7

Never elide inclusive numbers when the first number ends in 00.

> 100–103   *not*   100–03   *and not*   100–3
> 300–329   *not*   300–29

In other numbers, do not omit the tens digit from the higher number. *Exception:* Where the tens digit of both numbers is zero, write only one digit for the higher number.

> 234–37   *not*   234–7
> 3,824–29   *not*   3,824–9
> 605–7   *not*   605–07

13. Units of measurement expressed in words or abbreviations are usually used only after the second element of an inclusive number. Symbols, however, are repeated.

> ten to fifteen dollars
> 30 to 35 degrees Celsius
> an increase in dosage from 200 to 500 mg
>   *but*
> 45° to 48° F
> $50–$60 million
>   *or* $50 million to $60 million

14. Numbers that are part of an inclusive set or range are usually styled alike: figures with figures, spelled-out words with other spelled-out words.

from 8 to 108 absences
five to twenty guests
300,000,000 to 305,000,000
   not 300 million to 905,000,000

Specific Styling Conventions

The following paragraphs, arranged alphabetically, describe styling practices commonly followed for specific situations involving numbers.

Addresses

1. Numerals are used for all building, house, apartment, room, and suite numbers except for *one,* which is usually written out.

6 Lincoln Road	Room 982
1436 Fremont Street	Suite 2000
Apartment 609	One Bayside Drive

   When the address of a building is used as its name, the number in the address is often written out.

   the sophisticated elegance of Ten Park Avenue

2. Numbered streets have their numbers written as ordinals. Street names from First through Tenth are usually written out, and numerals are used for all higher-numbered streets. Less commonly, all numbered street names up to and including One Hundredth are spelled out.

   167 Second Avenue
   19 South 22nd Street
     or less commonly 19 South Twenty-second Street
   145 East 145th Street
   in the 60s
     or in the Sixties [streets from 60th to 69th]
   in the 120s [streets from 120th to 129th]

When a house or building number immediately precedes the number of a street, a spaced hyphen may be inserted between the two numbers, or the street number may be written out, for the sake of clarity.

> 2018 - 14th Street
> 2018 Fourteenth Street

3. Arabic numerals are used to designate highways and, in some states, county roads.

> Interstate 90   *or*   I-90
> U.S. Route 1   *or*   U.S. 1
> Texas 23
> County 213

Dates

4. Year numbers are written as figures. If a year number begins a sentence, it may be left as a figure but more often is spelled out; the sentence may also be rewritten to avoid beginning it with a figure.

> the 1997 edition
> Nineteen thirty-seven marked the opening of the Golden Gate Bridge.
>   *or*   The year 1937 marked the opening of the Golden Gate Bridge.
>   *or*   The Golden Gate Bridge opened in 1937.

5. A year number may be abbreviated to its last two digits when an event is so well known that it needs no century designation. In these cases an apostrophe precedes the numerals.

> the blizzard of '88
> class of '91   *or*   class of 1991
> the Spirit of '76

6. Full dates are traditionally written in the sequence month-day-year, with the year set off by commas that precede and follow it. An alternative style,

used in the military and in U.S. government publications, is the inverted sequence day-month-year, which does not require commas.

traditional: July 8, 1976, was a warm, sunny day in Philadelphia.

the explosion on July 16, 1945, at Alamogordo

military: the explosion on 16 July 1945 at Alamogordo

the amendment ratified on 18 August 1920

7. Ordinal numbers are not used in full dates. Ordinals are sometimes used, however, for a date without an accompanying year, and they are always used when preceded in a date by the word *the*.

December 4, 1829
on December 4th   *or*   on December 4
on the 4th of December

8. All-figure dating, such as 6-8-95 or 6/8/95, is usually avoided in formal writing. For some readers, such dates are ambiguous; the examples above generally mean June 8, 1995, in the United States, but in almost all other countries mean August 6, 1995.

9. Commas are usually omitted from dates that include the month and year but not the day. The word *of* is sometimes inserted between the month and year.

in October 1997
back in January of 1981

10. References to specific centuries may be either written out or expressed in figures.

in the nineteenth century   *or*   in the 19th century
a sixteenth-century painting
   or   a 16th-century painting

11. The name of a specific decade often takes a short form, usually with no apostrophe and uncapitalized. When the short form is part of a set phrase, it is capitalized.

> a song from the sixties
> *occasionally*   a song from the 'sixties
> *or*   a song from the Sixties
> tunes of the Gay Nineties

The name of a decade is often expressed in numerals, in plural form. The figure may be shortened, with an apostrophe to indicate the missing numerals; however, apostrophes enclosing the figure are generally avoided. Any sequence of such numbers is generally styled consistently.

> the 1950s and 1960s   *or*   the '50s and '60s
>   *but not*
> the '50's and '60's
> the 1950s and '60s
> the 1950s and sixties

12. Era designations precede or follow words that specify centuries or numerals that specify years. Era designations are unspaced abbreviations, punctuated with periods. They are usually typed or keyboarded as regular capitals, and typeset in books as small capitals and in newspapers as full-size capitals. The abbreviation B.C. (before Christ) is placed after the date, while A.D. (*anno Domini*, "in the year of our Lord") is usually placed before the date but after a century designation. Any date given without an era designation or context is understood to mean A.D.

> 1792–1750 B.C.
> between 600 and 400 B.C.
> from the fifth or fourth millennium to c. 250 B.C.
> between 7 B.C. and A.D. 22
> c. A.D. 100 to 300

the second century A.D.
the 17th century

13. Less common era designations include A.H. (*anno Hegirae*, "in the year of [Muhammad's] Hegira," or *anno Hebraico*, "in the Hebrew year"); B.C.E. (before the common era; a synonym for B.C.); C.E. (of the common era; a synonym for A.D.); and B.P. (before the present; often used by geologists and archaeologists, with or without the word *year*). The abbreviation A.H. is usually placed before a specific date but after a century designation, while B.C.E., C.E., and B.P. are placed after both a date and a century.

the tenth of Muharram, A.H. 61 (October 10, A.D. 680)
the first century A.H.
from the 1st century B.C.E. to the 4th century C.E.
63 B.C.E.
the year 200 C.E.
5,000 years B.P.
two million years B.P.

Degrees of Temperature and Arc

14. In technical writing, a quantity expressed in degrees is generally written as a numeral followed by the degree symbol (°). In the Kelvin scale, neither the word *degree* nor the symbol is used with the figure.

a 45° angle
6°40'10"N
32° F
0° C
Absolute zero is zero kelvins or 0 K.

15. In general writing, the quantity expressed in degrees may or may not be written out. A figure may be followed by either the degree symbol or the word *degree;* a spelled-out number is always followed by the word *degree*.

latitude 43°19″N
latitude 43 degrees N
a difference of 43 degrees latitude
The temperature has risen about thirty degrees.

Fractions and Decimal Fractions

16. In nontechnical prose, fractions standing alone are usually written out. Common fractions used as nouns are usually unhyphenated, although the hyphenated form is also common. When fractions are used as modifiers, they are hyphenated.

    lost three quarters of its value
      or lost three-quarters of its value
    had a two-thirds chance of winning

    Multiword numerators and denominators are usually hyphenated, or written as figures.

    one one-hundredth of an inch *or* 1/100 of an inch

17. Mixed fractions (fractions with a whole number, such as $3\frac{1}{2}$) and fractions that form part of a modifier are usually expressed in figures in running text.

    waiting $2\frac{1}{2}$ hours
    a $\frac{7}{8}$-mile course
    $2\frac{1}{2}$-pound weights

    Fractions that are not on the keyboard or available as special characters on a computer may be typed in full-sized digits; in mixed fractions, a space is left between the whole number and the fraction.

    a 7/8-mile course
    waiting 2 3/4 hours

18. Fractions used with units of measurement are usually expressed in figures, but common short words are often written out.

$\frac{1}{10}$ km	half a mile
$\frac{1}{3}$ oz.	a half-mile walk
$\frac{7}{8}$ inch	a sixteenth-inch gap

19. Decimal fractions are always set as figures. In technical writing, a zero is placed to the left of the decimal point when the fraction is less than a whole number; in general writing, the zero is usually omitted. Commas are not used in numbers following a decimal point.

> An example of a pure decimal fraction is 0.375, while 1.402 is classified as a mixed decimal fraction.
> a .22-caliber rifle
> 0.142857

20. Fractions and decimal fractions are usually not mixed in a text.

> weights of 5½ lbs., 3¼ lbs., and ½ oz.
> *or* weights of 5.5 lbs., 3.25 lbs., and .5 oz.
> *not* weights of 5.5 lbs., 3¼ lbs., and ½ oz.

Lists and Outlines

21. Both run-in and vertical lists are often numbered. In run-in numbered lists—that is, numbered lists that form part of a normal-looking sentence—each item is preceded by a number (or, less often, an italicized letter) enclosed in parentheses. The items are separated by commas if they are brief and unpunctuated; if they are complex or punctuated, they are separated by semicolons. The entire list is introduced by a colon if it is preceded by a full clause, and often when it is not.

> Among the fastest animals with measured maximum speeds are (1) the cheetah, clocked at 70 mph; (2) the pronghorn antelope, at 61 mph; (3) the lion, at 50 mph; (4) the quarter horse, at 47 mph; and (5) the elk, at 45 mph.

The new medical dictionary has several special features: *(a)* common variant spellings; *(b)* examples of words used in context; *(c)* abbreviations, combining forms, prefixes, and suffixes; and *(d)* brand names for drugs and their generic equivalents.

22. In vertical lists, each number is followed by a period; the periods align vertically. Runover lines usually align under the item's first word. Each item may be capitalized, especially if the items are syntactically independent of the words that introduce them.

The English peerage consists of five ranks, listed here in descending order:

1. Duke (duchess)
2. Marquess (marchioness)
3. Earl (countess)
4. Viscount (viscountess)
5. Baron (baroness)

The listed items end with periods (or question marks) when they are complete sentences, and also often when they are not.

We require answers to the following questions:

1. Does the club intend to engage heavy-metal bands to perform in the future?
2. Will any such bands be permitted to play past midnight on weekends?
3. Are there plans to install proper acoustic insulation?

Items that are syntactically dependent on the words that introduce them often begin with a lowercase letter and end with a comma or semicolon just as in a run-in series in an ordinary sentence.

Among the courts that are limited to special kinds of cases are

1. probate courts, for the estates of deceased persons;
2. commercial courts, for business cases;

3. juvenile courts, for cases involving children under 18; and

4. traffic courts, for minor cases involving highway and motor vehicle violations.

A vertical list may also be unnumbered, or may use bullets (•) in place of numerals, especially where the order of the items is not important.

> Chief among the important advances in communication were these 19th-century inventions:
> > Morse's telegraph
> > Daguerre's camera
> > Bell's telephone
> > Edison's phonograph

> This book covers in detail:
> > • Punctuation
> > • Capitalization and italicization
> > • Numbers
> > • Abbreviations
> > • Grammar and composition

23. Outlines standardly use Roman numerals, capitalized letters, Arabic numerals, and lowercase letters, in that order. Each numeral or letter is followed by a period, and each item is capitalized.

> III. The United States from 1816 to 1850
> > A. Era of mixed feelings
> > > 1. Effects of the War of 1812
> > > 2. National disunity
> > B. The economy
> > > 1. Transportation revolution
> > > > a. Waterways
> > > > b. Railroads
> > > 2. Beginnings of industrialization
> IV. The Civil War and Reconstruction, 1850–77

Money

24. A sum of money that can be expressed in one or two words is usually written out in running text, as

is the unit of currency. But if several sums are mentioned in the sentence or paragraph, all are usually expressed as figures and are used with the unspaced currency symbol.

> The scalpers were asking eighty dollars.
> Grandfather remembered the days of the five-cent cigar.
> The shoes on sale are priced at $69 and $89.
> Jill wanted to sell the lemonade for 25¢, 35¢, and 45¢.

25. Monetary units of mixed dollars-and-cents amounts are expressed in figures.

> $16.75
> $307.02

26. Even-dollar amounts are often expressed in figures without a decimal point and zeros. But when even-dollar amounts appear near amounts that include cents, the decimal point and zeros are usually added for consistency. The dollar sign is repeated before each amount in a series or inclusive range.

> They paid $500 for the watercolor.
> The price had risen from $8.00 to $9.95.
> bids of $80, $90, and $100
> in the $80–$100 range

27. Sums of money in the millions or above rounded to no more than one decimal place are usually expressed in a combination of figures and words.

> a $10-million building program
> $4.5 billion

28. In legal documents a sum of money is usually written out fully, often capitalized, with the corresponding figures in parentheses immediately following.

> Twenty-five Thousand Dollars ($25,000)

Organizations and Governmental Entities

29. Ordinal numbers in the names of religious organizations and churches are usually written out.

> Seventh-Day Adventists
> Third Congregational Church

30. Local branches of labor unions and fraternal organizations are generally identified by a numeral, usually placed after the name.

> Motion Picture Studio Mechanics Local 476
> Loyal Order of Moose No. 220
> Local 4277 Communications Workers of America

31. In names of governmental bodies and electoral, judicial, and military units, ordinal numbers of one hundred or below are usually written out but often not.

> Second Continental Congress
> Fifth Republic
> First Congressional District
> Court of Appeals for the Third Circuit
> U.S. Eighth Army
> Twelfth Precinct *or* 12th Precinct
> Ninety-eighth Congress *or* 98th Congress

Percentages

32. In technical writing, and often in business and financial writing, percentages are written as a figure followed by an unspaced % symbol. In general writing, the word *percent* normally replaces the symbol, and the number may either be written out (if it does not include a decimal) or expressed as a figure.

> *technical:*   15%
>   13.5%

> *general:*   15 percent
>   87.2 percent
>   Fifteen percent of the applicants were
>   accepted.
>   a four percent increase
>   *or* a 4% increase

33. In a series or range, the percent sign is usually included with all numbers, even if one of the numbers is zero.

> rates of 8.3%, 8.8%, and 9.1%
> a variation of 0% to 10% *or* a 0%–10% variation

Plurals

34. The plurals of written-out numbers, including fractions, are formed by adding *-s* or *-es.*

> at sixes and sevens
> divided into eighths
> ever since the thirties
> still in her thirties

35. The plurals of figures are formed by adding *-s* or less commonly *-'s,* especially where the apostrophe can prevent a confusing typographic appearance.

> in the '80s
> since the 1980s [*or less commonly* 1980's]
> temperatures in the 80s and 90s [*or* 80's and 90's]
> the *1*'s looked like *l*'s

Ratios

36. Ratios are generally expressed in figures, usually with the word *to;* in technical writing the figures may be joined by a colon or a slash instead. Ratios expressed in words use a hyphen (or en dash) or the word *to.*

> odds of 10 to 1
> a proportion of 1 to 4

a 3:1 ratio
29 mi/gal
a fifty-fifty chance
a ratio of ten to four

Time of Day

37. In running text, the time of day is usually spelled out when expressed in even, half, or quarter hours or when it is followed by *o'clock*.

> around four-thirty
> arriving by ten
> planned to leave at half past five
> now almost a quarter to two
> arrived at nine o'clock

38. Figures are generally used when specifying a precise time.

> an appointment at 9:30 tomorrow morning
> buses at 8:42, 9:12, and 10:03 a.m.

39. Figures are also used when the time of day is followed by *a.m.* and *p.m.* These are usually written as punctuated lowercase letters, sometimes as small capital letters. They are not used with *o'clock* or with other words that specify the time of day.

> 8:30 a.m.   *or*   8:30 A.M.
> 10:30 p.m.   *or*   10:30 P.M.
> 8 a.m.   *or*   8 A.M.
> home by nine o'clock
> 9:15 in the morning
> eleven in the evening

With *twelve o'clock* or 12:00, it is helpful to specify *midnight* or *noon* rather than the ambiguous *a.m.* or *p.m.*

> The third shift begins at 12:00 (midnight).

40. Even-hour times are generally written with a colon and two zeros when used in a series or pairing with any times not ending in two zeros.

> started at 9:15 a.m. and finished at 2:00 p.m.
> worked from 8:30 to 5:00

41. The 24-hour clock system—also called *military time*—uses no punctuation and omits *o'clock, a.m., p.m.,* or any other additional indication of the time of day. The word *hours* sometimes replaces them.

> from 0930 to 1100
> at 1600 hours

Units of Measurement

42. In technical writing, all numbers used with units of measurement are written as numerals. In nontechnical writing, such numbers often simply follow the basic conventions explained on pages 133–34; alternatively, even in nontechnical contexts all such numbers often appear as numerals.

> In the control group, only 8 of the 90 plants were affected.
> picked nine quarts of berries
> chugging along at 9 [*or* nine] miles an hour
> a pumpkin 5 [*or* five] feet in diameter
> weighing 7 pounds 9 ounces
> a journey of 3 hours and 45 minutes

The singular form of units of measurement is used in a modifier before a noun, the plural form in a modifier that follows a noun.

> a 2- by 9-inch board *or* a two-inch by nine-inch board
>   *or* a two- by nine-inch board
> measured 2 inches by 9 inches   *or*   measured two inches by nine inches
> a 6-foot 2-inch man

is 6 feet 2 inches tall   *or*   is six feet two inches tall
is six feet two   *or*   is 6 feet 2

43. When units of measurement are written as abbreviations or symbols, the adjacent numbers are always figures. (For abbreviations with numerals, see the section on pages 131–32.)

6 cm	67.6 fl. oz.
1 mm	4′
$4.25	98.6°

44. When two or more quantities are expressed, as in ranges or dimensions or series, an accompanying symbol is usually repeated with each figure.

4″ × 6″ cards
temperatures of 30°, 55°, 43°, and 58°
$450–$500 suits

Other Uses

45. Figures are generally used for precise ages in newspapers and magazines, and often in books as well.

Taking the helm is Colin Corman, 51, a risk-taking
    high roller.
At 9 [*or* nine] she mastered the Mendelssohn Violin
    Concerto.
the champion 3[*or* three]-year-old filly
for anyone aged 62 and over

46. Figures are used to refer to parts of a book, such as volume, chapter, illustration, and table numbers.

vol. 5, p. 202
Chapter 8   *or*   Chapter Eight
Fig. 4

47. Serial, policy, and contract numbers use figures. (For punctuation of these numbers, see paragraph 3 on page 139.)

Serial No. 5274
Permit No. 63709

48. Figures are used to express stock-market quotations, mathematical calculations, scores, and tabulations.

Industrials were up 4.23.
$3 \times 15 = 45$
a score of 8 to 2   *or*   a score of 8–2
the tally: 322 ayes, 80 nays

6 Quotations

Writers and editors rely on two common conventions to indicate that a passage of prose or poetry is quoted directly from another source. Short quotations are usually run in with the rest of the text and enclosed by quotation marks. Longer passages are usually set off distinctively as separate paragraphs; these paragraphs, called *block quotations* or *extracts,* are the main subject of this chapter. For the treatment of short run-in quotations, see the sections beginning on page 43 (for punctuation) and page 54 (for capitalization).

For prose quotations, length is generally assessed in terms of either the number of words or the number of lines. Quoted text is usually set as a block when it runs longer than about 50 words or three lines. However, individual requirements of consistency, clarity, or emphasis may alter these limits. A uniform policy should generally be observed throughout a given work.

Running in longer quotations can make a passage read more smoothly; alternatively, setting even short quotations as extracts can make them easier for the reader to locate.

For quotations of poetry, different criteria are used. Even a single line of poetry is usually set as an extract, although it is also common to run one or two lines into the text.

Attribution of quotations to their author and

source (other than epigraphs and blurbs) is dealt with in Chapter 7, "Notes and Bibliographies." (The un-attributed borrowed quotations in this chapter are from William Shakespeare, the *Congressional Record*, Abraham Lincoln, the U.S. Constitution, Martin Lister, the Song of Songs, William Wordsworth, John Keats, T. S. Eliot, Walt Whitman, Ezra Pound, and Matthew Arnold.)

Styling Block Quotations

Block quotations are generally set off from the text that precedes and follows them by adding extra space above and below the quotation, indenting the quoted matter on the left and often on the right as well, and setting the quotation in smaller type with less leading.

Introductory Punctuation, Capitalization, and Indention

Block quotations are usually preceded by a sentence ending with a colon or a period, and they usually begin with a capitalized first word.

> Fielding hides his own opinions on the matter deep in *Tom Jones:*
>
> > Now, in reality, the world have paid too great a compliment to critics, and have imagined them men of much greater profundity than they really are. From this complaisance the critics have been emboldened to assume a dictatorial power, and have so far succeeded that they are now become the masters, and have the assurance to give laws to those authors from whose predecessors they originally received them.

If the quoted passage continues an obviously incomplete (unquoted) sentence that precedes it, a comma may be used instead, or no punctuation at all, depending on the sentence's syntax, and the following extract will usually begin with a lowercase letter.

According to Fielding,

> the critics have been emboldened to assume a dictatorial power, and have so far succeeded that they are now become the masters, and have the assurance to give laws to those authors from whose predecessors they originally received them.

When the beginning of a block quotation is also the beginning of a paragraph in the original, the first line of the quotation is normally indented like a paragraph, and any subsequent paragraph openings in an extract are similarly indented.

Expanding on his theme, his tone veers toward the contemptuous:

> The critic, rightly considered, is no more than the clerk, whose office it is to transcribe the rules and laws laid down by those great judges whose vast strength of genius hath placed them in the light of legislators, in the several sciences over which they presided. This office was all which the critics of old aspired to; nor did they ever dare to advance a sentence without supporting it by the authority of the judge from whence it was borrowed.
>
> But in process of time, and in ages of ignorance, the clerk began to invade the power and assume the dignity of his master. The laws of writing were no longer founded on the practice of the author, but on the dictates of the critic. The clerk became the legislator, and those very peremptorily gave laws whose business it was, at first, only to transcribe them.

Quotations within an Extract

If a block quotation itself contains quoted material, double quotation marks enclose that material. (In a run-in quotation, these would be set as single quotation marks.)

Davenport reports what may have been the last words Pound ever spoke in public:

> "Tempus loquendi," the frail voice said with its typical rising quaver, "tempus tacendi," quoting Ecclesiastes, Malatesta, and Thomas Jefferson simultaneously, and explaining, in this way, that he had said quite enough.

Dialogue in a block quotation is enclosed in quotation marks, and the beginning of each speech is marked by paragraph indention, just as in the original.

> Next O'Connor's hapless protagonist is collared and grilled by the retired schoolteacher in the second-floor apartment:
>
> "Florida is not a noble state," Mr. Jerger said, "but it is an important one."
>
> "It's important alrighto," Ruby said.
>
> "Do you know who Ponce de Leon was?"
>
> "He was the founder of Florida," Ruby said brightly.
>
> "He was a Spaniard," Mr. Jerger said. "Do you know what he was looking for?"
>
> "Florida," Rudy said.
>
> "Ponce de Leon was looking for the fountain of youth," Mr. Jerger said, closing his eyes.
>
> "Oh," Ruby muttered.

If a speech runs to more than one paragraph, open quotation marks appear at the beginning of each paragraph of the extract; closing quotation marks appear only at the end of the final paragraph.

For dialogue from a play or meeting minutes, the speakers' names are set on a small indention, in italics or small capitals, followed by a period or colon. Runover lines generally indent about an em space further.

> This vein of rustic drollery resurfaces in the scene where the transformed Bottom meets the fairies (act 2, scene 1):
>
> *Bottom.* I cry your worship's mercy, heartily: I beseech your worship's name.
> *Cobweb.* Cobweb.
> *Bottom.* I shall desire you of more acquaintance, good Master Cobweb: if I cut my finger, I shall make bold with you. Your name, honest gentleman?
> *Peaseblossom.* Peaseblossom.
> *Bottom.* I pray you, commend me to Mistress Squash, your mother, and to Master Peascod, your father.

> SEN. BAUCUS: Mr. President, I suggest the absence of a quorum.
> THE PRESIDING OFFICER: The clerk will call the roll.

The legislative clerk proceeded to call the roll.

SEN. WARNER: Madam President, I ask unanimous consent that the order for the quorum call be rescinded.

THE PRESIDING OFFICER: Without objection, it is so ordered.

Alterations and Omissions

Although absolute accuracy is always of first importance when quoting from another source, there are certain kinds of alterations and omissions that authors and editors are traditionally allowed to make. (The conventions described in this section are illustrated with block quotations; however, the conventions are equally applicable to run-in quotations.)

Obviously, the author must always be careful not to change the essential meaning of a quotation by making deletions or alterations or by putting quotations in contexts that may tend to mislead the reader.

Changing Capital and Lowercase Letters

If the opening words of a quotation act as a sentence within the quotation, the first word is capitalized, even if that word did not begin a sentence in the original version.

> Henry Fielding was already expressing identical sentiments in 1749:
>
>> The critics have been emboldened to assume a dictatorial power, and have so far succeeded that they are now become the masters. . . .

In situations in which meticulous handling of original source material is crucial (particularly in legal and scholarly writing), the capital letter would be placed in brackets to indicate that it was not capitalized in the original source.

> [T]he critics have been emboldened to assume a dictatorial power, and have so far succeeded that they are now become the masters. . . .

Even if the quotation's first word was capitalized in the original, it is generally not capitalized when the quoted passage is joined syntactically to the sentence that precedes it.

> Fielding asserts boldly that
>> the critic, rightly considered, is no more than the clerk, whose office it is to transcribe the rules and laws laid down by those great judges whose vast strength of genius hath placed them in the light of legislators, in the several sciences over which they presided.

Omissions at the Beginning or End of a Quotation

Since it is understood that most quotations are extracted from a larger work, ellipsis points at the beginning and end of the quotation are usually unnecessary. If a quotation ends in the middle of a sentence, however, the period following the omission is closed up to the last word and followed by three ellipsis points. Any punctuation that immediately follows the last quoted word in the original is generally dropped.

> We are met on a great battlefield of that war. We have come to dedicate a portion of that field, as a final resting place for those who here gave their lives. . . .

If the omission in the quoted passage ends with a question mark or an exclamation point, such punctuation follows the three ellipsis points. (Some style guides ask that these marks precede the ellipsis points.)

Omissions within Quotations

Omissions from quoted material that fall within a sentence are indicated by three ellipsis points.

The Place where it is kept . . . is a very Pit or Hole, in the middle of the Fauxbourg, and belongs to the Great Abbey of that Name.

Punctuation used in the original that falls on either side of the ellipsis points is often omitted; however, it may be retained, especially to help clarify the meaning or structure of the sentence.

We the People of the United States, in Order to . . . establish Justice, . . . provide for the common defence, . . . and secure the Blessings of Liberty . . . , do ordain and establish this Constitution for the United States of America.

If an omission includes one or more entire sentences, or the beginning or end of a sentence, within a paragraph, the end punctuation preceding or following the omission is retained and followed by three ellipsis points.

We can not dedicate—we can not consecrate—we can not hallow—this ground. The brave men, living and dead, who struggled here, have consecrated it, far above our poor power to add or detract. . . . It is for us the living, rather, to be dedicated here to the unfinished work which they who fought here have thus far so nobly advanced.

If a full paragraph or more is omitted, the omission is indicated by ellipsis points at the end of the paragraph that precedes the omission.

The words were written in 1915 by Hans Leip (1893–1983), a German soldier on his way to the Russian front parting from his sweetheart. His "Lili Marleen" was really a combination of two girls, his own, Lili, and his buddy's, Marleen. The poem was published in 1937 in a book of Leip's poems entitled *Die kleine Hafenorgel* ("The Little Harbor Organ"). Norbert Schultze (1911–), who would become the prominent composer of such propaganda titles as "The Panzers Are Rolling in Africa," set "Lili Marleen" the next year. . . .

It was Lale Andersen, a singer in literary cabarets in Munich and Berlin, whose record of the song was released in late 1939. It was not initially a success, but on August 18, 1941, a German shortwave radio station in Belgrade broadcast the song to Rommel's troops in North Africa.

If text is omitted from the beginning of any paragraph other than the first, three indented ellipsis points mark the omission. Note that they do not stand in for any omitted text preceding the paragraph.

> We were in Paris at the time of the Fair of St. Germain. It lasts six weeks at least: The Place where it is kept, well bespeaks its Antiquity; for it is a very Pit or Hole, in the middle of the Fauxbourg, and belongs to the Great Abbey of that Name. . . .
>
> . . . Knavery here is in perfection as with us; as dextrous Cut-Purses and Pick-Pockets. A Pick-Pocket came into the Fair at Night, extreamly well Clad, with four Lacqueys with good Liveries attending him: He was caught in the Fact, and more Swords were drawn in his Defence than against him; but yet he was taken, and delivered into the Hands of Justice, which is here sudden and no jest.

Other Minor Alterations

Archaic spellings and styles of type, punctuation, and capitalization should be preserved in direct quotations if they do not interfere with a reader's comprehension.

> Also he shewed us the *Mummy of a Woman* intire. The scent of the Hand was to me not unpleasant; but I could not liken it to any Perfume now in use with us.

If such archaisms occur frequently, the author may wish to modernize them, adding an explanation to this effect in a note or in the preface. (Several passages quoted in this chapter have been tacitly modernized.) Obvious typographical errors in modern works may be corrected without comment. Inserting *sic* in brackets after a misspelling in the original version is not necessary unless there is a specific reason for calling attention to the variant. The same holds for using *sic* for other small apparent errors of fact, grammar, punctuation, or word choice or omission.

Sometimes an author wishes to insert a brief explanation, clarification, summary of omitted material, or correction. These insertions, or *interpolations,* are enclosed in brackets. (For more on this use of brackets, see the section beginning on page 3.)

> For, lo, the winter is past, the rain is over and gone;
> The flowers appear on the earth; the time of the singing of
>   birds is come, and the voice of the turtle [i.e., turtledove]
>   is heard in our land.

Words that were not originally italicized may be italicized in the quoted passage for the sake of emphasis, as long as the author adds a bracketed notation such as "Italics mine," "Italics added," or "Emphasis added" immediately following the italicized portion or (more often) at the end of the passage.

> Both Russell and Ochs had noted the same reference: "Portions of the Feingold collection found their way into the hands of Goering and Hess; others would later surface in Romania, Argentina and Paraguay; and *the still unaccounted-for pieces were rumored to be part of a prominent Alsatian estate,* but no systematic effort was made to recover them." [Italics mine.]

Any footnote or endnote numbers or parenthetical references in the original version are usually omitted from short quotations; in their place authors often insert their own references.

Epigraphs and Blurbs

Thorough documentation is normally required only in scholarly writing, and even in scholarly contexts certain kinds of set-off quotations need not be exhaustively documented. These include quotations from classic sources—which will have been published in a number of different editions, and therefore have various possible publishing data—and casual allusions that are not essential to the author's central argument.

Such quotations may particularly be employed as *epigraphs*—short quotations from another source placed at the beginning of an article, chapter (where they may be placed above the title), or book. Other instances would include examples illustrating grammatical elements or word usage, and dictionaries of quotations.

For such quotations, the attribution is generally set by itself on the line below the quotation. Alternatively (and especially if space is a concern), it is run in on the last line of the quotation. When set on its own line, it is generally preceded by an em dash; somewhat less frequently, it is set without an em dash, often enclosed in parentheses. Whatever its punctuation, it is normally set flush right. When run in with the quotation, it usually follows the latter immediately with no intervening space, separated only by either an em dash or parentheses.

The name of the quotation's author is normally set roman, and the name of the publication in which it originally appeared is normally set italic. Either may instead be set in small caps. If all the attributions consist only of authors' names, they may be set in italics.

> I went to the woods because I wished to live deliberately, to front only the essential fact of life, and see if I could not learn what it had to teach, and not, when I came to die, discover that I had not lived.
>
> —Henry David Thoreau, *Walden*
> *or*
> (Henry David Thoreau)

Epigraph attributions are often very brief; this one, for example, could have read "H. D. Thoreau," "Thoreau, *Walden*," or simply "Thoreau."

Advertising *blurbs*—favorable quotations from reviewers or customers that appear on book jackets or advertising materials—are standardly enclosed in quotation marks, and the attribution is never enclosed in parentheses. But the latter's placement may vary, subject to the overall design of the jacket or advertisement. The attribution may appear on its own line or be run in with the blurb; it may be preceded by an em dash or unpunctuated, it may be set flush with the right margin of the quotation, run in with the quotation with no intervening space, centered on its own line, or aligned on a set indention.

> "Ms. Kingston finds the necessary, delicate links between two cultures, two centuries, two sexes. Seldom has the imagination performed a more beautiful feat."—*Washington Post*

When an attribution line follows a passage of poetry, the line may be set flush right, centered on the longest line in the quotation, or indented a standard distance from the right margin.

> Bring me my Bow of burning gold,
> Bring me my Arrows of desire,
> Bring me my Spear; O clouds unfold!
> Bring me my Chariot of fire!
>
> —William Blake, *Milton*

An attribution line following quoted lines from a play or the Bible may include the act and scene or the book and verse.

> All the world's a stage
> And all the men and women merely players;
> They have their exits and their entrances;
> And one man in his time plays many parts,
> His acts being seven ages.
>
> (*As You Like It*, 2.7)

> A feast is made for laughter, and wine maketh merry:
> but money answereth all things.
>
> (Ecclesiastes, 10:19)

(For details on documenting other sources of quotations, see Chapter 7, "Notes and Bibliographies," and the section beginning on page 178.)

Quoting Verse

The major difference between quotations of prose and poetry is that lines of poetry always keep their identity as separate lines. When run in with the text, the poetic lines are separated by a spaced slash.

> Was it Whistler, Wilde, or Swinburne that Gilbert was mocking in the lines "Though the Philistines may jostle, you will rank as an apostle in the high aesthetic band, / If you walk down Piccadilly with a poppy or a lily in your medieval hand"?

When poetic lines are set as extracts, the lines are divided exactly as in the original.

> Dickinson describes this post-traumatic numbness as death in life:
> This is the Hour of Lead—
> Remembered, if outlived,
> As Freezing persons, recollect the Snow—
> First—Chill—then Stupor—then the letting go—

Up to three or four short lines of poetry are occasionally run in if they are closely integrated with the text.

> In the thoroughly miscellaneous stanza that follows—"He has many friends, lay men and clerical, / Old Foss is the name of his cat; / His body is perfectly spherical, / He weareth a runcible hat"— Lear seems to bestow new meaning on his older coinage *runcible*.

However, quotations of as few as one or two lines are usually set off from the text as extracts.

> He experienced the heady exaltation of Revolutionary idealism:
> Bliss was it in that dawn to be alive,
> But to be young was very Heaven!

The horizontal placement of a poetry excerpt is normally determined by its longest line, which is centered horizontally, all the other lines aligning accordingly.

The relative indentions of an excerpt's lines should always be preserved.

> The famous first stanza may have given the English-speaking world its lasting image of the Romantic poet:
>
> My heart aches, and a drowsy numbness pains
>   My sense, as though of hemlock I had drunk,
> Or emptied some dull opiate to the drains
>   One minute past, and Lethe-wards had sunk:
> 'Tis not through envy of thy happy lot,
>   But being too happy in thine happiness,—
>   That thou, light winged Dryad of the trees,
>   In some melodious plot
> Of beechen green, and shadows numberless,
>   Singest of summer in full-throated ease.

If the quotation does not start at the beginning of a line, it should be indented accordingly.

>   I do not find
> The Hanged Man. Fear death by water.

If the lines of a poem are too long to center, the quotation may be set using a standard indention, with runover lines indented further.

> As it nears its end, the poem's language becomes increasingly evocative:
>
> The last scud of day holds back for me,
> It flings my likeness after the rest and true as any on
>   the shadowed wilds,
> It coaxes me to vapor and the dusk.

In a speech that extends over several lines, quotation marks are placed at the beginning and end of the speech. If a speech extends beyond one stanza or section, quotation marks are placed at the beginning of each stanza or section within the speech.

> In the cream gilded cabin of his steam yacht
> Mr. Nixon advised me kindly, to advance with fewer
> Dangers of delay. "Consider
>   Carefully the reviewer.
>
> "I was as poor as you are;
> When I began I got, of course,
> Advance on royalties, fifty at first," said Mr. Nixon,

It was formerly common to begin every line within a speech with quotation marks, but these added quotation marks are now standardly removed without comment by modern editors.

When a full line or several consecutive lines of poetry are omitted from an extract, the omission is indicated by a line of ellipsis points extending the length of either the preceding line or the missing line.

> Ah, love, let us be true
> To one another! for the world, which seems
> To lie before us like a land of dreams,
> . . . .
> Hath really neither joy, nor love, nor light,

Poetry extracts that do not end in a period or other terminal punctuation may be followed by ellipsis points; alternatively, the original punctuation (or lack of it) may be left by itself.

> This royal throne of kings, this scepter'd isle,
> This earth of majesty, this seat of Mars,
> This other Eden, demi-paradise, [. . .]

7 Notes and Bibliographies

A writer who borrows a quotation, idea, or piece of information from another work is traditionally required to acknowledge the borrowing in some way, and in serious nonfiction writing such acknowledgment is normally done by means of reference notes, usually in tandem with a bibliography. Thorough documentation of this kind is the distinguishing mark of scholarly writing. Scholarly documentation accomplishes several things: (1) it gives proper credit for work done by others and makes plagiarism more difficult, (2) it directs the reader to sources that may be of interest, (3) it may take the place of a lengthy explanation, (4) it can strengthen an argument by marshaling respectable published support, (5) it indicates the extent and quality of the writer's research, and (6) it can guide the interested reader to other relevant works that may not actually have been cited.

Most published nonfiction omits bibliographic references altogether. Most readers are somewhat put off by references, and omission of references tends to be conducive to a more relaxed tone. Articles in popular magazines, for example, never employ reference notes, relying instead on casual mentions of any sources within the running text itself (e.g., "As Hawking observed in his *Brief History of Time*, . . . ," "At a symposium in New York in March 1948, Margaret Mead criticized Kinsey's report, complaining that . . .").

Not all notes are simple bibliographic citations. So-called *substantive* or *content notes* may be used for discussions of subjects ancillary to the main topic being discussed. Such discussions, which might otherwise simply appear within parentheses, are usually moved out of the main text whenever they are long enough or digressive enough to represent an undesirable interruption of the main line of discussion.

Source documentation is widely dreaded, especially by younger writers, who may regard the practice as almost impossibly arcane, difficult, and time-consuming. However, much of the difficulty is often simply the result of disorganized research. The demands of documentation become much easier if the researcher has been systematic and meticulous about jotting down a complete and accurate bibliographic record of each work studied at the time it is first looked at (as well as being painstakingly accurate in copying the passages themselves). Once the complete record is in hand, formatting—and, if necessary, reformatting—the data usually becomes a relatively simple task.

Nevertheless, there indeed exists a bewildering variety of conceivable types of citations, and the unlucky researcher will from time to time encounter unusual and exacting citation problems. If an analogous citation cannot be found in the endnote lists in a scholarly journal, the best advice is often simply to provide the reader with all genuinely relevant information in a concise form broadly consistent with the style of the other citations. The accuracy and adequacy of the information are always more important than achieving some "perfectly" consistent form, especially when there may well be no other comparable entry with which the problematic entry truly need be absolutely consistent.

Since no style manual can describe in detail more

than a fraction of the bibliographic styles now in use, the writer submitting an article to a particular journal should always follow any instructions to authors in the journal's front or back matter and study carefully the references in its articles, the latter being unquestionably the most efficient way of learning its particular (and possibly unique) style. If a manuscript prepared on computer must be submitted to more than one journal (after an initial rejection), the original can be changed easily from one journal's style to another's, each different form being preserved as a separate electronic file. Within a given discipline, such changes will usually be minor. Book publishers, unlike journals, generally permit a reasonable range of different documentation styles, though they can be expected to require (or impose) internal consistency just as rigorously as do journals.

Several style manuals have established themselves as the standard guides to bibliographic form and other style issues in the various disciplines. In the humanities particularly, but also importantly in the social and natural sciences, *The Chicago Manual of Style* has long held a privileged position, especially in book publishing, and its treatment of bibliographic citation is the most comprehensive of all. In the life sciences and physical sciences, *Scientific Style and Format: The CBE Manual for Authors, Editors, and Publishers* is the most widely followed authority. In the social sciences, the *Publication Manual of the American Psychological Association* (APA) is commonly relied on. College and university departments usually prescribe certain manuals for use by undergraduates and generally by graduate students as well: those most often assigned are perhaps Kate Turabian's *Manual for Writers of Term Papers, Theses, and Dissertations* and (especially in the humanities) the *MLA Handbook for Writers of Research Papers*. In the business office, the *Gregg Reference Manual* has been standard for many years.

Ordinary word-processing programs now make the

job of inserting references far simpler than it was in the precomputer era. Their important functions include automatic renumbering of notes whenever new notes are added or existing ones are deleted, automatic reformatting of pages to accommodate footnotes, and automatic changing of footnotes to endnotes (or vice versa) throughout. These functions take only a few minutes to master and can save the user immense amounts of time.

Special software programs today provide automatic formatting of the elements of bibliographic citations in any of a large number of styles used in the humanities, social sciences, and natural sciences. Using an on-screen template, the user types each element into its appropriate box, and the program automatically creates the format in the chosen bibliographic style. For many students and scholars, this capacity can be of modest assistance. However, the main task will still lie in what precedes the formatting of the elements—that is, the careful gathering of all the essential documentation data and the judicious deployment of the source material within the new text.

References usually take one of three forms: footnotes, endnotes, or parenthetical references. Footnotes, set at the bottom of the page, can be more convenient than notes at the end of an article, chapter, or book for the serious reader, who is thereby spared the need of constantly flipping back and forth. Computer programs have largely freed typists and typesetters from the arduous task of calculating text-block lengths to accommodate footnotes of varying lengths, thus largely neutralizing an older argument against footnotes. However, footnotes are often disliked by more casual readers accustomed to a relaxed style of presentation. They may also be felt to make pages less attractive, and a heavily footnoted work may have ungainly pages that consist as much of footnotes as of normal text. Partly for these reasons, endnotes have become increasingly common in recent decades, and are now sometimes even employed with no actual reference numbers in the text (see "White-Copy System" on page 197).

Scholarly works in the natural sciences and to a somewhat looser extent in the social sciences and humanities employ parenthetical references, highly condensed bibliographic references set within parentheses right in the running text. Parenthetical references have been found to be extremely efficient in scientific writing, where professionals expect to encounter them frequently. Since the scientific articles cited tend to be short and highly focused on a single research finding, bald citations devoid of page references or any accompanying discussion are usually felt to be adequate. In the social sciences and especially the humanities, parenthetical references—which do not allow for even brief "content" discussions—must generally be at least supplemented by footnotes or (more commonly) endnotes.

In the humanities, footnotes and endnotes have traditionally been preferred throughout, but in recent years there has been a trend in the humanities toward using parenthetical references where appropriate. The name of the cited text's author is often worked smoothly into the text itself, so such references tend to shrink to mere parenthesized page references that hardly disturb the flow of the text. This extreme concision is nevertheless often inappropriate to the types of references a humanities scholar is likely to cite and the kinds of points the scholar is likely to make, and it is thus usually necessary to combine the two modes of citation. In writing intended for a more general public, parenthetical references are almost never seen, since they inevitably break up a text in a way that most people reading primarily for pleasure dislike.

The choice of reference type is actually rarely left to the writer. For term papers and theses, professors often require a specific reference style that is standard in their field; scholarly journals almost always impose a house policy for all their articles; a publisher of books for a professional audience may apply a general policy on documentation to all its books; a large corporation may specify a single mode of documentation for its reports; law firms generally follow the standard style of the legal profession; and so on.

Rules for documentation in serious writing were developed to ensure thoroughness and internal formal consistency. But as this variety of treatment reminds us, documentation data may be deployed in a variety of ways without losing any of its content or scholarly value.

This chapter seeks to provide an introduction to every significant issue of documentation and to provide consensus versions—versions that can be translated readily into the special style of any given journal or authority—of citation style in the humanities and sciences. Since most aspects of documentation style are more easily comprehended through examples than through discussion, a number of details will be found in the examples themselves but not otherwise referred to.

Note: Wherever alternative ways of styling particular elements are mentioned in this chapter, such alternatives should not be randomly mixed. Instead, one or the other style alternative should be adopted and maintained throughout a given work.

Footnotes and Endnotes

Footnotes and endnotes—the traditional modes of scholarly documentation, though they have waned in use in all disciplines in recent decades—use sequential superscript numbers to key bibliographic information about sources (author, title, place of publication, publisher, date, and page number) or ancillary discussions to specific text passages. Notes that appear at the bottom of the page are called *footnotes;* otherwise identical notes that appear at the end of an article, chapter, or book are called *endnotes.*

The superscript numbers are generally placed immediately after the material to be documented, whether it is an actual quotation or a paraphrase of language used in the source, or sometimes after the name of the source's author. The number is normally placed at the end of a paragraph, sentence, or clause, or at some other natural break in the sentence; it follows all punctuation marks except the dash.

> As one observer noted, "There was, moreover, a degree of logic in the new LDP-SDPJ axis, in that the inner cores of both parties felt threatened by the recent electoral reform legislation";[7] this opinion seems to have been shared by various other commentators.[8]

The numbering is consecutive throughout a paper or article. In a book, it almost always starts over with each new chapter.

The note itself, usually set in type one or two points smaller than the text type, begins with the corresponding number. The number may either be set as a superscript or set on the line and followed by a period; the latter is now more common in typeset material.

[4] I. L. Allen, *The City in Slang* (Oxford, 1993), 156.

or

4. I. L. Allen, *The City in Slang* (Oxford, 1993), 156.

Both footnotes and endnotes normally provide full bibliographic information for a source the first time it is cited. In subsequent references to the source, the information is abridged (see "Subsequent References to Books and Articles" on page 187).

Whenever data that would normally appear in a note—particularly the author's name or the source's title—appears in the text itself, adequately identified as the source of the quotation or information, it may be omitted from the note.

When endnotes are employed in a book, the task of locating a particular endnote should be made as easy as possible for the reader by providing running heads on each page of endnotes that individually specify which pages of the main text are covered by that page of endnotes—for example, "Notes to pp. 305–316," "Notes to pp. 317–330," etc. In addition, the endnotes for each book chapter or section should be preceded by a bold heading ("Chapter 1," "Chapter 2," etc.).

Superscript letters (used in alphabetical order, and always lowercase) or superscript marks are occasionally substituted for reference numbers when footnotes are employed. Both are commonly employed for table footnotes to indicate that they are not part of the larger chapter reference sequence. In tables of technical data, use of letters will avoid the risk that numerical superscripts will be mistaken for mathematical exponents, and use of marks will avoid the smaller risk that letters could similarly be taken for exponents. The traditional marks are listed below in the order normally used.

*	(asterisk)
†	(dagger)
‡	(double dagger)
§	(section mark)
‖	(parallels)
¶	(paragraph mark)
#	(number or pound sign)

This sequence usually begins anew with each page. If more than seven notes are needed in a sequence, numbers or letters should be used instead. When less than five are needed, the asterisk and dagger may be used in the order *, **, †, ††.

The following paragraphs describe the various elements of initial references.

Books

The basic elements of book citations are (1) the author's name, (2) the book's title, (3) the place of publication, publisher, and date of publication, and (4) the page or pages where the information appears.

Author's name The author's name is written in normal order, and followed by a comma. The names of two or more authors are listed in the sequence shown on the book's title page. If there are more than three authors, the first author's name is followed by *et al.* (for *et alii* or *et aliae,* "and others"), set in roman type. If a publication is issued by a group or organization and no individual is mentioned on the title page, the name of the group or organization (sometimes called the *corporate author*) may be used instead. If the corporate author is the same as the publisher, or if for any reason no name appears on the title page, the name may be omitted and the book title may begin the note.

4. Elizabeth Bishop, *One Art,* ed. Robert Giroux (New York: Farrar, Straus & Giroux, 1994), 102.

15. Bert Hölldobler and Edward O. Wilson, *The Ants* (Cambridge, Mass.: Belknap–Harvard Univ. Press, 1990), 119.

8. Gerald J. Alred, Charles T. Brusaw, and Walter E. Oliu, *The Business Writer's Handbook,* 6th ed. (New York: St. Martin's, 2000), 182–84.

22. Randolph Quirk et al., *A Comprehensive Grammar of the English Language* (London: Longman, 1985), 135.

12. New York Times Staff, *The White House Transcripts* (New York: Bantam, 1974), 78–79.

6. *The World Almanac and Book of Facts 2000* (Mahwah, N.J.: World Almanac Books, 1999), 763.

Title of the work The title is italicized in keyboarded and typeset manuscripts (underlined in typed or handwritten material). Each word of the title and subtitle is capitalized except for internal articles, coordinating conjunctions, and prepositions. A colon separates the title from any subtitle even if no colon is used on the title page. In hyphenated compounds, the second (third, etc.) element is generally capitalized as if there were no hyphen. Prepositions of four or more letters are often capitalized.

> 44. Alan Lloyd, *The Wickedest Age: The Life and Times of George III* (London: David & Charles, 1971), 48.
>
> 20. *The Post-Physician Era: Medicine in the Twenty-First Century* (New York: Wiley, 1976), 14.
>
> 3. Arthur Miller, *A View from [From] the Bridge* (1955; New York: Viking, 1987), 11.

Editor, compiler, or translator If no author is mentioned on the title page, the name of the editor, compiler, or translator is placed first in the note, followed by the abbreviation *ed.* (or *eds.*), *comp.* (*comps.*), or *trans.* In works listing the original author and title, the name of an editor, compiler, or translator is preceded by the abbreviation *ed., comp.,* or *trans.* or some combination of them.

> 7. Arthur S. Banks and Thomas C. Muller, eds., *Political Handbook of the World, 1999* (Binghamton, N.Y.: CSA Publications, 1999), 293–95.
>
> 14. Simone de Beauvoir, *The Second Sex,* trans. and ed. H. M. Parshley (1953; New York: Knopf, 1993), 446.

Part of the book If a reference is to one part of a book (such as an article, short story, or poem in a collection), the part's title is enclosed in quotation marks. Titles of chapters of a work by a single author are usually ignored.

> 4. Grace Paley, "Dreamer in a Dead Language," *Later the Same Day* (New York: Farrar, Straus & Giroux, 1985), 9–36.
>
> 10. G. Ledyard Stebbins, "Botany and the Synthetic Theory of Evolution," *The Evolutionary Synthesis: Perspectives on the Unification of Biology,* ed. Ernst Mayr and William B. Provine (1980; reprint, Cambridge, Mass.: Harvard Univ. Press, 1998), 382–89.

Name of a series If a book belongs to a series, the series name should be included. If the book is a numbered volume in the series, the volume number is also included. The series name is capitalized headline-style but not italicized.

> 4. George W. Stocking, Jr., ed., *Functionalism Historicized: Essays on British Social Anthropology,* History of Anthropology Series, vol. 2 (Madison: Univ. of Wisconsin, 1984), 173–74.

Edition If a work is other than the first edition, the number or the nature of the edition is shown.

> 11. Albert C. Baugh and Thomas Cable, *A History of the English Language,* 4th ed. (Englewood Cliffs, N.J.: Prentice Hall, 1992), 14.
>
> 29. *A Handbook for Scholars,* 2nd ed. (New York: Oxford, 1992), 129.

Volume number If a work has more than one volume, the total number of volumes follows the title and edition, and the number of the volume cited precedes the page number, with an unspaced colon between them.

> 3. Ronald M. Nowak, *Walker's Mammals of the World,* 6th ed., 2 vols. (Baltimore: Johns Hopkins Univ., 1999), 2:461.

Publication data The city of publication, the short name of the publisher, and the year of publication, in that order, follow next, enclosed in parentheses. A colon follows the city name, and a comma follows the publisher's name. If the city is a small one, the abbreviated state name (or country name) should be included; state names should all take either their older traditional form or the official post-office form. If the city or publisher is not known, use *n.p.* (for *no place* or *no publisher*); if the year is not given, use *n.d.* (for *no date*); if the pages are unnumbered, use *n. pag. (no pagination).*

Publishers' names are now commonly abbreviated, in both notes and bibliographies, to the most concise form that will still remain unambiguous for the reader. Thus, University of Oklahoma Press may be cited as "Univ. of Oklahoma," "U of Oklahoma P,"or even simply "Oklahoma"; W. W. Norton & Co. becomes simply "Norton"; and so on. The writer should adopt a basic level and style of abbreviation for publishers' names and observe it throughout.

> 13. Vitalij V. Shevoroshkin and T. L. Markery, *Typology, Relationship and Time* (Ann Arbor, Mich.: Karoma [Publishers, Inc.], 1986), 15.
> 28. Dan Sperber, *On Anthropological Knowledge: Three Essays* (New York: Cambridge [University Press], 1985), 20.

Reprint A reprint of an older work should include the original year of publication (if known) followed by a semicolon, the word "reprint," and the reprint data.

> 36. Douglas C. McMurtrie, *The Book: The Story of Printing and Bookmaking*, 3d ed. (1943; reprint, New York: Dorset, 1990), 235.

Page number The number of the page or pages on which the cited material can be found is preceded by a comma and followed by a period; the abbreviation *p.* or *pp.* is usually omitted. For inclusive numbers, either the elided style (see paragraphs 11–12 on pages 141–42) or the unelided style should be used consistently.

> 33. Roland Barthes, *Writing Degree Zero,* trans. Annette Lavers and Colin Smith (New York: Farrar, Straus & Giroux, 1977), 106–8 [or 106–108].

Articles

The following paragraphs describe specific elements of first references to articles in periodicals. Their basic elements are (1) the author's name, (2) the article's title, (3) the periodical's name and issue, and (4) the page or pages referred to. As with book references, any of this data included in the text itself can be omitted from the note.

Author's name The author's name is treated like that of a book author. Writers of book reviews or letters to the editor are treated like authors.

> 10. Renato Rosaldo, "Doing Oral History," *Social Analysis* 4 (1980): 89–90.
>
> 7. Gordon A. Craig, review of *The Wages of Guilt: Memories of War in Germany and Japan*, by Ian Buruma, *New York Review of Books*, 14 July 1994: 43–45.

Article title The article's title is capitalized headline-style, enclosed in quotation marks, and not italicized.

> 5. Richard Preston, "A Reporter at Large: Crisis in the Hot Zone," *New Yorker*, 26 Oct. 1992: 58.

Periodical name The periodical's name is italicized and capitalized like the title of a book. If the word *The* begins the name, it is generally omitted.

> 31. Richard Harris, "Chicago's Other Suburbs," *[The] Geographical Review* 84, 4 (Oct. 1994): 396.

Periodical volume, number, and date If a periodical identifies its issues by both volume and number, both may be specified (in Arabic rather than Roman numerals); a comma separates the two elements, but no punctuation precedes the volume number. However, a periodical whose pages are numbered consecutively through an annual volume actually needs only the volume number. The volume number is followed by the year, in parentheses; if the season, month, or precise date appears on the journal, it may optionally be included as well. Popular weekly and monthly magazines, including those that bear a volume-and-number designation, are normally referred to only by date. The name of the month is usually abbreviated (*Jan., Feb., Mar., Apr., May, June, July, Aug., Sept., Oct., Nov., Dec.*), and a precise date, as for a weekly or a newspaper, should be inverted (e.g., "29 Feb. 1996"). When no volume number is used, the date is preceded by a comma and followed by a colon.

> 6. John Heil, "Seeing Is Believing," *American Philosophical Quarterly* 19 (1982): 229.

> 15. John Lukacs, "The End of the Twentieth Century," *Harper's,* Jan. 1993: 40.

> 10. Sam Dillon, "Trial of a Drug Czar Tests Mexico's New Democracy," *New York Times,* 22 Aug. 1997: A4.

> 8. Harold S. Powers, "Tonal Types and Modal Categories in Renaissance Polyphony," *Journal of the American Musicological Society* 34 (1981) [*or* 34, 3 (Fall 1981)]: 428–70.

Page number The number of the page or pages on which the cited material can be found is always included. The page number is separated from the issue date by a colon and a space, and the abbreviation *p.* or *pp.* is omitted. As in book citations, inclusive numbers should employ either the elided or the unelided style throughout.

Unpublished materials

When an unpublished work is cited, the title (if any) follows the author (if known) and is enclosed in quotation marks and capitalized like a book or article title. If the work is untitled, a descriptive title, not enclosed in quotation marks, should be used instead. The date (if known), any identification or cataloging number, and the name and location of the institution where it can be found, should follow. If the pages are numbered, a page reference should be included. A thesis or dissertation citation should include the granting institution and the year.

> 14. "Pedigree of the Lister family of Ovenden and Shibden Hall," SH:3/LF/27, Calderdale Archives Dept., Halifax, West Riding, Yorkshire.

7. Clive Johnson, letter to Elizabeth O'Hara, 9 Nov. 1916, Johnson Collection, item 5298, California State Historical Society, San Marino, Calif.

1. "Noster ceus psallat letus," MS 778, Fonds Latin, Bibliothèque Nationale, Paris.

30. Linda R. Spence-Blanco, "Structure and Mode in the Lassus Motets," Ph.D. dissertation, Indiana Univ., 1995, 132–35.

Subsequent References to Books and Articles

Later references to a previously cited source employ a shortened form of the data in the first note. This may include the author's last name, a shortened form of the title, and a page reference; it never includes a periodical name, the publisher's name or location, or the publication year. As with initial references, if the author's name or the title appears in the running text introducing the quoted material, they need not be repeated in the note.

9. Bishop, 68.

22. Hölldobler and Wilson, 19–20.

31. Quirk et al., 450.

If more than one work by a given author has been cited, the author's name should be followed by the name of the book, usually shortened, unless the title has just been mentioned in the text.

9. Bishop, *One Art,* 68.

A shortened reference to an article in a periodical should include the author's last name, the title of the article (often shortened), and the page number.

14. Lukacs, "End," 41.

Though the shortened style is almost universally employed in footnotes and endnotes today, a few writers still use the traditional Latin abbreviation *ibid.*

where appropriate. *Ibid.* (for *ibidem,* "in the same place") is used only when referring to the work cited in the immediately preceding note. It may be used several times in succession. When used without a page number, it indicates the same page of the same source as in the note immediately preceding.

> 10. Simone de Beauvoir, *The Second Sex,* trans. and ed. H. M. Parshley (1953; reprint, Knopf, 1987), 600.
> 11. Ibid., 609.
> 12. Ibid.

The Latin abbreviations *op. cit.* (for *opere citato,* "in the work cited") and *loc. cit.* (for *loco citato,* "in the place cited") are very rarely used today but are often encountered in older works. *Op. cit.* refers to the source cited earlier (with other notes intervening) but not to the identical page or pages.

> 19. Sheldon and Eleanor Glueck, *Unraveling Juvenile Delinquency* (New York: Commonwealth Fund, 1950), 23.
> 20. Don C. Gibbons, *Delinquent Behavior* (Englewood Cliffs, N.J.: Prentice-Hall, 1972), 341.
> 21. Glueck, op. cit., 30–34.

Loc. cit. refers strictly to the same page or pages of the same source cited earlier, with references to other sources intervening.

> 13. W. T. Sanders, *Cultural Ecology of the Teotihuacan Valley* (Pennsylvania State Univ., 1965), 312–13.
> 14. Sabloff and Andrews, op. cit., 160.
> 15. Sanders, loc. cit.

Substantive Notes

Substantive or *content notes*—notes providing additional information, commentary, or cross-references—are provided when the author desires to supply a piece of nonessential information, usually not primarily bibliographic, without interrupting the main flow of the text.

Such notes are keyed to the text in the same sequence as bibliographic notes, as in the following list.

1. Lyon Richardson, *A History of Early American Magazines* (New York: Thomas Nelson, 1931), 8.

2. Total average circulation per issue of magazines reporting to the Bureau of Circulation rose from 96.8 million in 1939 to 147.8 million in 1945.

3. For a particularly compelling account of this episode, see James P. Wood, *Magazines in the United States* (New York: Ronald Press, 1949), 92–108.

4. Richardson, 42.

5. For more details, see Appendix.

Texts that use parenthetical references (see below) for all purely bibliographic notes frequently simultaneously use footnotes or endnotes for substantive notes. Any note that refers to a book or article that is not the source of material used in the text (as in note 3 above) also becomes a footnote or endnote.

An unnumbered *source note* is frequently placed at the beginning of each part of a collection of works by different authors to provide information about the individual author or to state where the selection was originally published, and may also acknowledge those who assisted the author or provide other miscellaneous information. Source notes are normally not keyed to the text with a reference number or mark. (The logical place to put the mark would be on the title or the author's name, where most editors and designers are reluctant to use such symbols.) Such notes are conventionally placed at the bottom of the first page of the article or chapter, regardless of which style of documentation is being used in the text itself.

Dr. Muller holds the Rothbart Chair in Sociology at the University of Wisconsin, Madison. The research for this article was partly funded by a grant from the Ganz Foundation.

Reprinted, with permission, from the *Kansas Quarterly* 10 (1978), pp. 42–50.

Parenthetical References

Parenthetical references are highly abbreviated bibliographic citations enclosed in parentheses within the running text itself, which direct the reader to bibliography entries containing the full bibliographic data.

Parenthetical references have the advantage of providing essential information within the text without seriously impeding the reader. Such references originated in the natural sciences. Scientific research articles tend to be brief, sharply focused on a single survey or experiment, and readily summarizable; such articles obviously lend themselves well to bare parenthetical references. Parenthetical references are common in the social sciences as well. They are also often encouraged in the humanities, and even show up occasionally in writing for a broader general audience. However, they are not popular among readers reading for pleasure. Such stripped-down references are also often inadequate in the humanities, where nuances of meaning rather than hard experimental findings are often at issue. And substantive notes can rarely be handled by parenthetical references at all, and must take the form of footnotes or endnotes even if the bulk of a work's references are being treated parenthetically.

A parenthetical reference, like a superscript note reference, is placed either immediately after the quotation or piece of information whose source it refers to or after the author's name. It falls outside of quotation marks but inside commas, periods, semicolons, colons, and dashes. The following example (from Frank B. Gill's *Ornithology*) exemplifies the style used in the sciences:

> R. Haven Wiley (1974) suggests that this is the primary reason that open-country grouse display in leks whereas forest grouse tend to display solitarily. Birds-of-paradise that display in leks are species that inhabit forest borders and second-growth forest, where pre-

dation risk tends to be higher than in primary forest (Beehler and Pruett-Jones 1983). Conspicuous display on traditional sites, however, may attract predators and thereby counter any possible advantages. The Tiny Hawk of Central America, for example, seems to specialize on lekking hummingbirds as prey (F.G. Stiles 1978).

Note how the parenthetical shrinks to the year alone when an author's name appears in the text, and how initials are provided to distinguish F.G. Stiles from another Stiles in the bibliography. The corresponding bibliography entries read as follows:

Beehler, B.M., and S.G. Pruett-Jones. 1983. Display dispersion and diet of birds of paradise: A comparison of nine species. Behav. Ecol. Sociobiol. 13: 229–238.

Stiles, F.G. 1978. Possible specialization for hummingbird-hunting in the Tiny Hawk. Auk 95: 550–553.

Wiley, R.H. 1974. Evolution of social organization and life history patterns among grouse (Aves: Tetraonidae). Q. Rev. Biol. 49: 201–227.

Author-Date References

A parenthetical reference to a work normally consists simply of the author's last name followed by the year of the work's publication. This style, known as the *author-date* (or *name-year) system*, is the parenthetical style used universally in the natural sciences and widely in the social sciences. The alternative *author-page system* (see page 193) is seen in the field of literature and less often in other fields within the humanities. It should be noted that the two styles are often combined; especially in the social sciences, both year and page are very frequently included in the same parenthesis.

Unlike most texts employing footnotes and endnotes, those employing parenthetical references absolutely require a bibliography, since the author's last name followed by a year obviously does not adequately identify a source except for readers very familiar with the literature of their field. The bibliography, or reference list, will generally be alphabetically ordered by the authors' last names, so as to permit the reader to easily locate the source referred to. And in such bibliographies the author's name is usually followed immediately by the year of the work's publication, thereby matching the information given in the parenthetical reference and ensuring maximum ease of lookup.

Often a bibliography will contain works by more than one person with the same last name, or more than one work by a single author from the same year, with the result that a simplest form of author-date reference will be ambiguous. In cases of confusable last names, initials should be added to the last name in the reference (as in the "F.G. Stiles" reference above). Where a single author has published two cited works in the same year, a letter should follow each date: "(Wells 1992a)," "(Wells 1992b)," etc. Any such letters must also be attached to the date in the bibliographic entry.

If a work has two or more authors, the reference must reflect the style and order of the authors' names employed by the bibliography. A reference to a work by two authors will take the style "(Krieger and McCann 1997)"; a work with three authors might read "(Krieger, McCann, and Forster 1988)"; a work with four or more authors, "(Krieger et al. 1990)." A corporate-author name may be abbreviated—e.g. "(Amer. Chem. Soc. 1994)"—as long as abbreviating will not make the bibliographic listing hard to find. A work lacking an official author should be referred to by its title (shortened) if that is how the bibliographic entry will begin: for example, "(*Chicago Manual [of Style]* 1993)."

Two or more works by the same author can be shown within one parenthesis: "(Corelli 1988, 1990)." Citations to separate works by different authors can also be combined: "(Nilsson 1979; Flagstad and Melchior 1982)."

If a longer work is cited, it may be necessary to include a page reference, since page references are rarely permitted in the accompanying bibliography. A page number should be separated from the year by a comma or a colon and may be preceded by *p.* or *pp.:* "(Huizinga 1922, 424)," "(Huizinga 1922: 424)," or "(Huizinga 1922, p.424)." If a multivolume work is cited, the volume number can be included as well, separated from the page reference by a colon: "(Radcliffe and Laing 1985, 2:466)." A reference to an entry in a dictionary or encyclopedia should begin with the name of the actual entry if this will be the headword of its bibliography entry: "('Zoroastrianism and Parsiism,' *Ency. Britannica*)." References to classic literary works that have been published in various editions often cite stanzas, lines, verses, chapters, books, or parts rather than page numbers.

For unpublished or nonprint sources that will not be listed in a bibliography, such as telephone interviews or letters to the author, the reference must include all the data a bibliography entry would have included: the name of the source, the type of communication, the location if applicable, and the date: "(Clarissa Sackville, personal interview, Tunbridge Wells, Conn., 10 Sept. 1996)."

As with other types of references, whenever the running text immediately preceding the parenthetical reference provides any information that would normally appear in the reference, the parenthetical may omit that data.

Author-Page References

Since articles in the humanities tend to be longer and more discursively wide-ranging than scientific articles, and also less likely to be quickly superseded by articles of more recent date, a reference style that includes page references has traditionally been thought more desirable than a style that omits them in favor of a date.

Thus, the type of parenthetical reference most used in certain humanities fields provides the author's last name and a page reference but omits the year of publication. This style, prescribed by the influential *MLA Handbook for Writers of Research Papers,* is used very widely in college and graduate-school term papers and theses and in journals in the field of English. It is less common in the other humanities and infrequent in the social sciences. However, as mentioned, the addition of a page reference to an author-date citation, effectively melding the two systems, is now fairly common especially in the social sciences. Such author-date-page references are endorsed by the widely followed *Publication Manual of the American Psychological Association* (APA).

When more than one work by a given author is cited, references to those works must include a shortened version of their titles (which thus take the place of the date in sciences style). Such shortened titles almost always include (and may consist solely of) a noun. Thus, citations to Jan Tschichold's *The New Typography* and *The Form of the Book* might read "(Tschichold, *Typography* 45)" and "(Tschichold, *Form* 117–18)." Note that the APA manual would call instead for the style "(Tschichold, 1991, pp. 117–18)"—but only where a page reference seemed to be needed.

Otherwise, author-page references observe the same rules as author-date references. For example, they can accommodate multiple author names and diverse citations within a single parenthetical just as author-date references do. Like other parentheticals, they are normally placed immediately after the documented quotation or piece of information or after the author's name, outside any quotation marks but inside (i.e., to the left of) commas, periods, semicolons, colons, or dashes.

More often than in scientific writing, writers in the humanities try to mention the name of cited authors in the running text, a practice that reflects the generally more personal nature of humanities writing. This generally results in parentheticals that consist solely of a page number; such short references hardly interrupt the flow of the text, and most readers so inclined can readily learn to ignore brief numerical interpolations.

> In his *Autobiography* Yeats recalls telling Wilde, half in compliment, "I envy those men who become mythological while still living," and receiving the reply, "I think a man should invent his own myth" (87–88).

Other Systems

Number (Citation-Sequence) System

A newer style of citation, primarily employed in scientific journals (including *Science* and *Nature*), is the one sometimes known as the *citation-sequence system,* a method combining features of the endnote and parenthetical-reference styles.

In the citation-sequence system, each reference source is given a number corresponding to the order of its first appearance in the article. Less commonly, the numbering may reflect instead the alphabetical order of the authors' names. (When numbering according to alphabetical order, the author will be able to assign the final numbers only at the very end of the writing process.) The broader term *number system* covers both the citation-sequence and the alphabetical numbering methods. Regardless of which ordering is used, once a source has been cited, every subsequent citation employs the same number. The numbers are either set like superscript footnote references or set full-size and enclosed in parentheses or brackets. The sources are listed at the end in numerical order (which may reflect either alphabetical or citation sequence).

The example below (from the *New England Journal of Medicine*) illustrates how the method works.

> No antimicrobial drug given alone is adequate therapy for H. pylori. For example, bismuth or amoxicillin given alone eradicates H. pylori rapidly in just over 20

percent of patients.[48-50] H. pylori rapidly becomes resistant to metronidazole alone, resulting in very poor rates of eradication.[62] Treatment with clarithromycin alone may be more effective; in one study an eradication rate of 44 percent was achieved with a high dose (2 g daily) given for 14 days.[55]

The corresponding entries in the nonalphabetical reference list are as follows (note that these follow a style employing minimal punctuation and italicization):

48. Chiba N, Rao BV, Rademaker JW, Hunt RH. Meta-analysis of the efficacy of antibiotic therapy in eradicating Helicobacter pylori. Am J Gastroenterol 1992;87:1716–27.

49. Tytgat GNJ. Treatments that impact favourably upon the eradication of Helicobacter pylori and ulcer recurrence. Aliment Pharmacol Ther 1994; 8:359–68.

50. Penston JG. Helicobacter pylori eradication—understandable caution but no excuse for inertia. Aliment Pharmacol Ther 1994;8:369–89.

55. Peterson WL, Graham DY, Marshall B, et al. Clarithromycin as monotherapy for eradication of Helicobacter pylori: a randomized, double-blind trial. Am J Gastroenterol 1993;88:1860–4.

62. Rautelin H, Seppala K, Renkonen OV, Vainio U, Kosunen TU. Role of metronidazole resistance in therapy of Helicobacter pylori infections. Antimicrob Agents Chemother 1992;326:163–6.

(Since alphabetical order is irrelevant in the citation-sequence system, the authors' names actually need not be inverted as they are here. In addition, all dates follow the journals' names here, since there are no parenthetical references that would require the dates to be moved forward.)

Note the advantages of this system. The page re-

mains uncluttered by parenthetical references and
footnotes. Several citations can be combined incon-
spicuously in a single parenthesis or superscript (separated by commas). Ideally, the writer will feel encouraged to provide the authors' names in the running text
wherever the reader will find them useful and to omit
them wherever they seem unnecessary. The system allows for maximum concision, producing reference lists
of minimal length.

It also has some disadvantages. Like any endnotes,
notes in the citation-sequence system require the curious reader to turn to the end of the article whenever
the author or title is not named in the running text.
Like parenthetical references, citation-sequence notes
are intended only for purely bibliographic notes, and
any substantive notes must generally be handled as separate footnotes or endnotes, since such discussions will
generally relate to only one particular reference to a
given source rather than to all the references to that
source.

An exhaustive discussion of this and related systems
is provided in Mary-Claire van Leunen's *A Handbook for
Scholars.*

White-Copy System

When a serious book is seeking to reach both a scholarly audience and an audience of laypeople, the author
or editor will often choose a documentation style that
actually omits all references from the main text while
retaining complete documentation at the end of the
volume. This so-called *white-copy system* thereby allows
the layperson to read an entire work without being constantly reminded of its documentation. At the same
time, it permits the scholarly reader to seek out the documentation at will; though he or she is not alerted to
the existence of individual references, the assumption
is that any serious reader will sense which text passages
require documentation, and in any case will not be

looking for documentation except where it is of particular interest.

The system is fairly simple to employ, only slightly more laborious than normal endnotes. Consider the following example (from Kip S. Thorne's *Black Holes and Time Warps*):

> . . . As Robert Serber recalls, "Hartland pooh-poohed a lot of things that were standard for Oppie's students, like appreciating Bach and Mozart and going to string quartets and liking fine food and liberal politics."
>
> The Caltech nuclear physicists were a more rowdy bunch than Oppenheimer's entourage; on Oppenheimer's annual spring trek to Pasadena, Hartland fit right in. Says Caltech's William Fowler, "Oppie was extremely cultured; knew literature, art, music, Sanskrit. But Hartland—he was like the rest of us bums. He loved the Kellogg Lab parties, where Tommy Lauritsen played the piano and Charlie Lauritsen [leader of the lab] played the fiddle and we sang college songs and drinking songs. Of all of Oppie's students, Hartland was the most independent."
>
> Hartland was also different mentally. "Hartland had more talent for difficult mathematics than the rest of us," recalls Serber. "He was very good at improving the cruder calculations that the rest of us did." It was this talent that made him a natural for the implosion calculation.
>
> Before embarking on the full, complicated calculation, Oppenheimer insisted (as always) on making a first, quick survey of the problem. . . .

The corresponding endnotes read:

> 212 ["Hartland pooh-poohed . . . liberal politics."] Interview—Serber.
>
> 212 ["Oppie was extremely cultured; . . . most independent.] Interview—Fowler.
>
> 212 ["Hartland had more talent . . . rest of us did."] Interview—Serber.
>
> 212 [Before embarking . . . quick survey of the problem.] Here I am speculating; I do not know for sure

that he carried out such a quick survey, but based on my understanding of Oppenheimer and the contents of the paper he wrote when the research was finished (Oppenheimer and Snyder, 1039), I strongly suspect that he did.

As this example illustrates, the references can be keyed just as precisely as if superscripts appeared on the text page itself. (The accompanying reference list is divided into a section of taped interviews and a standard bibliography.) Notice that the list includes both substantive and bibliographic endnotes. If specific page references had been necessary, they could have been dealt with by an entry such as the following:

> 213 ["I miss terribly . . . in their absence."] Rabi et al. (p. 257).

The corresponding entries in the bibliography read as follows:

Fowler, William A. Taped interview. 6 August 1985, Pasadena, California.

Oppenheimer, J.R., and Snyder, H. (1939). "On Continued Gravitational Contraction," *Physical Review* **56**, 455.

Rabi, I.I., Serber, R., Weisskopf, V.F., Pais, A., and Seaborg, G.T. (1969). *Oppenheimer.* Scribners, New York.

Serber, Robert. Taped interview. 5 August 1985, New York City.

White-copy endnotes may include either full initial references or (as here) a condensed style similar to that of parenthetical references, pointing the curious reader to a bibliography for the rest of the data.

Like standard endnotes, white-copy endnotes usually benefit from running heads that indicate which text pages are covered by each page of endnotes.

The white-copy system seems unlikely to be adopted by scholarly journals or for books exclusively aimed at a scholarly readership. But it is increasingly favored by authors and editors of fairly weighty books that are seen to have the potential to attract a large audience if presented to readers in a palatable form.

Bibliographies

Works in which sources are documented generally end with an alphabetized list of the work's references, which also often includes works not specifically referred to. Such a bibliography, often helpful in footnoted works, is essential in works with parenthetical references, since these brief references only point the reader toward the complete data in a bibliography.

Works with footnotes or endnotes traditionally provide full bibliographic data in initial references, so a bibliography will generally be somewhat redundant in such works; however, even in footnoted works a bibliography will enable the serious reader to scan the writer's sources rapidly, identify useful sources for further reading, and survey the significant publications in a general field at a glance. Annotated bibliographies, with their helpful descriptions, serve additionally to guide the reader to recommended sources. Thus, footnoted (or endnoted) books generally include bibliographies. Footnoted articles, on the other hand, frequently forgo bibliographies altogether, since it is usually so easy for the reader to scan the notes themselves.

Broadly speaking, there are two different styles for bibliography entries: one for the the humanities and general writing, and one for the natural and social sciences. In recent years, some academic journals and publishers have adopted elements of scientific style for documentation in the humanities.

Bibliography entries in the humanities essentially repeat the data contained in the initial footnote to each source, simply inverting the author's name and altering some of the punctuation. Entries in science bibliographies include all the data that humanities entries include but with various differences in style and format.

In sciences style the year of publication immediately follows the author's name; this places the same data included in the parenthetical references right at the beginning of each entry, and thus permits the reader to quickly identify the source cited in a given parenthetical reference. The other differences between the two styles are these: In the sciences, (1) initials (not separated by spaces) are generally used instead of the author's first and middle names, (2) all words in book and article titles are lowercased except the first word, the first word of any subtitle, and proper nouns and adjectives, and (3) article titles are not enclosed in quotation marks. Increasingly in scientific publications, (4) the author's first and middle initials are closed up without any punctuation, and (5) book and journal titles are not italicized.

In each set of examples below, the first group illustrates humanities style and the second illustrates sciences style. These examples, like the examples of in-text references described earlier, by no means exhaust the possible variations on these two basic systems; variant styles are recommended by various professional organizations and academic disciplines. An examination of the references in a professional or scholarly journal will reveal the minor ways in which its preferred style differs from the examples here. (The discussions preceding these examples inevitably repeat some of the information provided earlier in the "Footnotes and Endnotes" section.)

Books

A bibliography entry for a book should include all the following elements that are relevant. (Note that most of the humanities entries in the sample bibliography entries beginning on page 202 match those shown under "Footnotes and Endnotes" beginning on page 181.)

Author's name   The author's name comes first. Names of coauthors are listed in the same order as on the title page. The name of the first author is inverted so that the surname comes first and serves as the basis for alphabetization. The names of additional authors are generally not inverted (though scientific style varies in this respect). In humanities style, names are shown as they appear on the title page. In sciences style, the first and middle names are always abbreviated. In humanities style, if there are more than three authors, only the first author's name is generally shown, followed by *et al.* (set in roman type); in sciences style, either the first three names are listed and followed by *et al.* or as many as six names are listed. A period follows the final name.

In sciences style, the year of publication (with a period after it) normally follows the author's name.

<table>
<tr><td>*Humanities*</td><td>Bishop, Elizabeth, *One Art.* Ed. Robert Giroux. New York: Farrar, Straus & Giroux, 1994.</td></tr>
<tr><td></td><td>Hölldobler, Bert, and Edward O. Wilson. *The Ants.* Cambridge, Mass.: Belknap–Harvard Univ. Press, 1990.</td></tr>
<tr><td></td><td>Alred, Gerald J., Charles T. Brusaw, and Walter E. Oliu. *The Business Writer's Handbook.* 6th ed. New York: St. Martin's, 2000.</td></tr>
<tr><td></td><td>Quirk, Randolph, et al. *A Comprehensive Grammar of the English Language.* London: Longman, 1985.</td></tr>
<tr><td></td><td>New York Times Staff. *The White House Transcripts.* New York: Bantam, 1974.</td></tr>
<tr><td></td><td>*The World Almanac and Book of Facts: 2000.* Mahwah, N.J.: World Almanac Books, 1999.</td></tr>
<tr><td>*Sciences*</td><td>Chandrasekhar, S. 1983. *The mathematical theory of black holes.* New York: Oxford.</td></tr>
<tr><td></td><td>Mayr, E., and P.D. Ashlock. 1991. *Principles of systematic zoology.* 2d ed. New York: McGraw-Hill.</td></tr>
<tr><td></td><td>Morris, M.S., K.S. Thorne, and U. Yurtsever. 1988. Wormholes in spacetime and their</td></tr>
</table>

use for interstellar travel. *Amer. J. of Physics* 56, 395.

Lorentz, H.A., A. Einstein, H. Minkowski, et al 1923 *The principle of relativity*. Reprint, New York: Dover, 1952.

Work in America Institute. 1980. *The future of older workers in America*. New York: Work in America Institute.

McGraw-Hill yearbook of science and technology 2000. 1999. New York: McGraw-Hill.

Title In the humanities, the title of a book or journal is generally italicized. In the sciences, such a title is usually italicized but often not. In the humanities, headline-style capitalization (all words capitalized except for internal articles and prepositions) is standard; in the natural and social sciences, both headline-style and sentence-style capitalization (only the first word and proper nouns and adjectives capitalized) are used. (The titles of sample book references in the sciences in this chapter are set italic and use sentence-style capitalization.) Titles in the humanities include any subtitles, whereas subtitles are often omitted in science bibliographies.

Humanities	Maxmen, Jerrold S. *The Post-Physician Era: Medicine in the Twenty-First Century*. New York: Wiley, 1976.
Sciences	Hartshorne, C. 1973. *Born to sing[: An interpretation and world survey of bird song]*. Bloomington: Indiana Univ. Press.

Editor, compiler, or translator In entries for books that have an author, the name of an editor, compiler, or translator—preceded or followed by the abbreviation *ed.*, *comp.*, or *trans.* or some combination of these—follows the title. If no author is listed, the name of the editor, compiler, or translator is placed first, followed by a comma and *ed.*, *comp.*, or *trans.*

Humanities	Beauvoir, Simone de. *The Second Sex.* Trans. and ed. H. M. Parshley. 1953; New York, Knopf, 1993.
	Banks, Arthur S., and Thomas C. Muller, eds. *Political Handbook of the World, 1999.* Binghamton, N.Y.: CSA Publications, 1999.
Sciences	Robinson, I., A. Schild, and E.L. Schucking, eds. 1965. *Quasi-stellar sources and gravitational collapse.* Chicago: Univ. of Chicago Press.

Part of the book   When a bibliography entry cites only one part of a book, such as an essay in a collection or an article from a symposium, the name of that part is given first as a title in roman type. In humanities style, it is enclosed in quotation marks; in sciences style, it is not. The book title follows. Titles of chapters of nonfiction works by a single author are omitted.

Humanities	Culler, Jonathan. "Derrida." *Structuralism and Since: From Levi-Strauss to Derrida,* ed. John Sturrock. New York. Oxford Univ. Press, 1981: 154–80.
Sciences	Stebbins, G.L. Botany and the synthetic theory of evolution. 1980. *The evolutionary synthesis: Perspectives on the unification of biology,* ed. E. Mayr and W.B. Provine. Reprint, Cambridge, Mass.: Harvard Univ. Press, 1998.

Name of a series   If the book is part of a series, the series name (unitalicized) should be included, as well as the volume number if any.

Humanities	Stocking, George W., Jr. *Functionalism Historicized: Essays on British Social Anthropology.* History of Anthropology Series, vol. 2. Madison: Univ. of Wisconsin Press, 1984.
Sciences	Genoway, H.H. 1973. *Systematics and evolutionary relationships of spiny pocket mice,*

genus Liomys. Special Publications of the Museum 5. Lubbock: Texas Tech Univ. Press.

Edition

If a book is other than the first edition, the number or other description of the edition ("2d ed.," "1992 ed.," "Rev. ed.," etc.) follows the title.

Humanities   Baugh, Albert C., and Thomas Cable. *A History of the English Language.* 4th ed. Englewood Cliffs, N.J.: Prentice Hall, 1992.

Sciences   Gill, F.B. 1995. *Ornithology.* 2nd ed. New York. W. H. Freeman.

Volume number or number of volumes

In an entry that cites a multivolume work, the total number of volumes (e.g., "9 vols.") comes next. There is usually no need to cite the volumes actually used, since this will appear in a note or parenthetical reference. If only one volume was consulted, that volume alone is listed as an entry so that the text references can omit volume numbers.

Humanities   Boyd, Brian. *Vladimir Nabokov.* 2 vols. Princeton, N.J.: Princeton Univ. Press, 1990–91.

Sciences   Nowak, R.M. 1999. *Walker's mammals of the world.* 6th ed. 2 vols. Baltimore: Johns Hopkins Univ. Press.

Publication data

The city of publication (with the state abbreviation if necessary) and the name of the publisher follow; in humanities style, the year of publication follows the publisher.

A colon follows the city name. In humanities style, a comma follows the publisher's name, and a period follows the date. In the sciences, a period follows the publisher's name, the date having already appeared after the author's name. If the place or publisher is unknown, use *n.p;* if the date is unknown, use *n.d.* However, any part of the publication data that is known but not printed on the title page may be added in brackets.

If the title page lists more than one city, only the first appears in the bibliography. If a special imprint name appears above the publisher's name, it may be joined to the publisher's name with an en dash (e.g., "Golden Press–Western Publishing"). Short forms of publishers' names (e.g., "Wiley" for "John Wiley & Sons, Inc.," "Dover" for "Dover Publications, Inc.") are now fairly standard in bibliographies just as in notes; the abbreviated style, if used, should be used consistently. The word *and* and the ampersand (&) are equally acceptable within publishers' names; one or the other should be used consistently for all publishers.

For a multivolume work published over a period of several years, inclusive numbers are given for those years. For works about to be published, "in press" is substituted for the date.

> *Humanities*   Shevoroshki, Vitalij V., and T. L. Markery. *Typology, Relationship and Time.* Ann Arbor, Mich.: Karoma [Publishers, Inc.], 1986.
>
> Sperber, Dan. *On Anthropological Knowledge: Three Essays.* New York: Cambridge [Univ. Press], 1985.
>
> *Sciences*   Kuhn, T.S. 1996. *The structure of scientific revolutions.* 3rd ed. Chicago: [Univ. of] Chicago [Press].

Reprint   A citation of a reprint should specify the original publication year (if known).

> *Humanities*   McMurtrie, Douglas C. *The Book: The Story of Printing and Bookmaking.* 3d ed. 1943. Reprint, New York: Dorset, 1990.
>
> *Sciences*   Lorentz, H.A., A. Einstein, H. Minkowski, et al. 1922. *The principle of relativity.* Reprint, New York: Dover, 1952.

Page references   Page numbers are normally added to book entries in a bibliography only when the entry cites a discrete portion, such as an article or story in a collection, in which case inclusive page numbers for the complete piece are shown. If that portion is in a volume of a multivolume work, both volume and page number are given.

> *Humanities* Fernandez, James W. "The Argument of Images and the Experience of Returning to the Whole." *The Anthropology of Experience,* ed. Victor W. Turner and Edward M. Bruner, 159–87. Urbana: Univ. of Illinois Press, 1986.
>
> *Sciences* Briggs, J.C. 1986. Gobiesocidae. *Fishes of the North-eastern Atlantic and the Mediterranean,* ed. P.J.P. Whitehead et al. 3:1351–59. Paris: UNESCO.

Articles

Citations to journals, like citations to books, follow a style parallel to that used in footnotes.

Author's name The author's name follows the same style as for book entries. Writers of signed reviews or of letters to the editor are treated like authors.

> *Humanities* Rosaldo, Renato. "Doing Oral History." *Social Analysis* 4 (1980): 89–90.
>
> Craig, Gordon A. Review of *The Wages of Guilt: Memories of War in Germany and Japan,* by Ian Buruma. *New York Review of Books,* 14 July 1994: 43–45.
>
> *Sciences* Ho, P.T.C., and A.J. Murgo. 1995. Letter to the editor. *N. Eng. J. of Med.* 333:1008.

Article title In humanities style, the title and subtitle are enclosed in quotation marks and capitalized headline-style. In sciences style, article titles omit the quotation marks and use sentence-style capitalization; any subtitle is generally omitted. (A few journals in the natural sciences omit the article title altogether.)

Humanities   Preston, Richard. "A Reporter at Large: Crisis in the Hot Zone." *New Yorker*, 26 Oct. 1992: 58–81.

Sciences   Penrose, R. 1995. Gravitational collapse and spacetime singularities. *Phys. Rev. L.* 14: 57.

Periodical name   The periodical's name is italicized in the humanities and usually but not always in the sciences. Unlike book titles, periodical titles are capitalized headline-style in bibliographies in the sciences as well as the humanities. Any *The* at the beginning of a title is dropped. In the sciences, journal titles are generally abbreviated; each discipline has a standard set of abbreviations for its journals. (The citations in a scholarly or professional journal are the best source for such abbreviations in a given field.) Outside of the sciences, journal titles are generally not abbreviated. Titles that begin with the words *Transactions, Proceedings,* and *Annals* are traditionally inverted (thus, *Proceedings of the American Philosophical Society* becomes *American Philosophical Society Proceedings*). Names of newspapers are treated as they appear on the masthead, except that any initial *The* is omitted. A place-name is added in brackets if it is needed to identify the paper, and a particular edition ("Evening edition," "New England edition") may have to be identified.

Humanities   Harris, Richard. "Chicago's Other Suburbs." *[The] Geographical Review* 84, 4 (Oct. 1994): 396.

Perlez, Jane. "Winning Literary Acclaim, A Voice of Central Europe." *[The] New York Times*, New England Final ed., 9 Sept. 1997: B1–2.

Sciences   Goodwin, G.G., and A.M. Greenhall. 1961. A review of the bats of Trinidad and Tobago. *Bull. Amer. Mus. Nat. Hist. [Bulletin of the American Museum of Natural History]* 122:187–302.

Periodical volume, number, and date Periodicals whose issues are primarily identified by volume and number should be identified in that way in a bibliography. Those whose issues are instead identified primarily by date must be identified by date instead. Numbers are not commonly used unless the issue is paginated independently of the volume as a whole and the number is needed to identify the issue. If the volume number corresponds to a particular year, the year in parentheses follows the volume number. In the sciences, the year is omitted here, having already appeared next to the author's name.

Some periodicals use a seasonal designation in addition to a volume and number designation; the pages are often numbered independently of the volume as a whole. Popular monthly and weekly magazines are referred to by date, as are newspapers. Precise dates are given in day–month–year order. Names of months with more than four letters are usually abbreviated.

Some scientific journals print the volume number in boldface to distinguish it from adjacent page or issue numbers.

Humanities	Heil, John. "Seeing Is Believing." *American Philosophical Quarterly* 19 (1982): 224–48.
	Lukacs, John. "The End of the Twentieth Century." *Harper's*, Jan. 1993: 39– 58.
	Dillon, Sam. "Trial of a Drug Czar Tests Mexico's New Democracy." *New York Times*, 22 Aug. 1997: A4–5.
	Powers, Harold S. "Tonal Types and Modal Categories in Renaissance Polyphony." *Journal of the American Musicological Society* [or *JAMS*] 34, 3 (Fall 1981) [*or . . .* 34 (1981)]: 428–70.
Sciences	Glanz, W.E. 1984. Food and habitat use by two sympatric *Sciurus* species in central Panama. *J. Mammal.* 65:342–46.

> Conway, M.S., and H.B. Whittington. 1979. The animals of the Burgess Shale. *Scientific American* 240 (Jan.): 122–33.

Page numbers   Inclusive pages for *the whole article* are normally provided at the end of the entry, preceded by a colon and followed by a period. For newspaper entries, it may be necessary to add a section letter as well (e.g., "B6"). When an article is continued on later pages after a break, those pages should be cited as well (e.g., "38–41, 159–60"); alternatively, a plus sign following the opening page number ("38+") may take the place of all subsequent numbers.

Humanities	Friedrich, Otto. "United No More." *Time*, 4 May 1987: 28–37.
Sciences	Lemon, R.E., and C. Chatfield. 1971. Organization of song in cardinals. *Anim. Behav.* 19:1–17.

Unpublished Materials

Unpublished materials often itemized in source listings include not only theses and dissertations but also a bewildering variety of other documents, particularly those that may have come to be housed in archives—letters, receipts, reports, balance sheets, music manuscripts, legal briefs, evidentiary materials, memoranda, handwritten notes, speeches, book manuscripts, and so on. (Often the author will provide a separate list of archival documents.) It would hardly be possible to dictate a comprehensive set of guidelines for citing such documents. However, the writer who is careful to note down every identifiable cataloging or identification criterion on first being shown the materials and to reproduce these in a fairly consistent format in the bibliography is unlikely to be criticized.

The author's name should be treated just as for a book or article. Any formal title should appear just as it does on the work, enclosed in quotation marks and capitalized like the title of a book or article. If the work has no official title, a descriptive title, not enclosed in quotation marks, should be used instead.

If the work is dated, the date must be included. If the date is known but does not appear on the document, it should be enclosed in brackets.

The final essential information is the cataloging or identification number—or whatever information is necessary to identify and locate the document in its collection—along with the name of the collection, its parent institution (if any), and the city.

Humanities   "Pedigree of the Lister family of Ovenden and Shibden Hall." SH:3/LF/27. Calderdale Archives Dept., Halifax, West Riding, Yorkshire.

Johnson, Clive. Letter to Elizabeth O'Hara. 9 Nov. 1916. Item 5298, Johnson Collection, California State Historical Society, San Marino.

"Noster cetus psallat letus." MS 778, Fonds Latin, Bibliothèque Nationale, Paris.

Spence-Blanco, Linda R. "Structure and Mode in the Lassus Motets." Ph.D. dissertation. Indiana Univ., 1995.

Sciences   Maxwell, J.C. Letter to J.O. Hartwell, 9 June 1850. Bonneville Archive, King's College Library, Cambridge Univ., Cambridge, England.

Bibliography Order and Format

For ease of scanning, bibliographies are traditionally set with flush-and-hang indention—that is, with the initial line of each entry set flush left and the subsequent lines indented. All the entries are normally listed together alphabetically, whether the first word is an author's surname or the title of a book. (Initial articles in titles are ignored in determining alphabetical order.) Special types of entries—recordings, artworks, films, personal interviews, archival documents, etc.—may be segregated in separate lists. Bibliographies are occasionally divided into categories by subject matter; however, such divisions are usually desirable only for bibliographies that represent recommended-reading lists in a variety of discrete subject areas (as in this book's bibliography).

After the first listing of an entry by an author (or the coauthors) of more than one listed work, the name (or names) is replaced in succeeding adjacent entries by a long (three-em) underline or dash (usually typed as six hyphens). It is followed by a period, or by a comma and an abbreviation such as *ed.*, just as a name would be. The underline or dash substitutes for the author's or coauthors' full name or names. However, it may be used only when all the names are exactly the same in the adjacent entries; otherwise, all the names must be written out.

A work by a single author precedes a work by that author and another; and works *written* by an author usually precede works *edited* by the same person.

In the humanities, the various works by a single author or group of coauthors are ordered alphabetically by title. In the sciences, they are ordered by date; if an author has published more than one article during a year, each can be distinguished by a letter (often italicized) appended to the year (1995a, 1995b, etc.), which must also appear in any text references.

Depending on its scope, a list of sources may be headed "Bibliography," "List of References," "Literature Cited," "Works Cited," or "References Cited." (The term *bibliography* has been used broadly in this chapter to cover all these possibilities.) A list headed "Bibliography" traditionally lists all the works a writer has found relevant in writing the text. A "List of References" includes only works specifically mentioned in the text or from which particular quotations or pieces of information were taken. Writings in the sciences often use the heading "Literature Cited"; however, only "literature"—published works—actually cited can be included on such a list, and bibliographic information for unpublished works must be provided within the text itself. (Works in press may be considered literature.) The heading "References Cited" allows the inclusion of unpublished works. "Works Cited" allows the inclusion of the references described below under "Special Types of References."

In an *annotated bibliography,* entries are followed by a sentence or paragraph of description, in order to lead the reader to the most useful works for further study. A bibliography may be selectively annotated, or every single entry may include an annotation. The descriptive part may either be run in with the entry or be set off by spacing, indention, italics, or smaller type.

> Trow, George W. S. *Within the Context of No Context.*
> 1981; New York: Atlantic Monthly, 1997.
> A short, strange, elegant meditation on television and post–World War II American culture. After almost two decades, its aphoristic insights seem more uncannily prescient and disturbing than ever.

The elements and options of bibliography design can best be understood by studying the bibliographies in a variety of publications.

Special Types of References

Cited sources frequently include items that do not fit neatly into any of the categories described above. Several of these types of references (recordings, films, artworks, literary classics, etc.) appear almost exclusively in humanities writing, almost always identified concisely in the text itself. Thus, most of the illustrative examples below illustrate a single style of bibliography entry, from which the corresponding note or parenthetical reference can easily be generated.

Nonprint Sources

Nonprint entries will often be listed separately from standard bibliographic items. Many bibliographies omit nonprint entries altogether; however, if the decision is made to include them, it should be done systematically.

Personal communications The name of a person who supplied information in a personal communication is listed first, styled like an author's name. A descriptive word or phrase—"personal communication," "telephone interview," etc.—follows, unitalicized and without quotation marks. The place (if applicable) and date of the communication are also given.

> Sandage, Allen. Personal interview. Baltimore, 13 Sept. 1985.

Such sources are rarely included in a list of references; more often, the information is worked into the running text or provided exclusively as a footnote or endnote; in scientific publications it is usually given in the form of a parenthetical reference with no corresponding bibliography entry.

> . . . seemed a rather feeble construct (A. Sandage, pers. interview, 13 Sept. 1985).

Speeches Speeches and lectures are identified by (1) speaker's name, (2) speech title, in quotation marks (or a descriptive name if the speech has no formal title), (3) name of the meeting, sponsoring organization, or occasion, (4) place, and (5) date.

> Halcott-Sanders, Peter. "Armenia 1915—Rwanda 1994." LeSueur Memorial Address. Lafayette Hall, New Orleans. 2 November 1994.

Television or radio program Broadcast programs are occasionally cited in reference lists. The title of the program is usually listed first, in italics. If it is an episode of a series, the episode title is enclosed in quotation marks and the name of the series follows in italics. If the text reference is to a particular performer, director, or other person, that person's name may be listed first and thus determine the basis for alphabetization. The names of the performers, composer, director, or other participants may follow the title. The network, the local station and city, and the date of the broadcast complete the citation.

> "Goodbye, Farewell, and Amen." *M*A*S*H,* CBS. WFSB-TV, Hartford, Conn. 28 Feb. 1983.
>
> Burns, Ken. *Baseball.* 8 episodes. PBS. WGBY-TV, Springfield, Mass. 28 Sept.–16 Nov. 1994.

Sound recordings How recordings are listed in a discography frequently depends on the writer's focus. The participants in a recording may be numerous and various enough that it may sometimes be necessary to create entries for which no readily available model exists. A work devoted to performers will generally alphabetize a list of recordings by performers' names. (In orchestral recordings, this will usually be the conductor's name rather than the ensemble's.) Alternatively, a listing might alphabetize by composers' or songwriters' names. If a discography is entirely devoted to a single performer or composer, that person's name should naturally be omitted from all the entries. Common foreign terms (*Quatuor, Coro, Dirigent,* etc.) may be silently translated (as they have been in the first example below). The recording's title, the recording company's name, the year, and the catalog number follow, and other information may be added as needed.

> Abbado, Claudio, cond. Gustav Mahler, *Symphony No. 3.* Vienna Philharmonic Orch. and Chorus; Jessye Norman, soprano. 2-CD set. Deutsche Grammophon, 1982. 2741010.
>
> Cruz, Celia, with David Byrne. "Loco de Amor." On David Byrne, *Rei Momo.* Cassette tape. Luaka Bop/Sire Records, 1989. 925990-4.

Films and videotapes Films, film scripts, and videotapes are usually listed by either title or director. However, as with sound recordings, if such participants as
writers, performers, or composers are the focus of the
text, their names may be listed first, or such participants
may be listed subsequently in a consistent order. (As
with recordings, a filmography devoted to a single person will omit that person's name from all entries.) The
title (italicized) is usually followed by whatever other
names may be needed to identify the work. A descriptive term such as "Filmstrip," "Slide program," or
"Videocassette" should be added if appropriate, followed by the production company and the year. A catalog number and any other relevant information may
be added as appropriate.

> Tourneur, Jacques, dir. *Out of the Past.* With Robert
> Mitchum, Jane Greer, and Kirk Douglas. Screen-
> play: Geoffrey Homes (pseud. of Daniel Main-
> waring), James M. Cain, and Frank Fenton (both
> uncredited). Cinematography: Nicholas Musu-
> raca. RKO. 1947.

Artworks and crafts Artworks are occasionally cited
in reference lists. References to artworks generally
begin with the artist's name, which is followed by the
title (italicized), the year it was created, and the name
and city of the museum or collection. The work's
medium (or media) and sometimes its dimensions and
a catalog number may be included as well. If the artist
is unknown, the abbreviation "Anon." may begin the
entry; for crafts, "Anon." may more often be omitted
throughout. A descriptive title for an untitled work is
not italicized.

> Repin, Ilya Yefimovich. *Zaporozhian Cossacks.* Oil on
> canvas. 1891. State Russian Museum, St. Peters-
> burg.
> High chest. 1725–35. Boston, Mass. Pine, maple, tulip
> poplar. 69½ x 40¼ x 22½. Winterthur Museum,
> Wilmington, Del. 52.255.

Microforms Normally published material that has been microfilmed for storage is cited as if the actual works had been handled, with no mention of the microform process. Only materials that exist only or primarily on microfilm or microfiche—including archival materials, reports, privately printed works, and works published originally as microfiche sets—need to have that fact acknowledged. If they are available from a commercial service, it should be named. If the microphotography was done by the archive or library that is storing it, the latter's name and location must be given.

> Wiener Stadt- und Landesarchiv [Vienna City and Provincial Archives]. *Todten Protokoll* [List of Deceased Persons] (24 Oct. 1771). Microfilm.
>
> Russian Academy of Sciences Library, St. Petersburg (BAN). *Catalogue of Foreign Language Books and Periodicals to 1930.* 992 microfiche. London: Chadwyck-Healey.

Government and Legal Publications

If a publication by a government agency has a named author, that name may appear first. However, most government publications are officially authored by an agency rather than an individual. The name of the government (e.g., "U.S.," "Montana," "Chicago") usually comes first, then the names of the department (if applicable) and agency. The title (italicized) should be followed by any series or publication number used by the agency. Most U.S. government publications are published by the Government Printing Office, which is usually abbreviated *GPO;* however, references to congressional documents, and often other references to U.S. government sources, omit the GPO publication data altogether. Standardized abbreviations are often used in these references, but names may instead be spelled out, especially in works intended for a general audience.

U.S. Department of Labor. *Occupational Outlook Handbook, 2000–1.* Washington, D.C.: GPO, 2000.

U.S. Bureau of the Census. *Geographical Mobility, March 1994 to March 1995.* Current Population Reports, Series P-20, no. 37 (1996).

U.S. Office of Technology Assessment. *Informing the Nation: Federal Information Dissemination in an Electronic Age.* OTA-CIT-396 (1988).

Texas Dept. of Information Resources. *Video Conferencing Standards.* SRRPUB 5-1 (1995).

Congressional documents and bills Citations of Congressional documents normally list the following elements: (1) "U.S. House of Representatives" or "U.S. Senate" and the name of the committee or subcommittee, if applicable, (2) the document's title, (3) the document's number or other description, (4) the date, and (5) the page reference. The number and session of Congress are often included as well. The *Congressional Record* is identified only by date and page number.

U.S. House Special Committee on Aging. *The Early Retirement Myth: Why Men Retire before Age 62.* Publ. 97-298 (1981).

Cong. Rec. 2 Aug. 1996: S9466–69.

In citations of congressional bills, *H.R.* is the conventional abbreviation for "House of Representatives" and *S.* for "Senate." In citations of congressional reports, *H.* is used instead of *H.R.* For both bills and reports, the number and session of Congress follow the document title.

H.R. 898 (Balanced Budget Act), 105th Congress, 1st Session.

Laws, regulations, and constitutions References to laws, regulations, and constitutions should be documented in the notes and bibliography whenever complete data is not provided in the text.

The legal profession itself almost invariably follows

the citation forms stipulated in *The Bluebook: A Uniform System of Citation*, and almost anyone writing or editing legal books must be thoroughly familiar with the *Bluebook's* recommendations. However, its highly condensed forms, which are optimally efficient for professionals, are opaque to most laypeople. Thus, any author writing about a legal subject for a wider audience who intends to use *Bluebook* style should consider providing a guide to interpreting the citations in the prefatory matter or as a headnote to the endnotes or bibliography. Otherwise, any abbreviations should be limited to those readily understood by the public.

In general, federal laws are published in the United States Code (U.S.C.), and each state publishes its laws in its own series. In most series, the volume number precedes the name of the set. Wherever possible, the act's name (if it has one) should be included.

> Americans with Disabilities Act, 42 U.S.C. §1201 et seq. (1990).
>
> Minn. Stat. § 289.23.

Federal regulations codified in the *Code of Federal Regulations* or the *Federal Register* are identified by volume number, section or page number, and date.

> 32 C.F.R. § 199 (1994).
>
> 43 Fed. Reg. 54221 (1978).

Roman numerals are traditionally used for constitutional articles and amendments.

> Indiana Constitution, Art. III, sec. 2, cl. 4.

Court cases Titles of court cases are italicized within the text (e.g., *Surner* v. *Kellogg*, *In re Watson*) but not in bibliographies. The v. (for *versus*) is usually set roman.

A citation to a court case provides not only (1) the name of the case, but also (2) the number, title, and page of the volume in the multivolume set where it is recorded, and (3) the date. The name of the court that decided the case is usually included with the date if it is not mentioned in the running text. As in standard citations, the volume number precedes the abbreviated name of the multivolume series and the first page of the decision or regulation follows the name. (Inclusive page numbers are not used in legal references.)

> Turner Broadcasting System, Inc. v. Federal Communications Commission, 512 U.S. 622 (1997).
>
> Barker v. Shalala, 40 F.3d 789 (6th Cir. 1994).
>
> Palsgraf v. Long Island Railroad Co., 248 N.Y. 339 (1928).

Classic Literary Works

Since older classic literary works are usually available in different editions with different paginations, documentation of classic novels, stories, plays, and poems frequently includes the divisions of the work (chapter, book, part, act, scene, line) in addition to the page numbers of the edition being cited. (In long poems and verse plays with numbered lines, only the lines are cited.)

> This exchange closely resembles one in *Mansfield Park* (410; vol. 3, chap. 9).

Numerals alone are used in footnotes and endnotes and especially in parenthetical references whenever they can be easily understood without accompanying abbreviations or words such as *chap. (chapter)*, *v. (verse)*, *act, sc. (scene)*, or *l. (line)*, particularly in extended discussions of a given work. (Bear in mind that the abbreviations for *line* and *lines*, *l.* and *ll.* are easily mistaken for the numbers 1 and 11.) Frequently two numerals are used together, the first indicating a large division of the work and the second a smaller division, separated by a period or sometimes a comma: thus, "book 4, line 122" becomes "4.122." For the act and scene of a play, capital and lowercase Roman numerals may be used ("III.ii"), but Arabic numbers are now more common ("3.2").

> The redoubtable Mrs. Marwood has just pronounced that "For my part, my Youth may wear and waste, but it shall never rust in my Possession" (2.1).

Divisions of literary works are hardly ever cited specifically in bibliographies.

The Bible

The Bible is listed in bibliographies only when a particular edition is specified in the text; such editions follow standard bibliographic form. Whether or not an edition is specified, a standard text reference (whether provided as a note or a parenthetical) includes the name of the biblical book, set roman and often abbreviated, followed by Arabic numerals representing chapter and verse, separated by a colon (or, less often, a period). Such information commonly appears in parentheticals even in nonscholarly writing. If a book has two parts, an Arabic numeral precedes the book's name. Page numbers are never used in such citations.

> (Gen. 1:1)
> (Job 38:4-41)
> (2 Chron. 16:1-2)

Electronic Sources

Computer software References to computer software are normally treated just like book references except that the medium is added after the title. The city name is frequently dropped, and additional information, such as the operating system the software is designed for, may be added if appropriate.

> *Import/Export USA*. CD-ROM. Detroit: Gale Research, 1998. Windows.

British Library Map Catalogue on CD-ROM. Primary Source Microfilm, 2000.

On-line sources Since many on-line sources are highly subject to change or deletion, any on-line text likely to be cited—including personal E-mail messages—should always be either downloaded onto a disk or printed out and stored on paper (with a notation of the date accessed) as a permanent record.

There is no universally accepted standard for citing Internet sources, but since most such sources can now be accessed by using a Web browser, it is generally adequate to indicate the document's URL (uniform resource locator)—for materials available on Web, Gopher, FTP, or Telnet servers—somewhere in the citation, usually following the date on which the electronic document was published, posted, or last revised (if known). Thus a typical citation of an on-line source would show the author's name, the title of the document, the title of the complete work (such as the name of a periodical) in italics, the date, and the full URL. A URL is composed of the protocol used (*http, gopher, ftp,* or *telnet*), the server's identification, the directory path, and the file's name.

Agmon, Eytan. "Beethoven's Op. 81a and the Psychology of Loss." *Music Theory Online* 2, 4 (1996). http://boethius.music.ucsb.edu/mto/issues/mto.96.2.4/mto.2.4.agmon.html

"Sacagawea." *Encyclopædia Britannica Online.* http://www.eb.com [12 May 1999].

Kinsley, Michael. "Totally Disingenuous." *Slate* 11 Sept. 2000. http://slate.msn.com/Readme/00-09-11/Readme.asp [13 Sept. 2000].

Davies, Al. 1997. Mitral Valvular Prolapse Syndrome. *Medical Reporter* 2, 11 (Feb.). http://www.dash.com/netro/nwx/tmr/tmr0297/valvular 0297.html

CERT. "The CERT Coordination Center FAQ." (Aug. 1997). ftp://info.cert.org/pub/cert_faq (3 Oct. 1997).

> Dalhousie, Duncan. "Scottish Clans On-Line." (19 May 1996). gopher://dept.english.upenn.edu:70/11/Scotts/Clan.txt (3 Oct. 1997).

It is usually desirable to include the date of access at the end of the citation, enclosed in brackets; this may often be the only date shown, since many on-line documents do not include dates.

> Avoiding Problems with Altitude Sickness. *Mayo Clinic Health Oasis* 8 May 2000. http://www.mayohealth.org/mayo/9702/htm/altitude.htm [12 Oct. 2000]

The widely followed MLA guidelines for styling electronic citations instead place the unenclosed date of access before the URL and enclose the document's URL in angle brackets.

> Avoiding Problems with Altitude Sickness. *Mayo Clinic Health Oasis* 8 May 2000. 12 Oct. 2000. <http://www.mayohealth.org/mayo/9702/htm/altitude.htm>.

When a document is accessible only through a proprietary on-line service, the name of that service should be included in the citation:

> "French Truckers Create Blockades." *AP Online.* 4 Sept. 2000. Lexis-Nexis [14 Sept. 2000].

Periodicals published on paper that happen to be accessed on-line may be cited just like normal periodicals, with no acknowledgment of their on-line status, if it is clear that the text has not been altered for the on-line version.

> Friskics-Warren, Bill. "Earl Scruggs, Still Pickin' Up a Storm." *The Washington Post.* 4 June 2000, final edition. [13 Aug. 2000].

References to mailing lists or newsgroup postings should begin with the author's name, include the subject line (or a made-up descriptive subject line), and provide the name and electronic address of the mailing-list server or newsgroup and the date posted. A personal E-mail message can be called "Personal communication" with no mention of its electronic medium.

> Marchand, Jim. "L'humour de Berceo." (1 Oct. 1997). Medieval Texts Discussion List. Medtext-1@postoffice.cso.uiuc.edu
>
> Massey, Neil. "Year 2000 and Sendmail 8.8.6." (1 Oct. 1997). comp.mail.sendmail

Many mailing-list discussions are archived after messages are posted. Archives are usually maintained on the mailing list's server and may also be available through a Web page. An archived message is cited in its original form unless the message was accessed through a Web server rather than the list server or newsgroup.

> McCarty, Willard. "Reading vs. Clicking vs. Life." 19 May 2000. Humanist Discussion Group. http://lists.village.virginia.edu/lists_archive/Humanist/v14/0021.html [23 July 2000].

8 Copyediting and Proofreading

This chapter describes the basic editorial steps that writers, copyeditors, and proofreaders go through in order to produce accurate and readable written or printed materials. For some people involved with writing not intended for publication as a bound book, some of the steps (such as writing specifications for typesetters and handling page proofs) will not be necessary. However, for anyone writing for publication, this chapter can serve as a basic introduction to the range of activities referred to as *editorial production*.

Editorial production may be handled by a large staff of specialists or by a single person. A large book publisher may employ a staff of acquisitions editors, developmental editors, general editors, production editors, copy editors, designers, and proofreaders. A small company may require only one editor to handle all production tasks. In this chapter, the tasks are somewhat arbitrarily allocated to an *in-house editor,* with overall responsibility for getting the author's manuscript into print; a *designer,* who designs the book's interior; a *copy editor,* who does the principal editing of the manuscript for style, consistency, and correctness; and a *proofreader,* who checks typeset proofs against manuscript copy.

Overview

The process of producing a bound book from a book manuscript usually encompasses at least the steps listed below.

1. The author submits a manuscript, generally in both electronic and printed form, which will often already have gone through one or more revisions or rewritings as a result of reviews by an agent, a high-level editor, or several academic experts, depending on the nature of the manuscript.

2. The manuscript (also called *typescript* or *copy*) is given to a copy editor for copyediting.

3. The copyedited manuscript is sent to the author for review.

4. A designer (sometimes the in-house editor) designs the book's interior, producing a set of *design specifications,* or *specs.*

5. The typesetter, or *compositor,* sets *sample pages* that show how the proposed design will look in print; these are reviewed in-house, and the specs are altered if necessary.

6. The typemarked (or electronically coded) manuscript, which now incorporates all editorial changes, is sent to a typesetter, who sets it according to the design specs.

7. The typesetter returns *first* or *galley proofs.*

8. The editor sends a set of proofs to the author for review, and another (or sometimes the same set when it is returned) to a proofreader. The author's own corrections are carried to the proofreader's *master proof,* which is then returned to the typesetter, accompanied by any illustrations, in camera-ready form.

9. The typesetter makes the corrections by reset-

ting parts of the copy, which is then combined with any art—sometimes initially in the form of a *dummy* of the book made from photocopies or on a computer—to produce *second* or *page proofs.*

10. The editor or proofreader checks the proof corrections (and may ask for several revised proofs) and returns them to the typesetter.

11. The typesetter, after incorporating any further corrections, sends high-quality prints *(repro proofs)* or film negatives or an electronic version of the final pages to the printer.

12. The printer uses film to create a complete set of film proofs *(book blues),* which are sent to the editor for review.

13. The editor carefully reviews the book blues and returns them to the printer with all necessary corrections marked.

14. The printer makes the corrections, creates the printing plates, and starts the print run. At the very beginning of the run, the printer sends an early set of actual book signatures—called *folded and gathered sheets (f and g's or F&G's)—* to the editor for review.

15. The printed signatures go to the binder to produce bound books.

Some of these steps may become complex, especially when there is a large amount of artwork or when the manuscript is divided into sections that go through each stage at a different time. Scheduling is extremely important. Since typesetters and especially printers try to schedule their jobs to take advantage of every working minute, an editor's missed deadline may mean that work may be put off for weeks while the typesetter or printer completes other previously scheduled jobs. Thus, the handling of manuscript and proof must be carefully scheduled so that deadlines can be met without sacrificing editing and proofing quality. Editors generally keep a wall chart listing each of their various projects and each editorial steps involved in turning manuscript into bound books. Each cell will often show a target date, next to which will be filled in the date each stage is actually completed. A complicated book being handled section-by-section may even require a separate chart on which each chapter or section occupies its own row or column.

The Manuscript

Author's Manuscript Checklist

The author's manuscript must be submitted in a form that will make the editing as efficient as possible. Most authors now prepare their manuscripts on computers and submit them on diskette with accompanying hardcopy printouts. The author is usually asked to submit at least two printed copies of the manuscript. The manuscript should be typed or keyboarded on good-quality paper, using one side of the page only. All the pages should be the same size; any tearsheets (pages taken from a previous edition or another published source) or other larger or smaller pieces should be taped or reproduced onto $8\frac{1}{2}'' \times 11''$ paper. To allow for editing, all copy must be double-spaced, including tables, footnotes, and bibliographies, and margins at least one inch wide must be left on all sides. Right margins should not be justified. The printout should be clear and easy to read; some publishers will not accept dot-matrix printing.

Ideally the manuscript should be typed with the "Show ¶" function activated, so that all spacing shows up in the form of dots on-screen. A single space should follow periods and other end punctuation, and the manuscript should be checked thoroughly for inadvertently added spaces elsewhere as well.

The manuscript should be complete, including its title page, dedication, table of contents, list of illustrations (tables, maps), foreword, preface, acknowledgments, tables and illustrations (with captions), glossary, bibliography, and appendixes as appropriate—everything that the author intends to appear in the printed book except the copyright page and index.

The author may be asked to add generic coding of text elements (paragraphs, headings, etc.), following a code list provided by the editor. More often, coding will be entered by the publisher or typesetter.

Some publishers prefer to deal only with hard copy in the actual editing stages. In such cases, the author submits only the paper manuscript, which must be identical to the retained diskette. The copyedited manuscript will be returned to the author, who then enters all the suggested emendations that are found acceptable and returns the hard copy along with the diskette. (This may provide an added incentive for accuracy and consistent styling by the author when originally submitting the manuscript.) Where extensive changes have been requested, the editor may ask that new paper manuscript reflecting the changes be returned.

The author should particularly ensure that all the following tasks have been done:

1. Number the text pages throughout in the upper right-hand corner. For any pages added subsequently, add sequential letters to the previous page number (e.g., 18A, 18B). Number the front matter with lowercase Roman numerals (i, ii, iii, iv, etc.). Use separate numbering sequences for tables or illustrations ("Table 1," "Table 2," etc.; "Figure 1," "Figure 2," etc.); if there are many, include the chapter number ("Table 2.1," "Table 2.2," etc.).

2. Include adequate bibliographic information for each source of quoted material.

3. Obtain permission for any copyrighted material quoted in the text or used in preparing ta-

bles or graphs and for photos and artwork, and include a file of completed permission forms obtained from each copyright holder. The publisher should have supplied blank permission forms and instructions.

4. Type all footnotes or endnotes on a sheet separate from the text, regardless of their intended eventual placement on the printed page. Check the sequence of note numbers in the text and the notes themselves. For the bibliography, follow a standard bibliographic style. (See Chapter 7, "Notes and Bibliographies.")

5. Review all cross-references for necessity and accuracy. Table and figure numbers (in separate sequences) must match their text references. Cross-references to pages should read "see page 000" or "see page ■■■" at this stage; add the actual manuscript page number (circled) in the margin for later use. Cross-references to headings rather than page numbers can reduce the potential for error and the cost of inserting page numbers in the page proofs. (For more on cross-references, see the section on pages 259–60.)

6. Place each table or graph on a separate page. Highlight their suggested placement within the text by a text reference (e.g., "As Figure 5.5 shows, . . ." or "The following table . . . "). If there is no text reference, include a circled note in the margin (e.g., "Insert Fig. 5.5 here") or on a separate line at the appropriate point in the text. Include a concise caption for each figure. Type a list of all tables or illustrations; such a list may be typeset to follow a table of contents in the printed book, or may instead be used only by the editor as a checklist (suggest which in a note on the copy).

7. Submit all art in a separate folder along with a list of the art in the order in which it will appear. Enclose the art in heavy cardboard for protection.

8. Send the manuscript well wrapped by an express courier service or by registered mail (always retaining a backup copy).

Copyediting the Manuscript

In book publishing, editorial work is generally divided into at least two tasks. An upper-level editor—frequently the same editor who has acquired the manuscript for the publishing house—reads the manuscript critically, focusing on such large issues as conception, organization, and tone. This higher-level editing is often known as *manuscript editing* or *line editing*, names which distinguish it from what is known as *copyediting*. This may follow similar work already done by an agent who proposed the book to the editor. (Increasingly, in-house editors are allowing agents to take over much of this responsibility.) If the manuscript is a textbook or a serious nonfiction work, it may also be sent to outside reviewers who are expert in the subject. The editor may send the manuscript back to the author more than once for revision.

Occasionally the principal editor will act as the copy editor as well. In fact, some regard the distinction between manuscript editing and copy editing as artificial, especially in cases where the in-house editor may give the manuscript only cursory attention and the copy editor finds it necessary to do extensive recasting and reorganizing. Nevertheless, for the sake of clarity we will treat the two jobs as if they were strictly segregated, and this chapter will devote itself largely to the job of the copy editor and the more easily distinguishable proofreader.

Copyediting is often the most important stage in preparing a manuscript for publication, especially at a time when in-house editors are feeling increasing pressure to acquire large numbers of books and have less and less time for properly vetting them. The copy editor will sometimes be more of a specialist in the subject matter than the in-house editor. It is therefore often left to a first-rate copy editor to turn an awkward, eccentric, incoherent manuscript into a cogent and creditable text. However, the copy editor is normally expected to consult with the in-house editor before attempting any editing that goes beyond the limits of standard copyediting.

Of the many things copyediting attempts to do, the most fundamental is to impose a thorough consistency and formal correctness on a manuscript. Systematic thoroughness is the greatest copyediting virtue. Errors and inconsistencies that elude the copy editor and are discovered only at the proofreading stage are expensive to correct.

A copy editor must naturally have mastered the standard rules of English style. But he or she should also be an avid reader of good prose, since wide and thoughtful reading is what most reliably produces the kind of taste and critical discrimination that form the solidest foundation for an editor's judgment.

Some manuscripts are still copyedited in-house. However, most are sent out to freelance copy editors, who, thanks to overnight courier service, may live 2,000 miles away from the publisher's offices. Most copy editors charge by the hour and submit a final bill at the end of a project; a few editorial projects are contracted on a flat-fee basis. The hourly rate will often assume an average editing speed of approximately six to seven pages an hour.

The copy editor should be supplied (usually by the in-house editor) with colored pens or pencils and special copyediting tags or flags. The latter are pieces of colored paper, about 2″ × 4″ in size, with a gummed edge that, when moistened, can be stuck firmly to the side of a manuscript page. (Pressure-sensitive tags, such as Post-its, are more prone to fall off and should not normally be used for serious copyediting—though they can be very useful for notes to oneself in the course of a project.) Notes and queries to the author or in-house editor are written on the side of the tag with the adhesive edge (often continuing to the other side), which is then stuck to the back edge of the page next to the text it discusses and folded over the front of the page. Depending on who is being addressed, "Au" (for "Author") or "Ed" (for "Editor") is then written on the side that shows when the tag is folded over; the manuscript page number should also be written at one corner of the tag. Alternatively, different-colored tags may be used for author and editor queries, or author queries may all be stuck on one side of the page and editor queries on the other. (Very brief queries may usually be written in the margins of the manuscript, though some editors discourage marginal queries.) (See Figure 8.1 for a copyediting tag.)

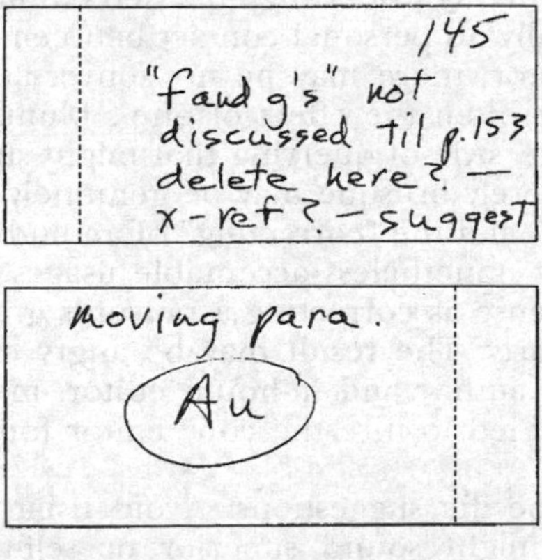

Figure 8.1 Copyediting Tag (both sides)

These tags remain in place until the in-house editor determines they should be removed. He or she will remove any tags addressed to "Ed" as soon as the issue addressed has been dealt with. The author should be instructed to address any queries directed to "Au"—either by making alterations to the manuscript or by writing brief answers on the tag itself—but not to remove the tags, since the in-house editor must make the final determination of how adequately each issue raised has been dealt with. All such tags should be removed by the editor before the manuscript goes to the typesetter, however. If a tag contains text to be inserted, it may be photocopied onto an $8\frac{1}{2}'' \times 11''$ sheet, along with instructions for insertion.

It goes without saying that the copy editor should make every effort to write clearly. If pencil is used, the pencils must be kept sharp; a dull pencil can make small handwriting very hard to read, and an in-house editor should never have to trace over such editing to make it clear enough for the typesetter.

Tact is of paramount importance for the copy editor. Authors vary greatly in their sensitivity to having their work edited, but many are quick to take offense at what they may consider high-handed editing. (Since there is usually no personal contact between copy editor and author, there may be no conversational opportunity to soften the effect of one's blunt editorial comments.) A style of querying that might strike most people as merely brusque may be genuinely insulting to an author, and the "correcting" of an author's idiosyncratic but nonetheless acceptable usages may give as much offense as correcting a person's grammar at a cocktail party. The result may be angry exchanges between the author and in-house editor, making the latter disinclined to hire the copy editor for the next project.

A few specific suggestions: Avoid using any language that might sound superior or self-righteous. Never use exclamation points in your messages to the author. Never simply write a question mark (or two or three) without explaining what it is you don't understand. Write frequent brief notes to accompany your emendations, generally worded as questions—such as "Au: OK?" or "Is this a bit clearer?" or "Maybe too informal?"—even where they may not be strictly necessary. And remain sensitive to the many legitimate style differences that continue to exist even among educated writers.

In conjunction with tact, a copy editor must cultivate a certain humility. He or she must always remember that the book is basically the author's, and that an attitude that regards a manuscript as a canvas on which to exercise one's own creative power is always inappropriate. The copy editor will rightly be faulted for permitting misspellings, inconsistencies, and flagrant errors to slip by, but it is the author who will receive near-exclusive credit or blame for the book as a whole.

An in-house editor may specify that a manuscript requires light editing, moderate editing, or heavy editing. Light editing may be quite cursory (and the copy editor's billable hours will be expected to reflect this), whereas authorization for heavy editing conveys broad latitude to shape the manuscript's prose. Moderate editing is naturally the norm, and this is the level that the present chapter basically addresses.

Basic Tasks

The copy editor is almost always obliged to do the following:

1. *Style the manuscript.* Most changes that a copy editor makes are "mechanical" or stylistic changes—in punctuation, capitalization, abbreviations, numbers, etc.—intended to conform the style of the text to a standard uniform style. Consistency is a major goal. Inconsistencies can easily appear even in the best writing, and removing those that might

prove misleading or distracting is often the copy editor's principal job. A style sheet is an essential aid; see "The Style Sheet" on page 240.

2. *Rewrite where necessary.* Rewriting the author's prose where its intention is unclear or its style awkward is a copyediting responsibility that must be handled judiciously, since it is all too easy to change the author's meaning inadvertently. The copy editor must always be careful not to appear to be substituting his or her own style for the author's. A query to the author may be preferable to attempting to rewrite passages that the copy editor may not completely understand.

3. *Rearrange content as needed.* Words, sentences, paragraphs, or whole sections may have to be transposed and sequences renumbered. Passages of text may have to be relegated to a note or an appendix, and vice versa. It is often best to alert the in-house editor if it appears that many such changes will be necessary.

4. *Verify data, as appropriate.* Freelance copy editors are generally responsible for verifying spelling of names and proper nouns, dates, foreignisms, and similar information. Query any odd-looking quotations, bibliographic references, dates, and names that cannot be verified. For a book in a specialist field, it is usually advisable to have on hand (perhaps from a library) several reputable and current reference books in the field, with which to check such information.

5. *Check headings.* Headings should be vetted for consistency and parallelism, organizational logic, and relevance to the text that follows them. Typing up the headings of each chapter in outline form is the best way of checking its organization. Check that the table of contents precisely reflects all the titles and headings.

6. *Verify all cross-references.* Check the author's cross-references and add new ones if necessary. (See "Cross-References" on page 259.)

7. *Check all sequences.* All numerical lists, all numbered footnotes or endnotes, all alphabetically arranged lists (such as bibliographies and glossaries), and all table or figure numbers must be in order.

8. *Regularize bibliographic style.* In general, the author's bibliographic style should be accommodated as far as possible; imposing consistency should be the copy editor's chief aim.

9. *Delete extra spacing.* On word-processed manuscripts, check that extra spaces have not been added inadvertently between words, and mark any such spacing for deletion. (If the manuscript is submitted to the typesetter on diskette, it is likely that such extra spacing will show up in the typeset proofs.)

10. *Review all tables.* Tables may need to be revised for accuracy, clarity, and consistency.

11. *Review the artwork.* If the content of any illustrations or charts seems unclear or inadequately related to the text, bring the problem to the author's attention. Be sure all captions are styled and worded consistently.

12. *Check for possible instances of copyright violation, plagiarism, libel, or other potential legal problems.* Query the author as to whether permission has been obtained to reproduce any materials potentially protected by copyright. Tactfully query the author or alert the editor about passages written in a different—and usually superior—style that you suspect have been plagiarized. Point out any potentially libelous statements; these may include negative claims of dubious veracity about named individuals

in nonfiction and even recognizable depictions of public figures in fiction.

13. *Keep a list of items that may require permission.* These may include quotations, illustrations, tables, and even data reedited from a given source. Include page references on the list. Alternatively, each item may be flagged. As a general rule, material more than 75 years old is in the public domain.

14. *Remove sexual and other bias.* Rewrite the copy to remove potentially offensive bias if you have permission to do so from the in-house editor.

15. *Renumber the pages if necessary.* Page numbers should appear on all copy except tables and illustrations, which usually are numbered sequentially by themselves.

16. *Typemark the manuscript.* If instructed to do so, add all the marks and notations that the typesetter will need to set the text in accordance with the design specifications. (Typemarking requires that the in-house editor provide a list of text elements and their abbreviations; see "Typemarking" on pages 263–64.)

Because of this variety of duties, the copy editor always goes through a manuscript more than once. A quick first read, perhaps without even a pen or pencil in hand, will acquaint the editor intimately with the text's organization, tone, vocabulary, and general problems. A slow and painstaking second pass will be the main occasion for fixing most errors of spelling, punctuation, grammar, parallelism, order, and general consistency. For very simple texts, this much may be adequate. But in a text with various elements, it is often best to make a separate pass through the manuscript for each of them. In a text with tables, for example, making a separate pass looking only at the tables will ensure maximum focus on their format, content, consistency, and sequence. Separate passes for captions, footnotes, A- and B-heads, and so on—each of which will naturally go very quickly compared to the initial reading and markup—will be similarly useful.

Marking Up the Manuscript

Copy editors communicate with typesetters by using a set of standard conventions, symbols, and codes. Most of these are described and illustrated in the following section.

Manuscript page numbers must be complete and in sequence. They should appear at the upper right corner, where they can be readily scanned by anyone who handles the manuscript. Any pages inserted later should be identified with a letter following the number of the preceding page; pages 4A and 4B would thus fall between pages 4 and 5. The additional instruction on the bottom of page 4 "p. 4A follows" will alert the typesetter. For added clarity, the notation "follows p. 4" may be written at the top of page 4A. If the manuscript fills up with numerous lettered pages, however, the entire manuscript should be renumbered. If pages are deleted, change the number on the preceding page to include the missing pages. Thus, for example, if pages 15 and 16 were deleted, page 14 would be renumbered "14–16," which would tell the typesetter to expect page 17 to follow; the message "follows p. 14" can be added on page 17 as well.

Editorial revisions should be made as close as possible to normal reading order. In those frequent cases where they must be written several inches away, a line should be drawn connecting the inserted material to the insertion point.

Special instructions to the typesetter are often necessary but should be kept as brief as possible. These should be written in the margin rather than on flags. All such instructions should be circled to distinguish them from actual revisions. They may begin with the abbreviation "Comp" (for "Compositor") to make it clear who is being addressed (e.g., "Comp: Disregard horizontal lines").

Most longer text insertions are bracketed rather than fully circled. However, circled insertions that are clearly linked to their insertion points will not be confused with instructions.

The right margin may be reserved for editorial notations, and the left margin for typemarking. A heavily revised manuscript, however, will usually require editorial notations in both margins as well as between the lines.

Beginners understandably prefer using pencil rather than pen, though a fine-point pen is easier for the typesetter to read and will not smudge. If more than one person will be marking the copy, each should use a single identifying color. The copy editor's own mistakes should be whited out or erased rather than crossed out. Mistakes made by the author, in contrast, should never be erased but only crossed out; the author's original should always be visible behind the deletion marks.

The Style Sheet

Copy editors almost always work with a style sheet. There are two basic kinds. One is a list of preferred stylings which the in-house editor may give to the copy editor along with the manuscript reflecting the publisher's "house style." (These may even be full-fledged style manuals.) The other kind of style sheet, the subject of this section, is created by the copy editor while reading the manuscript. On it the copy editor notes his or her final style decision for each individual entry, whether it is based on the author's own preference, the editor's preference, or the publisher's style sheet. Though its principal use is often as a memory aid for the copy editor who creates it, it can also be useful for the in-house editor and the proofreader.

Many publishers provide their own printed blank style-sheet forms. In the absence of a standard form, a simple style sheet can be created easily by drawing a wide grid (perhaps six boxes per page) on two or three sheets of paper. Each of the first several boxes should be headed with three or four sequential letters of the alphabet; the remaining boxes may be given such headings as "Numbers," "Abbreviations," "Tables," "Captions," "Punctuation," "Notes," "Bibliography," "Cross-References," and "Miscellaneous." (See Figure 8.2.)

While working through the manuscript, the copy editor enters on the style sheet the preferred style for each word (phrase, abbreviation, etc.) about which there may be any doubt. It is not necessary to list words that appear in the general dictionary the editor will be following, except in cases where the author (or the specialized profession for which the book is being written) clearly has a strong preference for a different spelling or style than the one listed first in the dictionary. It is often helpful to include the number of the page where the word first appears; if the copy editor changes his or her mind late in the project, this will make it easier to comb the manuscript and change the word throughout.

When fiction is being edited, the style sheet is the best place to keep track of the spelling of characters' names and the identities of those bearing the names, since authors have often been known to change such names or characters inadvertently as a long novel progresses.

The entries should be brief. For example, if a hyphen will be used in the adjective *health-care*, the editor should write simply "health-care (adj)" in the H box. This will serve as a reminder throughout the editing project that the hyphen should always be included in the adjectival form, whereas the noun *health care* will probably remain unhyphenated (and perhaps need not be listed on the style sheet at all).

Some further examples will help illustrate the use

of the style sheet. The entry "résumé" would show that the word should always include the accent marks. The entry "President (U.S. only)" will show that in all references to the office of the U.S. president the word should be capitalized. The entry "west-northwest (text)—WNW (tables)" would illustrate the two styles to be followed for *all* compass directions. "Concours d'elegance (rom)" would show that the term is to be set in roman type rather than italics, and without its French accents. "W. E. B. Du Bois" shows that there will be a space between "Du" and "Bois" and that "Du" will be capitalized.

Under "Abbreviations," an entry might read "CIA," as a reminder that the periods should be removed wherever the form "C.I.A." appears and that full capital letters rather than small caps will be used. The entry "*e.g.*, *i.e.*" shows that these abbreviations will always be italicized.

Under "Captions," the entry "Brahms: Symphony No. 3, IV" could indicate that the standard caption form for all multimovement compositions would include the composer's last name, a colon, a standard simple styling of the composition's name, a comma, and the movement number written as a Roman numeral.

Under "Numbers," the entry "1980s" will indicate that all similar decade names will omit an apostrophe before the *s*, and the entry "5,200" announces that four-digit numbers use the optional comma. The simple entry "ten, 11" will indicate that all numbers up through ten are to be spelled out, while all higher numbers will be expressed in digits. The entry "one-half, one-fourth, three-fourths (in running text); all fractions with units smaller than tenths in running text set solidus" says that hyphens are to be used in the spelled-out form of fractions, and that fractions with large numerators or denominators will be set in digits as split or solidus fractions (e.g., "16/5") rather than as vertical or built-up fractions ("$\frac{3}{4}$"). Other entries can clarify the choice between such alternative forms as "2d" and "2nd," "1988–90" and "1988–1990," and "two million dollars" and "$2 million."

Under "Punctuation," the entry "series comma" will indicate that a comma is always to be used before *and* or *or* at the end of a series. "Set punc. following bold text rom in running text" would convey that boldface type should not normally extend to the punctuation that follows bolded words and phrases.

In the "Notes" and "Bibliography" sections, several sample footnotes or endnotes and their corresponding bibliography entries can illustrate the chosen style for a variety of types of bibliographic references.

Under "Cross-References," any standard form or forms for cross-references can be listed.

An experienced copy editor will need to make only a modest number of entries on a style sheet—perhaps no more than twenty for an undemanding book—since reliance on a standard dictionary and style manual will decide all but a small number of spelling and styling questions. However, a technical manuscript or a complex novel may well require many more.

When the style sheet is finished—after the copy editor's last reading of the manuscript—it is submitted with the manuscript, and may subsequently be copied and used by the author, the in-house editor, the typesetter, or the proofreader.

A style-sheet page is shown in Figure 8.2.

Copyediting Marks

The standard copyediting marks are illustrated in the example of a copyedited passage in Figure 8.3. The marks themselves are, for the most part, the same as proofreaders' marks; both are listed in Table 8.1.

Insertions and substitutions The symbol commonly used to indicate an insertion is a caret placed at the point of insertion; the addition is written over the

Figure 8.2 Style Sheet

HNOP	QRST	UVWXYZ
mid-1990s 23	St. Paul 34	Web 161
Midwestern 41	résumé 61	unequaled 189
ms. 49	re-create 86	
President 58 (U.S. only)	Quality Circle 117	
managed care (n., adj.) 64		
P/E ratio 128		

Abbrev.	Numbers	Punc.
WNW (table) 33	1990s	series ↗
kph 41	5,200	Jones's
CPA 59	ten, 11	
Sr., Jr. 103	2d	
e.g., i.e.	1988-90	

caret and above the line. If a character is added in mid-word, only a caret is needed below the insert. If a character is added to the beginning or end of a word, a close up sign may be added for clarity. Any large insertion should be enclosed in a brace extending from the caret. A long insertion that will not fit easily between the lines may be written in the margin, with a line drawn from the brace to the caret. Any additions within the margin must be written horizontally; the typesetter should not have to tilt the page in order to read any passage. Any insertion too long to fit in the margin should be typed on a separate sheet—never on a slip of paper stapled or stuck to the edge of the manuscript page. For a long insertion on page 24, a caret would be drawn at the insertion point, the instruction "Insert 24A" would be written and circled in the margin, and the new text would be typed on a sheet numbered 24A. Be sure it is obvious to the typesetter whether the insert should be run in with the preceding or following text or set as a separate paragraph. Several brief inserts can be typed on one sheet if they are all to be inserted on the same manuscript page and if each is clearly identified ("Insert A," "Insert B," etc.).

When words are substituted for the author's own, the original word or phrase is crossed out and the replacement text is written above the deleted passage, without a caret.

Deletions Material can be deleted by simply drawing a heavy line through the unwanted copy, being careful to begin and end the cross-out line precisely so that no characters or punctuation marks are missed, no extra characters are mistakenly deleted, and nothing is left ambiguous.

The delete sign, a line with a loop at the end, may be used to delete a single character, a word, or a whole line of copy. To cut a large section such as a paragraph, draw a box around it with the delete loop extending from one side, and draw a large X through the copy.

A single character may be crossed out with a simple slash whenever the deletion loop might interfere with an accompanying close-up sign.

To delete an underscore, attach a delete mark to its end; to delete only part of an underscore, divide it with a vertical line or lines and place delete marks only on the appropriate sections. If the copy is crowded, write "ital" or "rom" in the margin, circle the pertinent sections of the underscored material, and connect those sections and the margin notation with a line if necessary.

When the copy is heavily marked up, add close-up signs, run-in signs, or arrows to guide the typesetter from one part of the copy to another, and rewrite isolated single words and punctuation marks in their new positions so that they do not get lost. Most punctuation marks should normally appear immediately after the word they follow; however, a comma, semicolon, period, or other mark, written prominently, may be added at the beginning of an insertion or continuation if it cannot be written clearly next to the preceding text.

Close-up A close-up sign indicates a deletion of space. The close-up sign often consists of two arcs, but a single arc is usually adequate, especially if the copy is already heavily marked. It is frequently used to turn two or more separate words into a single word, or, with a deletion mark, to turn a hyphenated word into a closed-up word. Where a word breaks at the end of a line, deleting the hyphen and drawing close-up marks (which simply end in the margin) tells the typesetter that the hyphen is not properly part of the word. This generally only needs to be done where there is a realistic possibility of a mistake; however, some editors will ask that every end-of-line hyphen be marked for either retention or deletion.

When deleting several words—and especially wherever the next word being retained might possibly otherwise be overlooked by the typesetter—a large close-up mark can guide the typesetter from the beginning of a deletion to its end.

Capitals, small capitals, and lowercase letters Three underscores drawn below lowercase letters indicate a change to capital letters. A single lowercase letter can be capitalized by simply drawing the capital letter boldly over it so as to cover it. Any handwritten capitals that might be mistaken for lowercase can be reinforced with triple underscoring.

Small capitals are indicated by drawing a double underscore below capital or lowercase letters. A combination of three and two underscores indicates a combination of capitals and small capitals.

The lowercase symbol, a slash mark through a letter, is used to change a capital letter to lowercase. To change a word or phrase typed all in capitals to lowercase, slash the first letter to be lowercased and extend the top of the slash as a horizontal line across the top of the rest of the word or phrase. (Some copy editors simply slash the first letter for lowercasing and omit the horizontal continuation.)

In addition to the marks in the text, abbreviations such as "cap" (for "capitals"), "lc" ("lowercase"), "sm caps" ("small capitals"), and "caps/sc" ("capitals and small capitals") may be written in the margins if necessary for clarity.

Spaces The space symbol (#) instructs the typesetter to insert a word space, the amount of spacing between adjacent words on a line. To separate two words that were inadvertently closed up, draw a slash between them; the space symbol may be added to the upper end of the slash. Sometimes a *thin space*, smaller than a word space, may be needed—for example, on either side of operational signs in mathematics; this is usually indicated by a slash drawn where the space is desired and the note "thin #" circled in the margin. Occasionally a *hair space* ("hair #"), smaller than a regular thin space, is needed between two characters that might cause confusion when closed up entirely, such as a single quotation mark set next to a double quotation mark.

Italic, boldface, and roman type Italic type is indicated by a single underscore. (Italic capital letters thus require four separate underscores, with the note "ital caps.") For lengthy italic copy, simply write and circle "ital" in the margin and circle or bracket the passage. To change an italic word or phrase to roman, underscore or circle the italicized text and write and circle "rom" above it or in the margin. To mark a change from a large block of italic type, write "rom" in the margin as a precaution.

When marking already typeset copy, such as a tear sheet (a page torn from a printed book—often the previous edition of the book being edited—that will be reset), there is no need to underscore words that are already italicized.

Boldface is frequently used for headings and captions; design specifications usually dictate what text elements will be set bold, and the copy editor need not reiterate the specs by marking them up. To boldface a word or passage within the running text, draw a wavy underscore below it. If it is more than a line long, it may instead be clearly bracketed and the abbreviation "bf" written in the margin. To change boldface to roman, circle the affected words and write "lf" (for "lightface") in the margin. As always when writing *l*'s, make a distinct cursive loop.

Boldface italic type is indicated by a straight underscore with a wavy underscore below it (and if necessary the note "bold ital" in the margin).

Punctuation Punctuation marks can be added or changed to different marks as described below (in alphabetical order).

Apostrophe An apostrophe can be added by means of an inverted caret above the line at the insertion point.

Brackets Square brackets can usually be drawn in place. Parentheses can be converted to brackets by simply tracing the brackets heavily over the parentheses so as to obscure them.

Colon If a colon needs clarification or if it has been created from a period by drawing in the second point, a small circle or oval may be drawn around it. A semicolon can be changed to a colon by drawing two heavy dots over the semicolon so that the tail of its comma is obscured.

Comma A comma that is not clear—one inserted or retained next to a deletion, for example—should be highlighted by a caret drawn over it. Any added comma may be clarified by putting a caret above it.

Dashes The em dash, usually typed as two hyphens, is marked for the typesetter with a numeral 1 over the hyphens (or hyphen, if the author has typed just one) and a capital M below them. To call for dashes longer than one em, write a larger number over the hyphen—for example, 3 for a three-em dash. In print, the em dash is usually closed up tight to the text on both sides; close-up marks should be added if there is space between the hyphens and the surrounding text in the manuscript. (Newspaper style, and the house style for some book publishers, calls for spaces between the dash and the surrounding text.)

The en dash is usually represented in manuscript copy by a single hyphen. To change a hyphen to an en dash, write a 1 above the hyphen and a capital N below it. In an index, or in other types of copy that contain many en dashes, only the first one or two en dashes need be indicated, followed by a circled "etc."

Ellipsis points To add ellipsis points, simply draw three (or four) circled dots. Ellipsis points generally have spaces between them (except in newspaper text, where they are generally set without spaces). If they are closed up in the manuscript, the editor should simply make a series of vertical lines between them. Ellipsis points in mathematical copy are often raised off the baseline; to typemark these, place a caret above and an inverted caret below each point, or write "ctr points" in the margin.

Exclamation point   An added exclamation point should be written clearly so that it is not mistaken for other symbols (*l, 1, /,* etc.) that it may resemble.

Hyphen   Any hyphen inserted by the copy editor, and any hyphen that is part of an inserted word, should be doubled so that it looks like an equal sign. To ensure that the typesetter retains the hyphen in a hyphenated word or compound that breaks on its hyphen at the end of a line, such end-of-line hyphens should be doubled. As mentioned earlier, any end-of-line hyphen in the manuscript that denotes a syllabic break but might mistakenly be retained by the typesetter (and might represent a hyphen mistakenly keyboarded by the author) should be marked for deletion with a slash through it and a close-up mark (which simply extends out into the margin). End-of-line hyphenation that is not potentially ambiguous usually need not be marked for retention or omission, though some editors prefer it be done in every case.

Parentheses   Added parentheses should be drawn carefully, since handwritten parentheses can easily look like various other symbols. They should be slightly oversize. One or two tiny horizontal lines drawn through each handwritten parenthesis will help the typesetter recognize them.

Period   A point enclosed in a small circle denotes a period; it should be used whenever needed for clarity. To change a comma to a period, simply circle the typed comma. To change a colon or semicolon to a period, draw a circle around its lower half so that the circle goes through the upper point.

Question mark   Since question marks are used so frequently as shorthand for queries of various kinds, an added question mark can be clarified by the circled note "set ?"

Quotation marks An inverted caret under inserted quotation marks can help identify them when they might be misread. Potentially confusing combinations of single and double quotation marks can be clarified by putting separate inverted carets under the single and double quotes.

Semicolon A semicolon that might not be conspicuous should be highlighted by placing a caret over it. A comma can be changed to a semicolon by adding a point over it and a caret over the point. To change a semicolon to a comma, draw a caret over the comma so that it covers the point of the semicolon. To change a colon to a semicolon, draw a tail on the lower point and then a caret above the new semicolon.

Slash Since a handwritten slash can look confusingly like the number 1 or the letter *l*, it should be accompanied by the circled note "set slash."

Transposition The transposition sign—a line curving over one element and under another—is used to indicate transposition of characters, words, phrases, or sentences. Often the marginal note "tr" is added. To switch two words on either side of a word that will remain in place, the line should curve over the first word, under the second, and over the third.

When the material to be transposed is typed on more than one line, the editor usually circles one of the elements and shows its new position with a line leading from it to a caret or arrow at the insertion point. More complicated transpositions may have to be rewritten.

All transpositions must be marked with care and double-checked especially for punctuation of the re-ordered text. To delete punctuation when transposing, draw the curved line *through* the punctuation mark.

Run-in text The run-in sign—a sinuous line that leads from copy on one line to copy on another—is used to run them onto the same line. When a messy deletion of intervening material has been made, a run-in line can guide the typesetter to where the retained copy resumes.

Stet   The instruction "stet," Latin for "let it stand," is used to restore words mistakenly crossed out. Draw a series of heavy dots below the deleted material (erasing the cross-out line, if necessary, to make the text legible) and write "stet" in the margin.

Spell out or abbreviate   To indicate that a number is to be written out or an abbreviation is to be spelled in full, the editor simply circles the number or abbreviation, and may also write "sp" above it or in the margin. This should be done only when the intended change is unambiguous. For example, the circled fraction "1/2" could be set as either "one half" or "one-half," a circled "100" could be set as either "one hundred" or "a hundred," and the circled abbreviation "pt." could conceivably be spelled out as "point," "pint," "part," or something else. Thus, it is often better to cross out the abbreviation and spell out its replacement.

   Conversely, a spelled-out number may be circled to indicate that it should be set as digits—but again only where the intended form is absolutely clear. When a spelled-out word is to be abbreviated, however, the abbreviation should be written explicitly rather than left to the typesetter.

Align   Proper text alignment is usually more of a concern for proofreaders than for copy editors, but alignment of tables and other columns or lists may occasionally need to be clarified at the manuscript stage. To show vertical alignment, draw a pair of parallel vertical lines against the left or right side of the lines of copy that should be aligned left or right. To show horizontal alignment, draw two parallel horizontal lines under the type that must align. An additional instruction is usually written in the margin—for example, "Align stubhead left w/stub items" or "Align all figure cols right."

Diacritics and other special symbols Copy editors should know the names of special symbols, including the Greek alphabet, diacritics, and basic mathematical symbols, since any symbol that might be uncommon or confusing should be described or named in the margin the first time it appears. If the author has written > in a table, for example, it may be necessary to clarify the symbol by writing and circling "greater than" in the margin. Similarly, any odd spellings or stylings that are intentional but that the typesetter might misread or be tempted to "correct" should also be noted, either by placing stet points below the text or by writing "follow copy" in the margin. When there might be confusion between a zero and a capital *O*, or between the numeral 1 and the letter *l*, write in the margin "zero," "cap oh," "one," or "ell."

Diacritical marks should be added to foreign words if the author has omitted them. In the margin next to the line, either write and circle the name of the diacritic or rewrite the word, making the diacritics prominent. (A properly typed diacritic, or one that the author has drawn in clearly, usually does not require any further marking.) The most common diacritics (most of which are available in word-processing programs as special characters) are the following:

é	acute accent
è	grave accent
â	circumflex
ñ	tilde
ă	haček
ö	diaeresis
ç	cedilla
ō	macron
ŭ	breve

Subscript and superscript In handwritten or unclear copy, place a caret over any subscript (as in chemical symbols) and an inverted caret below any super-script (such as footnote numbers).

Indention and paragraphs Manuscript copy must sometimes be marked to tell the typesetter whether lines should be set flush left or right, centered, or indented, as well as the specific amount of indention.

In most publications the first lines of paragraphs are indented, except for those immediately following headings. Instructions on paragraph indention should be included in the design specifications.

When paragraph divisions are clear, there is no need to mark them further. However, when the starting point of a paragraph is obscure or when the editor wants to begin a new paragraph in midline, a paragraph symbol (¶) should be drawn next to its first word. A line-break symbol (see Table 8.1) may be inserted instead or additionally. In running text, it will be understood that the line-break symbol by itself denotes a new paragraph; in other contexts, the symbol may be ambiguous without clarification of its meaning.

To remove a paragraph's indention—for instance, for the first paragraph that follows a heading—draw the move-left symbol (which resembles an opening bracket) flush left on the text block. The move-right symbol (which resembles a closing bracket) is rarely used except to mark math copy or to reposition a credit line. Either symbol may be clarified by a note in the margin telling the typesetter to set the text flush left ("fl l"), flush right ("fl rt"), or flush with some particular part of the copy.

When marking a specific amount of indention for an item not covered by the design specs, *em quads* are often used. These tiny squares are placed just to the side of the line to be indented. The simple em quad indicates one em of space. A number written within the quad indicates a multiple of an em space (thus, a 3 in the quad tells the typesetter to set a three-em space); alternatively, the editor may draw in multiple empty quads, one for each space requested.

An *en quad*, drawn as a quad with a slash through it, is occasionally still used, mainly in numbered lists to indicate the amount of space between the period following each numeral and the text of the item. Such measurements will normally be stipulated in the design specs and usually need not be indicated on the manuscript.

An em quad or en quad can be extended vertically down the page by a vertical line descending from it. Em and en quads are usually drawn only at the beginning of an indented section to familiarize the typesetter with the desired format; the circled instruction "etc." will indicate that the spacing should continue in the same way.

Headings

In addition to running text, such text elements as headings, lists, cross-references, extracts, and bibliographic notes usually require special attention.

Almost any long piece of nonfiction can benefit from the inclusion of headings, since headings help the reader mentally organize the material and find specific passages. Thus, authors should be encouraged by their editors to employ headings in most manuscripts, and copy editors should feel free to suggest them where appropriate.

Headings should by themselves form an outline of the manuscript. To check the organization of a text, the copy editor will find it very helpful to copy out all the headings for each chapter in a vertical list resembling an outline. Any heading inconsistencies that are revealed by doing so—gaps, lack of parallelism, and so on—should be corrected or pointed out to the author.

Headings are usually nouns or concise noun phrases. (Newspaper headings, which usually describe events, will often use a complete sentence as a heading.) The copy editor should confirm that each heading accurately and concisely summarizes the text that follows. The text immediately following a heading

Table 8.1 Copyediting and Proofreading Marks

Text change	Copyediting example	Proofreading example
align or straighten	Venus: goddess of love Mars: god of war	Venus: goddess of love Mars: god of war (align)
apostrophe	cats dish	cats dish
boldface type	Warning: Not for internal use	Warning: Not for internal use (bf)
brackets	The Message Is the Medium [sic]	The Message Is the Medium [sic] [/]
capital letters	crossed the missouri River	crossed the missouri River (cap)
center	] My Thirteenth Year [	] My Thirteenth Year [(ctr)
close up	went for ward slowly	went for ward slowly
colon	as follows: rice, beans,	as follows, rice, beans, (:)
comma	peas, corn, carrots, celery	peas, corn, carrots, celery
deletion	attended this thee concert	attended this thee concert
diacritics	the entrée was entrecote	the entrée was entrecote é/ô
ellipsis	"Warm, winning, heart-breaking...	"Warm, winning, heart-breaking,
em dash en dash	That year—that is, the 1996-97 season	That year—that is, the 1996-97 season

Table 8.1 *(continued)*

Text change	Copyediting example	Proofreading example
em space en space	☐ C. Designations 2. Primary sources.	☐ C. Designations ☐ 2. Primary sources ▱
hyphen retain hyphen	a well-known scene- stealer	a well-known scene- stealer =/=
insertion	three pieces blueberry pie *of* *r*	three pieces blueberry pie of/r
italic type	"It was wunderbar!"	"It was wunderbar!" ital
line break (or paragraph)	end of line. New line. To read- it the manuscript	end of line. New line. To read- it the manuscript # lb
lowercase	The President was called at 3 A.M.	The President was called at 3 A.M. lc
move left move right	It was a dark and stormy night. --Shakespeare	It was a dark and stormy night. --Shakespeare
move up move down	Fungible Assets Unique Assets	Fungible Assets Unique Assets
paragraph	paragraph ends. New paragraph	paragraph ends. New paragraph ¶
parentheses	arrived Tuesday June 3	arrived Tuesday June 3 { }
period	That is enough Unbelievable It paused Nothing changed	That is enough Unbelievable ⊙/⊙ It paused Nothing changed ⊙/⊙
question mark	So he really wants it?	So he really wants it / set ?
quotation marks	liked the song Laura	liked the song Laura ᵛ/ᵛ

Table 8.1 *(continued)*

Text change	Copyediting example	Proofreading example
roman type	He *noticed* the mistake. (rom)	He *noticed* the mistake. (rom)
run in (no paragraph)	end of line. New line to be run in	end of line. New line to be run in (run in)
semicolon	Akron, Ohio; Ogden, Utah;	Akron, Ohio, Ogden, Utah, ;/;
slash	the team's owner/manager (slash)	the team's owner-manager (set slash)
small caps	from 423 B.C. to A.D. 310	from 423 B.C. to A.D. 310 (sc)(sc)
space	words that are runtogether///.	words that are runtogether ... #/#/#
spell out abbreviate	bought 3 apples on Mon. thirteen in the United States	bought 3 apples on Mon. (sp)(sp) thirteen in the United States 13/o/o
stet (let stand)	waved the white flag	waved the white flag (stet)
subscript superscript	CO2 C14	CO2 C14 2 14
substitution	the Van Dyke exhibit (Gogh)	the Van Dyke exhibit Gogh
transpose	beginning, end, middle cmoes after and before	beginning, end, middle (tr) cmoes after and before (tr)(tr)
wrong font		(Type Design) (wf)

should never depend on any words in the heading for an antecedent. All the headings at a given level should generally be grammatically parallel or otherwise consistent in form and style.

Lists

Lack of grammatical parallelism is perhaps the most common problem in lists, and copy editors will frequently have to recast list entries to achieve a necessary consistency.

Run-in lists—lists that occur as part of normal-looking sentences—may sometimes need to be clarified by the addition of parenthesized numbers, especially when the items are long or complex.

Displayed lists—that is, lists set off in vertical format—may be numbered, bulleted, or unnumbered and unbulleted. Numbered lists are usually desirable when the order or number of items is mentioned in the text or otherwise significant.

To change an author's run-in series to a vertical list, insert line-break symbols (deleting any commas or semicolons between the items by drawing the symbol through them), add initial capital letters if necessary, and change any numerals in parentheses to numerals with periods. To change an author's displayed list to run-in form, use run-in lines to connect the items, add punctuation after each item, change any capitalization as needed, and delete or restyle the numbering.

Cross-References

Cross-references will often have to be inserted for the sake of the reader's convenience where the author has not provided any, and those provided by the author may have to be rephrased for accuracy and stylistic consistency. Examples of cross-reference style (illustrating, for example, whether "chapter" is capitalized and whether "page" is abbreviated) should be included on the copy editor's style sheet.

Wherever the author refers to another page of the manuscript, the copy editor changes the number to 000 (or one or more small black squares) so that the manuscript page number will not be typeset. The 000 alerts the proofreader, editor, author, and typesetter to the fact that, later on when page proofs arrive, the appropriate cross-reference page numbers will have to be added. The copy editor writes the manuscript page number of the original reference in the margin to facilitate finding the new position of the original cross-reference at the later proof stages. The proofreader is responsible for carrying over all these notations to the margins of the proofs.

Cross-references that refer to chapters or sections rather than specific pages will avoid the necessity and expense of adding page references at the proof stage. However, the reader will usually be grateful for a precise page number.

Extracts

Extracts are quoted excerpts from other sources that are set off from the running text, usually by spacing, left (and often right) indention, smaller type size, or (usually) a combination of all three.

Excerpted text that runs to four lines or longer is generally set off as an extract, whereas shorter quotations are generally run in. Where longer quotations have been run in by the author, therefore, the copy editor may have to mark them to be set off. (More rarely, the editor may have to mark brief excerpts set off by the author to be run in instead.) This is done by simply inserting line-break symbols at the beginning and end of the extract, bracketing the passage with a vertical line in the margin, and adding the circled note "extract" (or, if the copy editor is typemarking the manuscript, the typemarking symbol for extracts instead). Any quotation marks enclosing the excerpt should be deleted, since setting text off makes such quotation marks redundant. The copy editor usually need not instruct the typesetter further about how to set extract text, since the design specs will cover extracts.

Notes and Bibliographies

For the formatting of notes and reference lists, the copy editor should be familiar with the various stylings discussed in Chapter 7. The author and in-house editor often agree on a particular format at the outset of a publishing project.

For ease of typesetting, many publishers prefer notes to be set as endnotes rather than footnotes. If the author has provided footnotes but the in-house editor desires endnotes instead, the copy editor must write in the margin next to the first footnote "Set all footnotes together at end of chapter [article, book]," and at the end of the chapter (or article or book) provide the new head "Notes" and write "Insert footnotes 1–00 here." If the author has typed endnotes when footnotes are desired instead, the copy editor should instruct the typesetter to "Set all endnotes as footnotes throughout."

A distinction is sometimes made between simple bibliographic notes, which are equally acceptable as footnotes or endnotes, and substantive or content notes, which are usually placed at the bottom of a page. In such cases, the substantive notes may employ a different set of reference symbols (*, †, etc.). The editor's job is made easier, in either case, if the author has been instructed to type all notes on pages separate from the text.

The copy editor should always be alert to the possibility that material in a given note might better be included in the body of the text, or vice versa, and should query the author wherever it seems desirable.

The copy editor should check the position of all reference symbols, moving them to more appropriate locations where necessary. Reference symbols in mathematical copy, in particular, may be mistaken for exponents or other symbols.

Reference symbols in the text usually appear as superscripts. Call the typesetter's attention to them by means of circled notations in the margin such as "fn 7," which will also be helpful to the copy editor making a late pass through the manuscript to recheck the notes alone. This late pass should include (1) checking numerical sequence, (2) confirming that the reference numbers correspond to the proper notes, (3) seeing that the publishing data in each note is complete, standard, and consistently styled (including consistency in any shortened forms), and (4) making sure all the references are signaled in the margin by hand so that the typesetter will spot them easily.

In editing bibliographies, the copy editor must be sure to (1) check alphabetical order, (2) compare each text reference with its bibliography entry to see that they correspond in every detail, (3) verify that the entries consistently follow a standard bibliographic style, and (4) query the author about any works that seem to have been overlooked.

Art and Tables

Any first reference to a piece of *art*—the term broadly used for any material not set by the typesetter—must be signaled, or called out, in a circled note in the manuscript margin, which should include the art's number (or, if it is unnumbered, a brief title).

The copy editor should be alert to the role the art is intended to play in the text. If an illustration does not seem to adequately illustrate its intended point, the author should be queried.

Any description of the art in the text must be completely accurate.

Any art apparently borrowed from another published source should be flagged with a query as to whether permission has been obtained. If the copy editor has the permission file, it should be systematically checked against the art file.

Hand-drawn diagrams may have labels that will have to be typeset. All such labels should be styled consistently (and otherwise edited if necessary) by the copy editor.

Any photographs or art that will become camera copy (as opposed to photocopies) must naturally be treated with great care. If a photograph must be numbered for identification, write the number on the back lightly in pencil. Keep all camera-copy art between protective cardboard, in a drawer if possible, and never set other materials on top of it.

All tables should be edited together for the sake of consistency. (It is thus helpful if the author has segregated them into a separate file.) The wording and styling of headings and stub entries should be regularized from table to table where the author has failed to do so, as should any terms and phrases that recur in the tables. Mark for alignment any table entries that have not been properly aligned horizontally or vertically. Query any tables that seem poorly conceived or structured. Text references to tables, like references to art, must be called out in the margin.

Typemarking

Typemarking is the marking of a manuscript with circled codes that identify its various type elements—headings of different levels, lists of different types, set-off material, chapter titles, and the like. By directing the typesetters to the appropriate item in the design specifications, these codes ensure that each element will be set according to the designer's wishes. It is often the copy editor who will be asked to typemark the manuscript, using a list of typemarking codes provided by the in-house editor. (Alternatively, typemarking may be done in-house, either before or after the copyediting phase.) This may be a standard list provided for every project, and the copy editor may have to select from its elements only those that actually are used in the manuscript being edited. There is generally no need for a copy editor to see the actual design specs, since basic typemarking has much more to do with analysis of the text than with actual design. The typemarking will usually be done in a color different from those used for editing. Some publishers, in fact, ask that each element be marked in its own color (as stipulated on an instruction sheet), the colors thereby becoming the primary signal for the element.

Though typemarking is largely mechanical and can go very fast, some pitfalls often lurk in a manuscript. If the copy editor has turned a run-in list into a set-off list, it must be given its appropriate mark; if the author has typed some of the headings incorrectly (if some typed as A-heads should instead be B-heads, for example), the copy editor must typemark them correctly; and so on.

The editor may request a memo from the copy editor that lists all the elements actually used, along with the page where each first appears, and possibly also the pages where any unusual examples of the element show up.

Copyedited Pages

Figure 8.3 shows two pages of copyedited text, illustrating the use of many of the marks described above.

Trafficking the Copyedited Manuscript

The copyedited manuscript will normally be returned to the editor, who will read all queries addressed to "Ed," and may also check the overall quality of the job and add further queries or marks (usually in different-colored pen). The editor then sends it on to the author, perhaps with a standard printed sheet of instructions on interpreting copyediting marks, responding to

Figure 8.3 Copyedited Text

John Wallis, a mathematician and Member of the Royal Society, published in 1658 a grammar, written in Latin, for the use of foreigners who ~~wanted to learn English~~. [stet] Wallis, according to George H. MacKnight, abandoned much of the method of Latin grammar. Wallis' grammar is perhaps best remembered for being the source of the much discussed distinction between "shall" and "will." Wallis grammar is also the one referred to by Samuel Johnson in the front matter of his 1755 dictionary. Dr. Ash deserves mention too. He defended the English of his time as an improvement over the English of Shakespeare and Johnson. He is the first person who worried about the preposition at the end of a sentence we know of. He eliminated many such prepositions from his own writings when revising his works for a collected edition. He seems to have decided the practice was wrong because it could not happen in Latin.

C. C. Fries tells us that 17th-century grammars in general were designed either for foreigners or for school use, in order to lead to the study of latin. In the 18th century, however, grammars were written predominately for English speakers, and although they were written for the purpose of instructing, they seem to find more fun in correcting. A change in the underlying philosophy of grammar had occurred, and in perhaps the first eighteenth-century grammar, A Key to the Art of Letters, published in 1700 it is made explicit by a schoolmaster named A. Lane. He thought it a mistake to view grammar simply as a means to learn a foreign language and asserted that "the true End and Use of Grammar is to teach how to speak and write well and learnedly in a language Already known, according to the unalterable Rules of right Reason." Gone was Ben Jonson's appeal to custom.

[Au: itals + cap OK?]

The 18th-Century Grammar

There was evidently a considerable amount of general interest in things grammatical among men of letters, for Addison, Swift, and Steele all treated grammar in one way or another in The Tatler and The Spectator in 1710, 1711,

Figure 8.3 *(continued)*

and 1712. In 1712 Swift published yet another proposal for an English academy (it came within a whisker of succeeding); John Oldmixon attacked Swift's proposal in the same year. Public interest must have helped create a market for the grammar books that began appearing with some frequency about this same time. And if controversy fuels sales, grammarians knew it; they were perfectly willing to emphasize their own advantages by denigrating their predecessors, sometimes in abusive terms.

We need mention here only a few of these productions. Pride of place must go to Bishop Robert Lowth's *A Short Introduction to English Grammar* (1762). Lowth's book is both brief and logical. Lowth was influenced by the theories of James Harris's *Hermes* (1751), a curious disquisition about universal grammar. Lowth apparently derived his notions about the perfectability of English grammar from Harris, and he did not doubt that he could reduce the language to a system of uniform rules.

His favorite mode of illustration is what was known as false syntax, examples of linguistic wrongdoing from the King James Bible, Shakespeare, Sidney, Donne, Milton, Swift, Addison, Pope, the most respected names in English literature. He was so sure of himself that he could permit himself a little joke; discussing the construction where a preposition comes at the end of a clause or sentence, he says, "This is an idiom, which our language is strongly inclined to."

Lowth's grammar was not written for children. Lowth's approach was strictly prescriptive; he meant to improve and correct, not describe. He judged correctness by his own rules — mostly derived from Latin grammar — which frequently went against established usage. But he did what he intended to so well that grammarians subsequently fairly fell over themselves in haste to get out versions of Lowth suitable for school use, and most subsequent grammars — including Noah Webster's first — were to some extent based upon Lowth's.

queries (with the injunction not to remove any flags or erase any marks), and generally dealing with the edited manuscript. The author will usually be encouraged to return the manuscript within a few weeks, as the sched ule requires.

When the manuscript returns, the editor will frequently have to reconcile the responses to the queries and clean up the manuscript for the typesetter. The flags are removed at this point (and may be saved in an envelope for possible later reference); the information on some of them may have to be transferred to the text. Where the author has decided to reject the copyeditor's or editor's suggestions, the editor will generally acquiesce. However, when these decisions seem to be the result of misunderstanding or when they may create problems of consistency, a call to the author may be necessary.

When the final issues have been resolved, the manuscript and diskette are sent to the typesetter, along with the specs (revised if necessary). Generally all changes will have been entered on the diskette by the publisher. Sometimes this task will be left to the typesetter, and sometimes, as mentioned earlier, the author will be asked to enter the changes. Camera-ready art is not usually included at this stage; however, if the editor expects to receive page-style first proofs, properly sized photocopies of the art may be sent, or the size of each art hole may be specified in the margin next to its text reference.

Electronic Editing

As mentioned, most manuscripts are created electronically and submitted on computer diskette or by E-mail attachment, often accompanied by a paper copy. Today most magazine and newspaper editing, as well as most editing of corporate communications, is probably done electronically. Most book editing, by contrast, continues to be done on paper, the marks on a copyedited manuscript being keyed into the electronic file (generally in-house, though the electronic file and paper manuscript may instead both be sent to the typesetter to have the corrections keyed in there) after they have been approved by the author and in-house editor.

The submission of electronic manuscripts has led to an increase in on-screen editing. Modern word-processing programs include editing functions that automatically preserve all the editing that has been done on a manuscript, clearly marked as such, and permit the easy acceptance or rejection of individual changes or of all the changes simultaneously. After an author or in-house editor has reviewed a copy editor's work, all the accepted changes exist in the form of keyboarded text and thus no further keyboarding step is necessary.

When these editing functions are activated, deleted text need not simply disappear but rather is generally struck through with a colored deletion line, while any added or substituted text appears underscored and in color (alternative display options are possible). Electronic editing is thus often referred to as *redlining*.

In this way, the manuscript's editorial "history" is preserved as it passes from hand to hand. At the end of the process, a copy of the file showing all the emendations and queries it has accumulated may be preserved for the record while a clean final file—from which all deleted text has in fact been discarded—is sent to the typesetter.

On-screen editing is valued by some because it permits use of a spell checker. If the user chooses the appropriate option, every keyboarded word not in the spell checker's dictionary will be highlighted in some way (with a wavy colored underline, for example) as soon as it appears on the screen. The editor can thereby deal with these real or apparent misspellings while progressing through the manuscript, avoiding the need for a separate spell-checking pass (using a dialogue box) through the entire document at the end of the job. If a manuscript repeatedly employs certain unusual or technical terms, names, or styling that the spell checker's dictionary doesn't recognize, the editor can either add the term to ("customize") the dictionary or simply click on the word and instruct the computer to ignore it throughout. Note that any copy editor who has been given the electronic manuscript file can make use of a computer's spell checking capacity even if he or she is actually marking up a paper copy.

Use of so-called grammar checkers is rarer among editors, since grammar checkers often highlight issues of composition that require a more nuanced approach than mechanical means can provide. Grammar checkers are most useful when they have been customized by the copy editor to highlight only those types of errors they have been demonstrably useful in identifying.

To take the place of paper flags, with their queries to editor or author, word-processing programs offer a Comments or Annotations feature. Positioning the cursor at the appropriate point in the text and clicking on the Comments or Annotations menu option causes a box to appear in which a query can be written ("Check use of term here," "Whose responsibility?" "Treatment too brief—expand," etc.). The box vanishes from the screen when closed, but a symbol identifying the editor who wrote the query automatically appears where the cursor was placed, and the next reader of the manuscript simply clicks on the symbol to read the electronic "flag." Since the symbols show up only on-screen and not in the printed manuscript, they can only be used when its subsequent readers will be looking at the on-screen version.

Two alternative methods will keep an editor's notes visible both on-screen and in print. One is to simply type any comments directly into the manuscript itself, enclosed in square brackets or curly braces. (At the end of the job, the search function can be used to ensure that all such comments have been removed.) The other is to set one's queries as footnotes or endnotes, using the Footnote function (similar to the Comments/ Annotations feature).

Most on-screen editors choose to leave their documents' editing history invisible as they work (by forgoing an option that reads, for instance, "Highlight changes on screen"). A "clean" screen makes it far easier to read the edited text, and the copy editor can proceed exactly as if he or she were revising, say, a personal letter on-screen and no record of the changes were even being kept.

When text has been electronically copyedited in a word-processing system other than the one used by the author or in-house editor, it may be difficult to convert it to the other system or systems while preserving its editorial markup. This need for compatibility with remote systems, along with authors' general lack of familiarity with on-screen editing, may be one reason why book publishing has been slow to embrace on-screen editing. However, compatibility is steadily increasing as users graduate to newer, more flexible versions of software.

Compatibility between word-processing software and typesetting systems, however, remains a serious issue in texts that are heavy with tables and mathematical equations, since formatting of tables and equations is generally lost in conversion to typesetting systems. For this reason, table- and equation-heavy manuscripts may be poor candidates for on-screen editing.

The in-house editor determines the form or forms in which the electronically copyedited manuscript will be returned to the author (marked-up printout only, marked-up printout with clean printout, clean printout with diskettes or E-mail attachment, etc.). Any electronic version returned to an author must be protected against having changes made on it that will not show up distinctively as new material.

The editing functions in word-processing programs were designed for work on small documents, particularly office documents that might need to go to various people for comments and additions. On larger projects they perform somewhat less well. Since very little text is ever visible on-screen, book editors may grow frustrated at lacking the browsing freedom that is so helpful for achieving a sense of perspective within a lengthy manuscript. Many book editors find on-screen editing to be alienating and counterintuitive and are far more comfortable working on paper.

To sum up: Electronic editing has been accepted far more quickly in newspaper and magazine publishing and corporate communications—where most pieces are short and where authorial review is a minor or nonexistent consideration—than it has in book publishing. Its principal advantage—that it renders unnecessary a separate keyboarding pass, whether in house or by the typesetter, when all editing is complete, and can thereby speed up the publishing process—often seems to be outweighed by its principal disadvantage—that it makes certain kinds of browsing and searching in long documents difficult and achieving a broad grasp of such documents elusive. However, some book publishers are now encouraging on-screen editing by their copy editors, and the shift toward electronic editing will likely continue in the coming years.

Proofs and Proofreading

The proofreader performs an indispensable role in the later stages of the publishing process, somewhat narrower than that of the copy editor but by no means lacking in scope for discrimination and judgment.

Book publishers generally make use of freelance proofreaders, though they will usually also have in-house proofreaders on the staff for smaller jobs. Magazines and especially newspapers more often keep all their proofreading in-house. (Typesetters almost always employ their own proofreaders, so most proofs that arrive at publishers' offices have already been proofread. However, publishers rarely rely solely on a typesetter's proofreading.)

Like copy editors, proofreaders normally work for an agreed-upon hourly fee. Since proofreading is a more "mechanical" task than copyediting, it usually goes faster, and proofreaders are often expected to work at a rate of approximately ten pages per hour—a rate that will vary considerably depending on the size of the pages and the type, as well as the technical difficulty of the material.

The proofreader's main job is to compare manuscript copy with proof—reading small sections of copy against the corresponding sections of proof, character by character—and to mark the proofs so that they follow the copy and the design specifications (a copy of which the editor will generally provide). In addition to typographical errors, the proofreader corrects obvious stylistic errors missed by the copy editor and points out to the editor or author any other possible problems.

In a second reading, the proofreader may focus on the grammar and sense of the material. However, most editors expect the proofreader to concentrate narrowly on discrepancies between manuscript and proofs and on the most basic issues of style and punctuation, and to ignore potential problems of any other kind if they were not noticed on a first reading.

As mentioned, the proofreader is responsible for knowing and applying the most standard rules of style and punctuation. Thus, if the copy editor failed to notice that a period was typed outside closing quotation marks, the proofreader would be remiss not to catch the error and automatically correct it (without bothering to ask "Ed: OK?" in the margin).

A proofreader's basic tools are minimal: several well-sharpened lead pencils, some editing tags or flags, a good dictionary, and a pica ruler with which to verify conformity to the design specifications. A small opaque ruler or an index card can be used to help the eyes focus on one line at a time.

First or Galley Proofs

Text sent to the typesetter as a manuscript returns to the publisher in the form of *first proofs,* on which the text is set the width of the type page. These proofs are often called *galley proofs* or *galleys,* named for the long strips of paper on which such proofs were usually printed. Traditional galley proofs omit art, captions, tables, and footnotes. However, first proofs today usually closely resemble book pages in almost every respect, having the same length of text block and including tentative folios and running heads or feet, and leaving room for art at the appropriate locations when they do not incorporate copies of the art itself. However, any page numbers and running heads or feet are usually only provisional, and footnotes and tables may all be segregated on separate pages rather than positioned as they will be in the bound book.

First proofs are usually sent out by the typesetter in batches so that proofreading can begin while typesetting continues on another batch of manuscript. Two or more copies are sent: one copy may be sent to the author for review (see below); another, designated the *master* proof, is the one that will be returned to the typesetter with all corrections marked on it, and is given to a proofreader.

Whenever more than one person works on a set of proofs, each should use an identifiable color of pencil or pen. Before the master copy is returned to the typesetter, the editor or proofreader must take special care that all revisions and instructions from all those who examined the proofs are properly transferred, or *carried,* to the master.

Most type proofs are merely photocopies; thus they will sometimes slightly distort the printed image and will often have physical flaws, such as faint type and small specks, which should not concern the proof-reader.

Revisions to proofs should be kept to a reasonable minimum, because it is expensive to make changes in typeset text. (The cost of alterations, usually stated in terms of the hourly cost of the typesetter's work, should be stated as part of the typesetter's job estimate.) For this reason, a proofreader is usually expected only to compare the proof with the manuscript copy and mark any necessary corrections but not to make other revisions. A proofreader who is concerned about some larger aspect of the typeset text should query the editor about it.

Author's Revisions

A fresh set of first proofs or a set of proofs that has already been proofread is usually sent to the author along with a request to proofread it and particularly to verify such details as the spellings of proper names, the accuracy of numerical data, and the content of bibliography and footnote items—things easily missed by a copy editor. A copy of the edited manuscript is included with the galleys to make comparison and checking easier. Authors are asked to keep new corrections to a minimum and are reminded about the cost of revision, which will often be charged to them. (Their contract will usually state that all author's alterations beyond a stated amount will be billed to the author.)

The proofreader's queries are usually written in the margin, preceded by "Au:" (for "Author")—assuming the proofreader has been told that the author will be seeing the proofread set—or "Qu:" (for "Query") or simply a question mark, and circled. When suggesting a correction that goes beyond a typographical error, the proofreader normally makes the correction and asks for confirmation in the margin by means of a simple note such as "Ed: ?" or "Au: OK?" The author is instructed, in a cover letter or a printed instruction sheet, to cross out such question marks and let the correction stand if it is acceptable. If it is not, the author is told to cross out the whole query, including the suggested change, and either write "OK as set" or provide an alternative revision. ("OK" by itself should be avoided, because it may not be obvious whether this applies to the original or the revision).

The author should be instructed not to erase any marks written on the galleys. Instead, an X drawn over a notation will indicate that it is unacceptable without obliterating it.

Proofreaders' Duties and Proofreading Marks

The correction marks used by proofreaders are shown above in Table 8.1. All proofreader's marks are written in the margin opposite the affected line rather than above the line, with only a corresponding caret, deletion strike-through, circle, or underscore in the text itself to show where the correction should be made. (All proofreading marks are traditionally written in the margin because typeset lines are single-spaced, leaving no room for the interlinear marks used by copy editors. Consequently, typesetters look for them only in the margins.) When two or more corrections occur in a single line, slash marks separate the symbols in the margin; the symbols are written in the same sequence as the errors in the line, reading from left to right. Proofreading symbols may be written in either margin. If several corrections must be made in a single line, they may begin in the left margin and continue to the right margin; however, a line with many errors should be deleted and rewritten correctly in the margin.

On first proofs, the proofreader's duties include confirming, at a minimum, the following aspects of the text:

1. Precise reproduction of every character in the edited manuscript, except where the copy editor failed to catch a standard error
2. Precise conformity of every element to the design specs throughout
3. Numerical and alphabetical sequences
4. Vertical and horizontal alignment of set-off text
5. Acceptable end-of-line word breaks

If first proofs arrive in the form of made-up pages with running heads and folios, the proofreader should additionally check the latter for correctness and sequence. (The specs should stipulate the content as well as the design of the running heads.) However, if the book will include art but no holes have yet been left for it, there is no point in checking the folios and running heads since addition of the art will alter the page makeup.

Any text references to missing tables or art of any kind should be repeated in a marginal note ("Fig. 8.1," "Einstein portrait," etc.).

Queries, as mentioned above, are usually kept as brief as possible and written right in the margin. A tag or flag, with the page number on it, may be used for longer queries.

In order that the publisher may allocate the costs of typesetting changes at the proof stage, the proofreader is traditionally (but not always) asked to assign responsibility for each marked alteration. These are classified as one of three types: (1) *printer's errors* (really *typesetter's* errors), errors that result from the typesetter's misreading of copy, careless keyboarding, or careless misunderstanding of design specs; (2) *author's alterations*, changes requested by the author as a result of discovering errors made in the manuscript or late changes in desired wording; and (3) *editor's alterations*, corrections that the copy editor failed to make or other changes requested by the proofreader. The proof-reader identifies these alterations by writing and cir-cling the abbreviation "PE," "AA," or "EA" in the mar-gin by each requested change. If the proofreader is not reading proofs that the author has already marked up, only "PE" and "EA" will be needed; assigning the au-thor's responsibility may be left to the in-house editor as one of the tasks of conflating the author's and proof-reader's marks onto a single set of proofs. The proof-reader should never label an error "PE" unless the copy and the instructions were absolutely clear; the typeset-ter should not be held responsible for misspelling a name as a result of an editor's bad handwriting or styling a text element wrong as a result of an ambigu-ously worded spec.

If the publisher will be absorbing the costs of the author's changes (this will generally be stipulated in the author's contract), only "PE" and "EA" need be used at all. The proofreader should always be told at the outset of each project what the PE (AA, EA) policy will be.

The following paragraphs describe (in alphabetical order) the standard proofreading marks, all of which are shown in the preceding table.

Align   Use the symbol in the text to show where type (usually in tables or lists) should be aligned. In the mar-gin, write "align" or provide a specific instruction such as "Align col heads."

Boldface   Draw a wavy line below the text, and write and circle "bf" in the margin.

Capital letter   Draw three lines under lowercase type in the text, and write "cap" or "uc" in the margin.

Center   Enclose the text to be centered between reverse brackets. Repeat the symbols in the margin, or write and circle "ctr." If clarification seems necessary, include an instruction such as "Ctr below head of col 1."

Centered dot   In the text, put a caret above the dot and an inverted caret below it, and draw the dot with both carets in the margin.

Change or add punctuation   To change punctuation, draw a slash through the incorrect punctuation mark and write the correct mark in the margin. To add punctuation, draw a caret at the text insertion point and write the punctuation in the margin, using the punctuation symbols in the table.

Close up   Place a close-up sign at the appropriate point in the text, and repeat it in the margin.

Deletion   Cross out the word or passage (use a slash to delete a single letter), and draw a delete sign in the margin. To substitute new text for deleted text, line out the deleted text and write the new text in the margin but omit the delete sign. To delete a paragraph or more, draw a box around the section, drawing a large X through it, and put a delete sign in the margin. To delete letters from the middle of a word, line them out (for a single letter, use a slash) and draw the delete sign within a close-up sign in the margin.

Em or en dash   Indicate the insertion point with a caret, and draw the appropriate symbol in the margin.

Em space   Draw the symbol or a caret in the text, and draw the symbol in the margin. To indicate more than one em, insert a 2 (3, 4, etc.) within the square or repeat the symbol for each em space required. To extend the indention downward, draw a vertical line descending from the em quad.

Hyphen   Indicate the insertion point with a caret, and draw a double hyphen in the margin.

Imperfect character   To mark an imperfectly printed character, circle it and put a circled X in the margin.

Insertion   Use a caret to show the insertion point in the text, and write the text for insertion in the margin.

Italic Underline the text, and write and circle "ital" in the margin.

Lowercase Draw a diagonal line through the capital letter in the text, and write and circle "lc" in the margin.

Move left or right Draw the move-left or move-right mark in both text and margin.

Paragraph To indicate a new paragraph, draw either a paragraph symbol or a line-break symbol (or both) in the text and put the paragraph symbol in the margin. To join two paragraphs into a single paragraph, connect the end and beginning of the separated paragraphs with a curving line and write "no ¶" in the margin.

Question mark Indicate the insertion point with a caret, and write and circle "set ?" in the margin.

Roman Circle italicized text, and write and circle "rom" in the margin. Circle boldface text, and write and circle "lf" ("lightface") in the margin.

Slash Indicate the insertion point with a caret, and write and circle "set slash" in the margin.

Small capitals Mark the text with a double underscore, and write and circle "sm cap" or "sc" in the margin.

Space Use a caret or a slash in the text to show where space should be added, and write the space symbol in the margin. This symbol may also be used to ask for added space between lines. To separate two letters that are crashing, specify "hair #" in the margin.

Spell out Circle the typeset number or abbreviation, and write "sp" in the margin. To avoid possible ambiguity, spell out the number or abbreviation in the margin instead.

Stet Place dots below inadvertently deleted material in the text, and write "stet" in the margin.

Subscript Circle the affected number in the text, and write the number with a caret above it in the margin. To add a superscript number (or change a number to a subscript), place a caret in the text (or circle the affected number) and write the number in the margin with a caret above it. To add a comma, use a caret in the text and draw a comma with a caret above it in the margin.

Superscript To add a superscript number (or to change a larger number to a superscript), place an inverted caret in the text (or circle the affected number) and write the number in the margin with an inverted caret below it. Add quotation marks and apostrophes by means of an inverted caret in the text and the appropriate mark with an inverted caret below it in the margin.

Transpose Use the curving line within the text, and write "tr" in the margin.

Figure 8.4 shows a page of text on which a number of the marks listed above are illustrated.

Word division Computer typesetting systems break words as commanded by their own internal dictionaries; these usually produce acceptable breaks, but may not be able to deal with names, odd punctuation, symbolic language, or unusual, technical, or foreign words. To correct any faultily divided words, insert a line-break symbol within the word (or between words) and repeat the symbol or write "bb" (for "bad break") in the margin.

Paragraph endings Most publishers and typesetters avoid dividing the last word of a paragraph at the end of the line or allowing a very short word to appear by itself on the last line of a paragraph. To correct any such runovers that may have been typeset, the proofreader may simply insert a line-break symbol near the end of

Figure 8.4 Proofread Text

John Wallis, a mathematician and Member of the Royal Society, published in 1658 a grammar, written in Latin for the use of foreigners who wanted to learn English. Wallis, according to George H. MacKnight, abandoned much of the method of Latin grammar. Wallis's grammar is perhaps best remembered for being the source of the much discussed distinction between *shall* and *will*. Wallis's grammar is also the one referred to by Samuel Johnson in the front matter of his 1755 dictionary. Dryden deserves mention too. He defended the English of his time as an improvement over the English of Shakespeare and Johnson. He is the first person who worried about the preposition at the end of a sentence (we much know of) He eliminated many such prepositions, his own writings when revising his works for a collected edition. He seems to have decided the practice was wrong because it could not happen in Latin.

C.C. Fries tells us that 17th century grammars in general were designed for foreigners or for school use, in order to lead to the study of Latin. In the 18th century, however, grammars were written predominately for English speakers, and although they were written for the purpose of instructing, they seem to find more fun correcting. A change in the underlying philosophy of grammar had occurred, and it is made explicit in perhaps the first eighteenth century grammar, A Key to the Art of Letters . . . , published in 1700 by a schoolmaster named A. Lane. He thought it a mistake to view grammar simply as a means to learn a foreign language and asserted that "the true End and Use of Grammar is to teach how to speak and write well and learnedly in a language Already known, according to the unalterable Rules of right Reason." Gone was Ben Jonson's appeal to custom.

The 18th-Century Grammar

There was evidently a considerable amount of general interest in things grammatical among men of letters, for Addison, Swift and Steele all treated grammar in one way or another in *The Tatler* and The Spectator in 1710, 1711, and 1712. In 1712 Swift published yet another proposal for an English academy (it came within a whisker of succeeding); John Oldmixon attacked Swift's proposal in the same year. Public interest must have helped create a market for the grammar books which began appearing with some frequency about this same time. And if controversy fuels sales, grammarians knew it, they were perfectly willing to emphasize their own advantages by denigrating their predecessors, sometimes in abusive terms.

the preceding line to force a word or part of a word to run over. If this would produce an awkward result, the editor may instead insert a word or two in the next-to-last line, but will probably simply choose to ignore the problem.

Headings   Runover lines in a heading should break at a logical point when possible. Words within headings should not be divided except where it is unavoidable. (The design specs should have stipulated this.)

Footnotes, tables, and illustrations   If the text will have footnotes (rather than endnotes), note where the footnote references occur, write a note in the margin ("fn 1," "fn 2," etc.) next to where a footnote reference occurs. Any notations in the margins of the manuscript that concern tables and illustrations ("Insert Islands chart about here," "fn 2 here," "Fig. 3.1," etc.) must be carried to the galley margins by the proofreader.

Lengthy insertions   The proofreader will occasionally have to insert lengthy material that the typesetter has inadvertently omitted or will have to carry to the master proof some addition from the author. In the case of omitted material, the typesetter can simply be instructed to "Set omitted text on msp. 133." Added material that does not fit at the bottom of the proof may be typed or photocopied on a separate page and identified as "insert A," "insert B," and so on. The point of insertion should be marked with a caret, and a note such as "insert A attached; run in" should be written in the margin.

Carryover instructions   All instructions from the editor to the typesetter that remain pertinent at this stage must be carried from the manuscript to the proofs.

If the galley proofs are of the traditional long kind that do not resemble finished pages, it may be necessary to include instructions about how to handle elements that present page-makeup problems—for example, long tables that could extend onto a second page (e.g., "Comp: Repeat title and col heads on new page")—but only if such instructions are not included in the specs, as they should have been.

For all cross-references that include page numbers (the number 000 or an eye-catching symbol will normally have been set in place of any actual numbers at this stage), the proofreader should carry over in the margin the number of the manuscript page where the discussion appears (e.g., "msp 47"), so that at the page-proof stage the proper text material can easily be located and confirmed by comparing the manuscript and the page proofs before writing in the final page reference. To make the task still easier at the future page-proof stage, the proofreader may provide both the manuscript page number and the corresponding galley page number (e.g., "msp.47, galley p.31"). If the first proofs are in page-proof form, the author may have been asked to insert the correct page references on his or her copy of the proofs.

Checking Proofs against Design Specs

In addition to reading the proofs against the manuscript, the proofreader or in-house editor should make a special pass through the proofs to see that every element conforms to the design specifications, which the proofreader should normally have been given. This entails taking various measurements—the width of the text block (and its length, if the first proofs take the form of made-up pages), the spacing around various levels of headings and around lists and other set-off material, the indention of extracts, and so on—as well as checking the size, face, and style of the type in headings, captions, tables, and other elements. After verifying conformity with the specs at the initial appearance of each element, all its subsequent appearances can generally be checked merely visually.

Typesetters usually require some latitude in spacing in order to make up visually acceptable pages; therefore, the spacing above heads (particularly at the second-proof stage) will not invariably be identical throughout. The proofreader must use some personal judgment about how much variation is acceptable.

Sometimes variations also occur in the density of the typesetting—that is, the amount of spacing between letters—and in the heaviness or darkness of the type itself. Typesetting machines allow for various density settings, or *tracks,* and the overall density setting is called the *tracking.* The proofreader should mark any striking examples of variable density on a given line (e.g., "Line set too tight" or "Line set too loose") or larger passage ("Match tracking density of earlier text") and should query the typesetter about any marked variation in heaviness, which will sometimes be merely the result of bad photocopying.

Second or Page Proofs

The master set of marked-up first proofs is returned to the typesetter, along with the camera-ready artwork and instructions as to where and how to insert the illustrations into the text. (For highly designed books, the editor may have had a dummy made from the proofs, which will be enclosed with them when they are returned to the typesetter.)

After the typesetter makes the requested revisions, the revised text is re-output as *second proofs,* traditionally known as *page proofs,* which show just what each page of the book will look like. (Since first proofs today usually take the form of pages, the term *page proofs* has become somewhat ambiguous, and *second proofs* is now the preferred name.) If the book contains artwork, it is normally at this stage that film or proofs of the illustrations, which have been photographed from the camera-ready artwork, are combined with film or proof of the text.

The typesetter sends back the marked-up first

proofs along with copies of the new second proofs, including a master proof for the editor and a copy for the indexer. The indexer should be sent copies of each batch as it arrives, since there will usually be minimal time in the schedule for creating the index.

Second proofs present a much easier proofreading job than first proofs, since there will be many fewer errors and the proofreader need not even reread sections of material for which no corrections were requested. The task will therefore often be assigned to an in-house proofreader rather than a freelancer, or the in-house editor may even personally proofread the second proofs.

The proofreader compares the marked-up first proofs with the new second proofs to confirm that all the requested alterations were carried out. Wherever a correction was made, the proofreader must check not only the line with the correction but any subsequent lines that were altered by the correction; though computer typesetting hardly ever introduces actual errors when text is simply repositioned because of changes elsewhere in the paragraph, undesirable character spacing and bad end-of-line breaks may sometimes result. The proofreader should also *slug* the second proofs against the first proofs—that is, hold corresponding sections of first and second proofs next to each other as a quick check that no lines were unintentionally deleted between the two stages. If so instructed, the proofreader again labels any new changes "PE" or "EA." As at the first-proof stage, the proofreader will only use "AA" when consolidating the author's marks on proofs that the author has already reviewed. Any errors marked in the first proofs (whether as "PE," "EA," or "AA") but not corrected by the typesetter is marked "PE" at this stage; however, any error noticed for the first time only in the second proofs should not be marked "PE."

The conscientious proofreader may want to make a series of quick passes through the second proofs, each devoted to a separate aspect of the text. A checklist would include at least the following items.

Corrections Examine every correction marked on the galley to be sure that the copy has been corrected as requested without introducing unwanted alterations. Examine the copy that surrounds the correction, especially the lines below it, to be sure that no undesirable spacing or end-of-line breaks have been introduced.

Typesetting instructions Be sure that all other instructions to the typesetter written on the first proofs, in the design specs, or in a cover letter have been carried out.

Cross-references Check each cross-reference to see that it refers the reader to the correct place. If the cross-reference is to the title of a chapter or section, be sure the wording matches. If the reference is to a page number (probably typeset as "page 000"), insert the correct number. (Ideally this will be done by the author, who will usually have been sent a set of second proofs and asked to provide missing cross-references.) If the cross-reference is to a passage that has not yet been set in pages, make a note in the margin to insert the reference later.

Tables and illustrations If tables and illustrations are not referred to by number in the text, read the text carefully for phrases like "the figure above" and make sure each figure has been positioned accordingly. If there is a discrepancy, revise the phrase (e.g., to "the figure below") rather than asking that the figure be moved. Check that each illustration or table matches its text reference and is complete, properly oriented and positioned, and correctly identified by caption. When a table continues to a second page, check that its headings have been repeated on the new page and that any continuation line required by the specs has been set.

Notes Check the sequence of footnote or endnote numbers, and match each superscript number in the text with its note. Each footnote must begin on the same page with its text reference; a long footnote may run over to the following page, as long as two lines or more are carried over. Check the footnotes for conformity to design specifications.

Running heads and folios Read the running heads on each page to confirm that they are correct. If a long running head has not been shortened so as to fit comfortably on its line (any necessary shortened forms should have been specified by the editor before the manuscript was sent out), the editor must abridge it at this point. Remove any running heads mistakenly set on chapter-opening pages or on any other pages where the specs require that they be omitted (e.g., pages with full-page illustrations or tables). Check that the folios are complete and sequential.

Facing pages Make sure that the last line of type on each page aligns with that on the opposite page. If not, draw double horizontal lines to indicate alignment and write in the margin "Align bottom of page."

Top of page Avoid beginning a page with the short final line of a paragraph, known as a *widow,* or any single short indented item such as the final item in a list. Either instruct the typesetter to remake the page or add words to the widow to fill it out. (Typesetters usually automatically avoid widows even when the specs fail to mention them.)

Bottom of page A heading should never be set at the bottom of a page without at least two lines of text below it. Most typesetters will observe this rule even if the specs do not include it, but the designer should have specified it nonetheless. To fix a mispositioned head, use the techniques described below either to add lines below the head and cut some above, or to add lines above the head in order to move it to the next page.

Chapter-ending pages Make sure the last page of each chapter contains at least five lines of text. (Again, the typesetter will generally do this without being told.)

It is generally expensive to make corrections on second proofs, so only essential changes should be made, and only in places and in ways that will cause the fewest lines to be reset. If possible, every line added to or deleted from a page must be compensated for in some way on that page, either by deleting or adding another line or by reducing or expanding space somewhere, such as above or below a heading or list.

While it is generally acceptable to shorten or lengthen the text block by one line, a similar change should usually be made on the opposite page to balance the alignment. If an illustration or table is set at the bottom of a page, strict facing alignment is unnecessary. Whenever the editor chooses to alter the bottom margin, the typesetter should be notified that the change is intentional by means of a note such as "1 li short OK." The editor can suggest ways to alter the spacing in such situations—for example, by asking in a marginal note that space be added or deleted around illustrations, tables, footnotes, or displayed passages. Deleting or adding text may prove awkward, and usually requires approval from the author.

Since the typesetter may charge extra for every line affected by an author's or editor's alteration, the least costly way to gain a line is to extend the last line of a paragraph over to a new line by adding words. When lines must be cut, the cuts should ideally be made near the end of a paragraph.

When the marked-up second proofs return from the publisher, the typesetter makes the final corrections. The typesetter confirms any requested corrections by sending (often faxing) copies of the individual corrected pages to the editor, who calls back to approve them.

Printers' Proofs

At this point the typesetter will finally produce the pages in the form the printer will receive them. These often take the form of *reproduction* (or simply *repro*) *proofs*—high-quality, camera-ready positive prints on specially coated paper, which will be photographed to make film negatives, from which the book plates will be created. The typesetters may make the film themselves from their own repro proofs. Whether repro or film, it will usually be sent directly to the printer, though it may instead be sent to the publisher to be forwarded to the printer. The editor should check that all the pages are included, and may want to look them over for specks and other imperfections.

A third possibility is that the typesetter will send the printer nothing but an electronic version of the pages, and the printer will create any necessary media directly from it.

After a period of usually one to four weeks, the printer sends the publisher a last set of proofs, produced from the film itself. These *film proofs* are commonly known as *bluelines* or *book blues*—or simply *blues*—because they are usually printed in blue ink. They arrive already folded into signatures matching the signatures in the book-to-be.

Checking the blues is an extremely important task, since any errors the editor misses at this stage will almost certainly show up in the bound book itself. Thus, the following steps are essential:

1. Check that the correct identifying mark appears on the spine of each signature. The signatures should either be numbered sequentially or have a distinctive mark that indicates the signature's order, generally by being lower on the spine than those that precede it and higher than those that follow it, or vice versa.

2. Check that all the pages are present and in order. Scan every page—spend at least five seconds apiece—for specks, blotches, obscured type, and the like. If an entire page or part of a page has printed light, this likely will not reflect

the way the actual page will print, but it may be safer to mark such pages anyway. Circle each error prominently in ink; if the printer might be unsure what is wrong, describe the error in a note on the page itself.

3. Page through the set again, this time spot-checking the page backup. Hold up to the light a reasonable sample of the pages to see whether the running head, folio, and text block align with those on the reverse side. Wherever they do not, note this on the page itself; if the problem is common, instruct the printer to "Check page backup throughout."

4. Check that all art is in its correct place and has printed clearly with sharp outlines. Check that none of the art has been flopped (reversed in orientation so that it reads backwards). If any late-arriving art has not been sent to the printer, it must be included in the package with the returned blues, along with any necessary sizing or other instructions. Likewise, if the index was typeset too late to be included in the blues, its film or repro must be sent back with them, along with any necessary instructions.

5. If the Cataloging-in-Publication (CIP) data has not yet been added on the copyright page, it must be returned with the blues.

6. On the first page of blues, list all the pages where errors, changes, or omissions have been marked. The list may be repeated in a cover letter.

Because printers' schedules tend to be tight, blues usually have to be returned quickly, sometimes on the same day they arrive.

The very last form in which an editor sees a printed text before the bound books arrive is known as *folded and gathered sheets*, (*f and g's* or *F&G's*). F&G's are a com-

plete set of the actual signatures that will be bound—
that is, with the actual ink color and on the same paper
stock. F&G's are sent immediately to the publisher as
soon as the print run begins, they often arrive on an editor's desk while the run is under way. (They need not
be returned to the printer.) If the print run is a short
one, there may be no time to halt it even if a serious
error is discovered in the F&G's, though even if the
printing cannot be stopped the binding often can be.
Any interruption at this stage will always be disruptive
and costly, however, and is rarely resorted to except
when a disastrous error is discovered.

If all the previous stages have been properly
checked, the bound books themselves should contain
no unpleasant surprises—or at least none that the editor can be held responsible for. Sometimes part of a
print run will be trimmed badly, so that the type block
comes too close to the edge of the page. Occasionally a
signature will be omitted. The editor should take a few
minutes to examine an advance copy before sending
one off to the author, and should alert the manufac-
turing manager about any faults.

Appendix A

Word Usage

Problems in Word Usage

The following list discusses words that present a variety of problems to writers. Review it from time to time to keep yourself alert to potential usage issues in your own writing. (See also the next section, which provides a list of easily confused words and clichés.)

aggravate *Aggravate* is used chiefly in two meanings: "to make worse" ("aggravated her shoulder injury," "their financial position was aggravated by the downturn") and "to irritate, annoy" ("The President was aggravated by the French intransigence"). The latter is not often seen in writing. However, *aggravation* usually means "irritation," and *aggravating* almost always expresses annoyance.

almost, most *Most* is often used like *almost* in speech ("Most everyone was there"), but it is rarely seen in writing.

alot, a lot *Alot* hardly ever appears in print and is usually regarded as an error.

alright Though the business community has been using the one-word *alright* since the 1920s, it is only gradually gaining acceptance and is still often regarded as an error. It is rarely seen in published works outside of newspaper writing.

amount, number *Number* is normally used with nouns
that can form a plural and can be used with a numeral ("a large number of orders," "any number of
times"). *Amount* is mainly used with nouns that denote a substance or concept that can't be divided and
counted up ("the annual amount of rainfall," "a large
amount of money"). The use of *amount* with count
nouns, usually when the number of things can be
thought of as a mass or collection ("a substantial
amount of job offers"), is often criticized; and many
people will regard it as an error.

apt, liable Both *liable* and *apt*, when followed by an infinitive, are used nearly interchangeably with *likely*
("more liable to get tired easily," "roads are apt to be
slippery"). This use of *apt* is widely accepted, but
some people think *liable* should be limited to situations risking an undesirable outcome ("If you speed,
you're liable to be caught") and it is generally used
this way in writing.

as, as if, like *Like* used as a conjunction in the sense of
as ("just like I used to do") or *as if* ("It looks like it will
rain") has been frequently criticized, especially since
its use in a widely publicized cigarette commercial
slogan. Though *like* has been used in these ways for
nearly 600 years, it is safer to use *as* or *as if* instead.

as far as "As far as clothes, young people always know
best" is an example of *as far as* used as a preposition.
This use developed from the more common conjunction use ("As far as clothes are concerned . . .")
by omitting the following verb or verb phrase; it is
very widely used in speech but is often regarded as an
error in print.

awful It has been traditional to criticize any use of
awful and *awfully* that doesn't convey the original
sense of being filled with awe. However, *awful* has
long been acceptable in the meanings "extremely ob-

jectionable" ("What an awful color") and "exceedingly great" ("an awful lot of money") in speech and casual writing. Use of *awful* and *awfully* as intensifiers ("I'm awful tired," "he's awfully rich") is likewise common in informal prose, but it is safer to avoid them in formal writing.

between, among It is often said that *between* can only be used when dealing with two items ("between a rock and a hard place"), and that *among* must be used for three or more items ("strife among Croats, Serbs, and Muslims"). However, *between* is actually quite acceptable in these latter cases, especially when specifying one-to-one relationships, regardless of the number of items ("between you and me and the lamppost").

can, may Both *can* and *may* are used to refer to possibility ("Can the deal still go through?" "It may still happen"). Since the possibility of someone's doing something may depend on someone else's agreeing to it, the two words have become interchangeable when they refer to permission ("You can [may] go now if you like"). Though the use of *can* to ask or grant permission has been common since the last century, *may* is more appropriate in formal correspondence. However, this meaning of *may* is relatively rare in negative constructions, where *cannot* and *can't* are more usual ("They can't [may not] use it without paying").

comprise The sense of *comprise* meaning "to compose or constitute" ("the branches that comprise our government") rather than "to include or be made up of" ("Our government comprises various branches") has been attacked as wrong, for reasons that are unclear. Until recently, it was used chiefly in scientific and technical writing; today it has become the most widely used sense. But it still may be safer to use *compose* or *make up* instead.

contact Though some regard *contact* as only a noun and an adjective, its use as a verb, especially to mean "get in touch with" ("Contact your local dealer"), has long been widely accepted.

data *Data* has firmly established itself with a meaning independent of its use as the plural form of *datum*. It is used in one of two ways: as a plural noun (like *earnings*), taking a plural verb and plural modifiers (such as *these* or *many*) but not cardinal numbers ("These data show that we're out of the recession"); or as an abstract mass noun (like *information*), taking a singular verb and singular modifiers (such as *this, much,* or *little*) ("The data on the subject is plentiful"). Both constructions are standard, but many people are convinced that only the plural form is correct, and thus the plural form is somewhat more common in print. What you want to avoid is mixing in signs of the singular (like *this* or *much*) when you use a plural verb.

different from, different than Both of these phrases are standard; however, some people dislike the latter and will insist that, for example, "different than the old proposal" be changed to "different from the old proposal." *Different from* works best when you can take advantage of the *from* ("The new proposal is very different from the old one"). *Different than* works best when a clause follows ("very different in size than it was two years ago").

disinterested, uninterested *Disinterested* has basically two meanings: "unbiased" ("a disinterested decision," "disinterested intellectual curiosity"), and "not interested," which is also the basic meaning of *uninterested*. Though this second use of *disinterested* is widespread, some people object to it and it may be safer to avoid it.

due to When the *due* of *due to* is clearly an adjective ("absences due to the flu") no one complains about the phrase. When *due to* is a preposition ("Due to the holiday, our office will be closed"), some people object and call for *owing to* or *because of.* Both uses of *due to* are entirely standard, but in formal writing one of the alternatives for the prepositional use may be safer.

each other, one another The traditional rules call for *each other* to be used in reference to two ("The two girls looked at each other in surprise") and *one another* to be used in reference to three or more ("There will be time for people to talk with one another after the meeting"). In fact, however, they are employed interchangeably.

finalize Though avoided by many writers, *finalize* occurs frequently in business and government contexts ("The budget will be finalized," "finalizing the deal"), where it is regarded as entirely standard.

good, well Both *good* and *well* are acceptable when used to express good health ("I feel good," "I feel well"), and *good* may also connote good spirits. However, the adverb *good* has been much criticized, with people insisting that *well* be used instead ("The orchestra played well this evening"), and this adverbial use should be avoided in writing.

hardly *Hardly* meaning "certainly not" is sometimes used with *not* for added emphasis ("Just another day at the office? Not hardly"). *Hardly* is also used like *barely* or *scarcely* to emphasize a minimal amount ("I hardly knew her," "Almost new—hardly a scratch on it"). When *hardly* is used with a negative verb (such as *can't, couldn't, didn't*) it is often called a double negative, though it is really a weaker negative. *Hardly* with a negative is a spoken form, and should be avoided in writing (except when quoting someone directly).

hopefully When used to mean "I hope" or "We hope" ("Hopefully, they'll reach an agreement"), as opposed to "full of hope" ("We continued our work hopefully and cheerfully"), *hopefully* is often criticized, even though other similar sentence adverbs (such as *frankly, clearly,* and *interestingly*) are accepted by everyone. Despite the objections, this sense of *hopefully* is now in standard use.

I, me In informal speech and writing, such phrases as "It's me," "Susan is taller than me," "He's as big as me," "Who, me?" and "Me too" are generally accepted. In formal writing, however, it is safer to use *I* after *be* ("It was I who discovered the mistake") and after *as* and *than* when the first term of the comparison is the sentence's subject ("Susan is taller than I," "He is as big as I").

imply, infer *Infer* is mostly used to mean "to draw a conclusion, to conclude" and is commonly followed by *from* ("I infer from your comments that . . . "). *Imply* is used to mean "to suggest" ("The letter implies that our service was not satisfactory"). The use of *infer,* with a personal subject, as a synonym of *imply* ("Are you inferring that I made a mistake?") is not widely accepted in print and is best avoided.

irregardless *Irregardless,* though a real word (and not uncommon in speech), is still a long way from general acceptance; use *regardless* (or *irrespective*) instead.

lay, lie Though *lay* has long been used as an intransitive verb meaning "lie" ("tried to make the book lay flat," "lay down on the job"), it is generally condemned. In writing it is safer to keep the two words distinct, and to keep their various easily confused forms *(lie, lying, lay, lain; lay, laying, laid)* distinct as well.

lend, loan Some people still object to the use of *loan* as a verb ("loaned me the book") and insist on *lend.* Nevertheless, *loan* is in standard use. *Loan* is used only literally ("loans large sums of money"), however, while *lend* can be used both literally ("lends large

sums of money") and figuratively ("Would you please
lend me a hand?").

less, fewer   The traditional view is that *less* is used for
matters of degree, value, or amount, and that it modifies nouns that refer to uncountable things ("less
hostility," "less clothing") while *fewer* modifies numbers and plural nouns ("fewer students," "fewer than
eight trees"). However, *less* has been used to modify
plural nouns for centuries. Today *less* is actually more
likely than *fewer* to modify plural nouns when dis-
tances, sums of money, and certain common phrases
are involved ("less than 100 miles," "less than $2000,"
"in 25 words or less") and just as likely to modify periods of time ("in less [fewer] than four hours"). But
phrases such as "less bills," "less vacation days," and
"less computers" should be avoided.

like, such as   Should you write "cities like Chicago and
Des Moines" or "cities such as Chicago and Des
Moines"? You are in fact free to use either one, or
change the latter to "such cities as Chicago and Des
Moines."

media   *Media* is the plural of *medium*. With all the references to the mass media today, *media* is often used
as a singular mass noun ("The media always wants a
story"). But this singular use is not as well established
as the similar use of *data,* and, except in the world of
advertising, you will probably want to keep *media*
plural in most writing.

memorandum   *Memorandum* is a singular noun with
two acceptable plurals: *memorandums* and *memoranda.*
Memoranda is not yet established as a singular form.

neither   the use of *neither* to refer to more than two
nouns, though sometimes criticized, has been standard for centuries ("Neither the post office, the
bank, nor City Hall is open today"). Traditionally, the

pronoun *neither* is used with a singular verb ("Neither is ideal"). However, when a prepositional phrase follows *neither,* a plural verb is common and acceptable ("Neither of those solutions are ideal").

one The use of *one* to indicate a generic individual lends formality to writing, since it suggests distance between the writer and the reader ("One never knows" is more formal than "You never know"). Using *one* in place of *I* or *me* ("I'd like to read more, but one doesn't have the time") is common in British English but may be thought odd or objectionable in American English.

people, persons *People* is used to designate an unspecified number of persons ("People everywhere are talking about the new show"), and *persons* is commonly used when a definite number is specified ("Occupancy by more than 86 persons is prohibited"). However, the use of *people* where numbers are mentioned is also acceptable nowadays ("Ten people were questioned").

per *Per,* meaning "for each," is most commonly used with figures, usually in relation to price ("$150 per performance"), vehicles ("25 miles per gallon," "55 miles per hour"), or sports ("15 points per game"). Avoid inserting words like *a* or *each* between *per* and the word or words it modifies ("could type 70 words per each minute").

phenomena *Phenomena* is the usual plural of *phenomenon.* Use of *phenomena* as a singular ("St. Elmo's Fire is an eerie phenomena") is encountered in speech and now and then in writing, but it is nonstandard and it is safer to avoid it.

plus The use of *plus* to mean "and" ("a hamburger plus french fries for lunch") or "besides which" ("We would have been on time, but we lost the car keys.

Plus, we forgot the map") is quite informal and is avoided in writing.

presently   The use of *presently* to mean "at the present time" ("I am presently working up a report") rather than "soon" ("He'll be with you presently"), while often criticized, is standard and acceptable.

pretty   *Pretty*, when used as an adverb to tone down or moderate a statement ("pretty cold weather"), is avoided in formal writing, so using it in correspondence will lend an informal tone.

prior to   *Prior to*, a synonym of *before*, most often appears in fairly formal contexts. It is especially useful in suggesting anticipation ("If all specifications are finalized prior to system design, cost overruns will be avoided").

proved, proven   Both *proved* and *proven* are past participles of *prove*. Earlier in this century, *proved* was more common than *proven*, but today they are about equally common. As a past participle, either is acceptable ("has been proved [proven] effective"), but *proven* is more frequent as an adjective ("proven gas reserves").

providing, provided   Although *providing* in the sense of "if" or "on condition that" has occasionally been disapproved ("providing he finds a buyer"), both *providing* and *provided* are well established, and either may be used. *Provided* is somewhat more common.

real   The adverb *real* is used interchangeably with *really* only as an intensifier ("a real tough assignment"). This use is very common in speech and casual writing, but you should not use it in anything more formal.

set, sit   *Set* generally takes an object ("Set the lamp over there") and *sit* does not ("sat for an hour in the doctor's office"). There are exceptions when *set* is used intransitively ("The sun will set soon," "The hen was setting") and *sit* takes an object ("I sat her down by her grandfather"). When used of people, however, intransitive *set* is a spoken use that should be avoided in writing.

shall, will *Shall* and *will* are generally interchangeable in present-day American English. In recent years, *shall* has been regarded as somewhat affected; *will* is much more common. However, *shall* is more appropriate in questions to express simple choice ("Shall we go now?") because *will* in such a context suggests prediction ("Will the prototype be ready next week?").

slow, slowly *Slow* used as an adverb (meaning "slowly") has often been called an error. *Slow* is almost always used with verbs indicating motion or action, and it typically follows the verb it modifies ("a stew cooked long and slow"). *Slowly* can be used in the same way ("drove slowly"), but it also is used before the verb ("The winds slowly subsided"), with adjectives formed from verbs ("the slowly sinking sun"), and in places where *slow* would sound inappropriate ("turned slowly around").

so The use of the adverb *so* to mean "very" or "extremely" is widely disapproved of in formal writing, except in negative contexts ("not so long ago") or when followed by an explaining clause ("cocoa so hot that I burned my tongue"). The use of the conjunction *so* to introduce clauses of result ("The acoustics are good, so every note is clear") and purpose ("Be quiet so I can sleep") is sometimes criticized, but these uses are standard. In the latter case (when used to mean "in order that"), *so that* is more common in formal writing ("to cut spending so that the deficit will be reduced").

such Some people disapprove of using *such* as a pronoun ("such was the result," "sorting out glass and newspapers and such"), but dictionaries recognize it as standard.

Frequently Confused Words

Misusing one word for another in one's writing is a common source of confusion, embarrassment, and unintentional humor. Computer spell checkers will not identify a word that is being wrongly used in place of the proper word. Try to review the following list periodically in order to avert word confusions you may be overlooking.

abjure to reject solemnly
adjure to command

abrogate to nullify
arrogate to claim

abstruse hard to understand
obtuse dull, slow

accede to agree
exceed to go beyond

accent to emphasize
ascent climb
assent to agree to something

access right or ability to enter
excess intemperance

ad advertisement
add to join to something; to find a sum

adapt to adjust to something

adept highly skilled
adopt to take as one's child; to take up

addenda additional items
agenda list of things to be done

addition part added
edition publication

adjoin to be next to
adjourn to suspend a session
adjure to command

adverse unfavorable
averse disinclined

advert to refer
avert to avoid
overt unconcealed

advice counsel or information
advise to give advice

affect to act upon or influence
effect result; to bring about

agenda *see* ADDENDA

alimentary relating to nourishment
elementary simple or basic

allude to refer indirectly
elude to evade

allusion indirect reference
illusion misleading image

amenable accountable, agreeable
amendable modifiable

amend to alter in writing
emend to correct

ante- prior to or earlier than
anti- opposite or against

anymore any longer, now
any more more

appraise to set a value on
apprise to give notice of
apprize to appreciate or value

arraign to bring before a court
arrange to come to an agreement

arrogate *see* ABROGATE

ascent *see* ACCENT

assay to test for valuable content
essay to try tentatively

assent *see* ACCENT

assure to give confidence to
ensure to make certain
insure to guarantee against loss

aural relating to the ear or hearing
oral relating to the mouth, spoken

averse *see* ADVERSE

avert *see* ADVERT

bail security given
bale bundle of goods

base bottom
bass fish; deep voice

biannual usually twice a year; sometimes every two years
biennial every two years

bloc group working together
block tract of land

born produced by birth
borne carried

breadth width
breath breathed air
breathe to draw in air

callous hardened
callus hard area on skin

canvas strong cloth; oil painting
canvass to solicit votes or opinions

capital city that is the seat of government
capitol state legislature building
Capitol U.S. Congress building

casual not planned
causal relating to or being a cause

casually by chance or accident
casualty one injured or killed

censor to examine for improper content
censure to express disapproval of

cession a yielding
session meeting

cite to summon; to quote
sight payable on presentation
site piece of land

collaborate to work or act jointly
corroborate to confirm

collision act of colliding
collusion secret cooperation for deceit

complacent self-satisfied
complaisant amiable

complement remainder
compliment admiring remark

concert to act in harmony or conjunction
consort to keep company

consul diplomatic official
council administrative body
counsel legal representative; to give advice

corespondent joint respondent
correspondent one who communicates

corroborate *see* COLLABORATE

council *see* CONSUL

councilor member of a council
counselor lawyer

counsel *see* CONSUL

credible worthy of being believed
creditable worthy of praise
credulous gullible

currant raisinlike fruit
current stream; belonging to the present

cynosure one that attracts
sinecure easy job

decent good or satisfactory
descent downward movement
dissent difference of opinion

decree official order
degree extent or scope

defuse to make less harmful
diffuse to pour out or spread widely

deluded misled or confused
diluted weakened in consistency

demur to protest
demure shy

deposition testimony
disposition personality; outcome

depraved corrupted
deprived divested or stripped

deprecate to disapprove of
depreciate to lower the worth of

descent *see* DECENT

desperate having lost hope
disparate distinct

detract to disparage or reduce
distract to draw attention away

device piece of equipment or tool
devise to invent, to plot

diffuse *see* DEFUSE

diluted *see* DELUDED

disassemble to take apart
dissemble to disguise feelings or intentions

disburse to pay out
disperse to scatter

discreet capable of keeping a secret
discrete individually distinct

disparate *see* DESPERATE

disperse *see* DISBURSE

disposition *see* DEPOSITION

dissemble *see* DISASSEMBLE

dissent *see* DECENT

distract *see* DETRACT

edition *see* ADDITION

effect *see* AFFECT

e.g. for example
i.e. that is

elementary *see* ALIMENTARY

elicit to draw or bring out
illicit not lawful

eligible qualified to have
illegible not readable

elude *see* ALUDE

emanate to come out from a source
eminent standing above others
immanent inherent
imminent ready to take place

emend *see* AMEND

emigrate to leave a country
immigrate to come into a place

eminence prominence or superiority
immanence restriction to one domain
imminence state of being imminent

ensure *see* ASSURE

envelop to surround
envelope letter container

equable free from unpleasant extremes
equitable fair

erasable removable by erasing
irascible hot-tempered

essay *see* ASSAY

every day each day
everyday ordinary

exceed *see* ACCEDE

excess *see* ACCESS

extant currently existing
extent size, degree, or measure

flaunt to display ostentatiously
flout to scorn

flounder to struggle
founder to sink

forego to precede
forgo to give up

formally in a formal manner
formerly at an earlier time

forth forward, out of
fourth 4th

gage security deposit
gauge to measure

gait manner of walking
gate opening in a wall or fence

generic general
genetic relating to the genes

gibe to tease or mock
jibe to agree
jive foolish talk

guarantee to promise to be responsible for
guaranty something given as a security

hail to greet
hale to compel to go; healthy

hearsay rumor
heresy dissent from a dominant theory

i.e. *see* E.G.

illegible *see* ELIGIBLE

illicit *see* ELICIT

illusion *see* ALLUSION

immanence *see* EMINENCE

immanent *see* EMANATE

immigrate *see* EMIGRATE

imminence *see* EMINENCE

imminent *see* EMANATE

imply hint, indicate
infer conclude, deduce

impracticable not feasible
impractical not practical

inapt not suitable
inept unfit or foolish

incite to urge on
insight discernment

incredible unbelievable
incredulous disbelieving, astonished

incurable not curable
incurrable capable of being incurred

inept *see* INAPT

inequity lack of equity
iniquity wickedness

infer *see* IMPLY

ingenious very clever
ingenuous innocent and candid

inherent intrinsic
inherit to receive from an ancestor

iniquity *see* INEQUITY

insight *see* INCITE

install to set up for use
instill to impart gradually

insure *see* ASSURE

interment burial
internment confinement or impounding

interstate involving more than one state
intestate leaving no valid will
intrastate existing within a state

irascible *see* ERASABLE

it's it is
its belonging to it

jibe *see* GIBE

jive *see* GIBE

lead to guide; heavy metal
led guided

lean to rely on for support
lien legal claim on property

lesser smaller
lessor grantor of a lease

levee embankment to prevent flooding
levy imposition or collection of a tax

liable obligated by law
libel to make libelous statements; false publication

lien *see* LEAN

material having relevance or importance; matter
matériel equipment and supplies

median middle value in a range
medium intermediate; means of communication

meet to come into contact with
mete to allot

meretricious falsely attractive
meritorious deserving reward or honor
meticulous extremely careful about details

militate to have effect
mitigate to make less severe

miner mine worker
minor one of less than legal age; not important or serious

moot having no practical significance

mute a person unable to speak; to tone down or muffle

naval relating to a navy

navel belly button

obtuse *see* ABSTRUSE

oral *see* AURAL

ordinance law, rule, or decree

ordnance military supplies

ordonnance compilation of laws

overt *see* ADVERT

parlay to bet again a stake and its winnings

parley discussion of disputed points

peer one of equal standing

pier bridge support

peremptory ending a right of action, debate or delay

preemptory pre-emptive

perpetrate to be guilty of

perpetuate to make perpetual

perquisite a right or privilege

prerequisite a necessary preliminary

persecute to harass injuriously

prosecute to proceed against at law

personal relating to a particular person

personnel body of employees

perspective view of things

prospective relating to the future

prospectus introductory description of an enterprise

perspicacious very discerning

perspicuous easily understood

pier *see* PEER

plain ordinary

plane airplane; surface

plaintiff complaining party in litigation

plaintive sorrowful

plat plan of a piece of land

plot small piece of land

pole long slender piece of wood or metal
poll sampling of opinion

pore to read attentively
pour to dispense from a container

practicable feasible
practical capable of being put to use

precede to go or come before
proceed to go to law

precedence priority
precedents previous examples to follow

preemptory *see* PEREMP-TORY

preposition part of speech
proposition proposal

prerequisite *see* PERQUISITE

prescribe to direct to use; to assert a prescriptive right
proscribe to forbid

preview advance view
purview part or scope of a statute

principal main body of an estate; chief person or matter
principle basic rule or assumption

proceed *see* PRECEDE

proposition *see* PREPOSI-TION

proscribe *see* PRESCRIBE

prosecute *see* PERSECUTE

prospective *see* PERSPEC-TIVE

prostate gland
prostrate prone; to reduce to helplessness

purview *see* PREVIEW

raise to lift, to increase
raze to destroy or tear down

reality the quality or state of being real
realty real property

rebound to spring back or recover
redound to have an effect

recession ceding back
recision cancellation
rescission act of rescinding or abrogating

respectfully with respect
respectively in order

resume to take up again
résumé summary

role part, function
roll turn

session *see* CESSION

shear to cut off
sheer very thin or transparent

sight *see* CITE

sinecure *see* CYNOSURE

site *see* CITE

stationary still
stationery writing material

statue piece of sculpture
stature natural height or achieved status
statute law enacted by a legislature

tack course of action
tact sense of propriety

tenant one who occupies a rental dwelling
tenet principle

therefor for that
therefore thus

tortuous lacking in straightforwardness
torturous very painful or distressing

track path or course
tract stretch of land; system of body organs

trustee one entrusted with something
trusty convict allowed special privileges

venal open to bribery
venial excusable

waive to give up voluntarily
wave to motion with the hands

waiver act of waiving a right
waver to be irresolute

who's who is
whose of whom

your belonging to you
you're you are

Appendix B

Grammar Glossary

This glossary provides definitions, and sometimes discussions, of grammatical and grammar-related terms, many of which appear in the text. Examples are enclosed in angle brackets. Cross-references to other glossary entries are shown in boldface.

abbreviation A shortened form of a written word or phrase used in place of the whole (such as *amt.* for *amount,* or *c/o* for *care of*).

   Abbreviations can be used wherever they are customary, but note that what is customary in technical writing will be different from what is customary in journalism or other fields. See also **acronym**.

absolute adjective An adjective that normally cannot be used comparatively <*ancillary* rights> <the *maximum* dose>.

   Many absolute adjectives can be modified by adverbs such as *almost* or *near* <an *almost fatal* dose> <at *near maximum* capacity>. However, many adjectives considered to be absolute are in fact often preceded by comparative adverbs <a *more perfect* union> <a *less complete* account>. In such cases, *more* means "more nearly" and *less* "less nearly."

absolute comparative The comparative form of an adjective used where no comparison is implied or stated, although in some cases comparison may be inferred by the reader or hearer <*higher* education> <a *better* kind of company> <gives you a *brighter* smile>

<an *older* woman>. See also **absolute adjective; comparison; double comparison; implicit comparative**.

acronym A word or abbreviation formed from the initial letter or letters of each of the major parts of a compound term, whether or not it is pronounceable as a word (such as *TQM* for *Total Quality Management,* or *UNPROFOR* for *United Nations Protection Force*); also called *initialism*.

active voice A verb form indicating that the subject of a sentence is performing the action <he *respects* the other scientists> <a bird *was singing*> <interest rates *rose*>; compare **passive voice**.

adjective A word that describes or modifies a noun <an *active* mind> <this is *serious*> <*full* and *careful* in its attention to detail>.

An adjective can follow a noun as a complement <the book made the bag *heavy*> and can sometimes modify larger units, like noun phrases <the *celebrated* "man in the street"> and noun clauses <it seemed *incomprehensible* that one senator could hold up the nomination>.

Adjectives can be described as *coordinate adjectives* when they share equal relationships to the nouns they modify <a *concise, coherent* essay> <a *soft, flickering, bluish* light>, and as *noncoordinate adjectives* when the first of two adjectives modifies the second adjective and the noun together <a *low monthly* fee> <the *first warm* day>.

An *indefinite adjective* designates unidentified or not immediately identifiable persons or things <*some* children> <*other* hotels>.

An *interrogative adjective* is used in asking questions <*whose* book is this?> <*which* color looks best?>.

A *possessive adjective* is the possessive form of a personal pronoun <*her* idea> <*its* second floor>.

A *relative adjective (which, that, who, whom, whose, where)* introduces an adjectival clause or a clause that functions as a noun <at the April conference, by *which* time the report should be finished> <not knowing *whose* lead she should follow>. See also **absolute adjective**; **attributive**; **demonstrative adjective**; **predicate adjective**.

adverb A word that modifies a verb, adjective, adverb, preposition, phrase, clause, or sentence.

   Traditionally adverbs indicate time, place, or manner <do it *now*> <*there* they remained> <she went *willingly*>. They can connect statements <a small bomb had been found; *nevertheless,* they were continuing their search> and can tell the reader what the writer thinks about what is being said in the sentence <*luckily* I got there on time>. They can modify verbs <ran *fast*>, adjectives <an *awfully* long speech>, participles <a *well*-acted play>, adverbs <doing *fairly* well>, particles <woke *right* up>, indefinite pronouns <*almost* everyone>, cardinal numbers <*over* 200 guests>, prepositional phrases <*just* out of reach>, and more. Sometimes they modify a preceding noun <the great city *beyond*>, and some adverbs of place and time can serve as the objects of prepositions <since *when*> <before *long*>.

   The notion that adverbs should not separate auxiliaries from their main verbs <you can *easily* see the river from here> <they should be *heartily* congratulated> is a false one, apparently based on fear of the split infinitive. See also **auxiliary verb**; **sentence adverb**; **split infinitive**.

adverbial genitive A form, or case, of some nouns used as adverbs of time, normally formed by adding *-s* <he worked *nights*> <the store is open *Sundays*>.

agreement A grammatical relationship that involves the correspondence in number either between the subject and verb of a sentence or between a pronoun and its antecedent; also called *concord*.

Subject-verb agreement for compound subjects joined by <u>and</u>: When a subject is composed of two or more singular nouns joined by *and,* the plural verb is usually used <*the sentimentality and lack of originality* which mark his writing> <*the bitterness and heartache* that fill the world>. Occasionally when the nouns form a single conceptual unit, the singular verb can be used <*the report's depth and scope demonstrates*> <*her patience and calm was* remarkable>. See also **notional agreement**.

Compound subjects joined by <u>or</u> (or <u>nor</u>): When singular nouns are joined by *or,* the singular verb is usually used <*the average man or woman was* not interested>; when plural nouns are so joined, the plural verb is used <*wolves or coyotes have* depleted his stock>. When the negative *neither . . . nor* is used with singular nouns, it usually takes a singular verb <*neither she nor anyone else is* fond of the idea>; when used with plural nouns, it takes a plural verb <*neither the proponents nor their adversaries are* willing to accept>. But when *neither . . . nor* is used with nouns of differing number, the noun closest to the verb usually determines its number <*neither he nor his colleagues were* present> <*neither the teachers nor the principal was* interested>. Similar rules apply to *either . . . or.*

Compound subjects joined by words or phrases like <u>with</u> or <u>along with</u>, or by punctuation: When a singular noun is joined to another by a word or phrase like *with, rather than,* or *as well as,* a singular verb is generally used <*that story, along with nine others, was* published> <*the battleship together with the destroyer was* positioned three miles offshore>. Parenthetical insertions set off by commas, dashes, or parentheses should not affect agreement <*this book, as well as various others, has* achieved notoriety> <*their management—and the company's balance sheets—has* suffered>.

Subject formed by a collective noun phrase: In constructions like "a bunch of the boys were whooping it up" or "a fraction of the deposits are insured," which make use of a collective noun phrase (*a bunch of the boys, a fraction of the deposits*), the verb is usually plural, since the sense of the phrase is normally plural. See also **collective noun**.

Subject expressing money, time, etc.: When an amount of money, a period of time, or some other plural noun phrase of quantity or measure forms the subject, a singular verb is used <*ten dollars is* all I have left> <*two miles is* as far as they can walk> <*two thirds of the area is* under water>.

Subject formed by <u>one in (out of)</u> . . . . : Phrases such as "one in five" or "two out of three" may take either a singular or a plural verb <*one in four union members was* undecided> <*one out of ten soldiers were* unable to recognize the enemy>, though grammarians tend to favor the singular.

Pronoun-antecedent agreement for nouns joined by <u>and</u>, <u>or</u>: When antecedents are singular nouns joined by *and,* a plural pronoun is used <*the computer and the printer* were moved because *they* were in the way>. But singular nouns joined by *or* can use either a singular or a plural pronoun, whichever sounds best <either *Fred or Marianne* will give *their* presentation after lunch> <*each employee or supervisor* should give what *he or she* can afford>.

Agreement for indefinite pronouns: The indefinite pronouns *anybody, anyone, each, either, everybody, everyone, neither, nobody, none, no one, somebody,* and *someone,* though some of them are conceptually plural, are used with singular verbs <*everyone* in the company *was* pleased> <*nobody is* responsible>, but are commonly referred to by *they, their, them,* or *themselves* <*nobody* could get the crowd's attention when *they* spoke> <*everybody* there admits *they* saw it>. Writing handbooks prescribe *he, she,* or *he or she,* or some other construction instead of the plural pronouns, but use of the plural *they, their,* or *them* has long been established and is standard.

antecedent A word, phrase, or clause to which a subsequent pronoun refers <*Judy* wrote to say *she* is coming> <they saw *Bob* and called to *him*> <I hear *that he is ill and it* worries me>.

appositive A word, phrase, or clause that is equivalent to an adjacent noun <a biography of *the poet Robert Burns*> <sales of *her famous novel, Gone with the Wind,* reached one million copies in six months > <*we grammarians* are never wrong>.

Restrictive and nonrestrictive appositives play different roles in a sentence and are traditionally distinguished by their punctuation. A nonrestrictive appositive <*his wife, Helen,* attended the ceremony> is generally set off with commas, while a restrictive appositive <he sent *his daughter Cicely* to college> uses no commas and indicates that one out of a group is being identified (in this case, one daughter from among two or more). Exceptions occur where no ambiguity would result <his wife Helen>. See also **nonrestrictive clause**; **restrictive clause**.

article One of three words (*a, an, the*) used with a noun to indicate definiteness <*the* blue car> or indefiniteness <*a* simple task> <*an* interesting explanation>.

attributive A modifier that immediately precedes the word it modifies <*black* tie, *U.S.* government, *kitchen* sink, *lobster* salad>.

Nouns have functioned like adjectives in this position for many centuries. In more recent years, some critics have objected to the proliferation of nouns used to modify other nouns: e.g., *language deterioration, health aspects, image enhancement.* While long or otherwise unexpected strings of this sort can occasionally be disorienting to the uninitiated (e.g., *management team strategy planning session*), the practice is flourishing and usually serves to compress information that the intended audience need not always have spelled out for it. Be sure, however, that the context and audience will allow for such compression.

A fairly recent trend toward using plural attributives has been attacked by some critics. There always had been a few plural attributives—*scissors grinder, physics laboratory, Civil Liberties Union, mathematics book*—but is it proper to use the more recent *weapons system, communications technology, operations program, systems analyst, earth-resources satellite, singles bar, enemies list*? The answer is that such plural attributives are standard. The plural form is chosen to stress plurality—more than one weapon, operation, enemy, etc.—or to otherwise distinguish its meaning from whatever the singular attributive might connote.

auxiliary verb A verb that accompanies another verb and typically expresses person, number, mood, or tense (such as *be, have, can, do*) <they *can* see the movie tomorrow> <she *has* left already>. See also **verb**.

cardinal number A number of the kind used in simple counting <*one, 1, thirty-five, 35*>; compare **ordinal number**.

case In English, a form of a noun or pronoun indicating its grammatical relation to other words in a sentence. See **nominative**; **objective**; **possessive**. See also **genitive**.

clause A group of words having its own subject and predicate but forming only part of a compound or complex sentence. A *main* or *independent clause* could stand alone as a sentence <*we will leave* as soon as the taxi arrives>; a *subordinate* or *dependent clause* requires a main clause <we will leave *as soon as the taxi arrives*>.

There are three basic types of clauses—all subordinate clauses—that have part-of-speech functions. An *adjective clause* modifies a noun or pronoun <the clown, *who was also a horse trainer*> <I can't see the reason *why you're upset*>. An *adverb clause* modifies a verb, adjective, or another adverb <*when it rains,* it pours> <I'm certain *that he is guilty*> <we accomplished less *than we did before*>. A *noun clause* fills a noun slot in a sentence and thus can be a subject, object, or complement <*whoever is qualified* should apply> <I don't know *what his problem is*> <the trouble is *that she has no alternative*>. See also **sentence**; **subordinate clause**.

collective noun   A singular noun that stands for a number of persons or things considered as a group (such as *team, government, horde*).

  Subject-verb agreement. Collective nouns have been used with both singular and plural verbs since Middle English. The principle involved is one of notional agreement. When the group is considered as a unit, the singular verb is used <the *government is* prepared for a showdown> <his *family is* from New England> <the *team has won* all of its home games>. When the group is thought of as a collection of individuals, the plural verb is sometimes used <her *family are* all staunch conservatives>. Singular verbs are more common in American English and plural verbs more common in British English, though usage remains divided in each case. See also **agreement**; **notional agreement**.

  A collective noun followed by *of* and a plural noun follows the same rule as collective nouns in general. When the notion is that of plurality, the plural verb is normally used <an *assemblage of rocks were* laid out on the table> <a *group of jazz improvisers were* heard through the window>. When the idea of oneness or wholeness is stressed, the verb is generally singular <this *cluster of stars is* the largest yet identified>.

  Pronoun agreement: The usual rule is that writers should take care to match their pronouns and verbs, singular with singular <the committee *is* hopeful that *it* will succeed>, plural with plural <the faculty *are* willing to drop *their* suit>. But in fact writers sometimes use a plural pronoun after a singular verb <the

audience *was* on *their* way out>. (The reverse combination—plural verb with singular pronoun—is very rare.)

Organizations as collective nouns: The names of companies and other organizations are treated as either singular <*Harvard* may consider *itself* very fortunate> or, less commonly, plural <the *D.A.R. are* going to do another pageant>. Organizations also sometimes appear with a singular verb but a plural pronoun in reference <*M-G-M hopes* to sell *their* latest releases> <*Chrysler builds their* convertible in Kentucky>. This usage is standard, though informal.

colloquial An adjective describing usage that is characteristic of familiar and informal conversation.

While not intended to carry pejorative overtones, the label *colloquial* often implies that the usage is nonstandard. See also **dialect**; **nonstandard**; **standard English**.

comma fault (comma splice, comma error) The use of a comma instead of a semicolon to link two independent clauses (as in "I won't talk about myself, it's not a healthy topic"). Modern style calls for the semicolon, but comma splices are fairly common in casual and unedited prose.

comparison Modification of an adjective or adverb to show different levels of quality, quantity, or relation. The *comparative* form shows relation between two items, usually by adding *-er* or *more* or *less* to the adjective or adverb <he's short*er* than I am> <her second book sold *more* quickly>. The *superlative* form expresses an extreme among two or more items, usually by adding *-est* or *most* or *least* to the adjective or adverb <the cheetah is the fast*est* mammal> <that's the *least* compelling reason> <the *most* vexingly intractable issue>. See also **absolute adjective**; **absolute comparative**; **double comparison**; **implicit comparative**.

complement An added word or expression by which a predicate is made complete <they elected him *president*> <she thought it *beautiful*> <the critics called her *the best act of her kind since Carmen Miranda*>.

compound A combination of words or word elements that work together in various ways (*farmhouse; cost-effective; ex-husband; shoeless; figure out; in view of* that; *real estate* agent; *greenish white* powder; *carefully tended* garden; *great white shark*).

Compounds are written in one of three ways: solid <*workplace*>, hyphenated <*screenwriter director*>, or open <*health care*>. Because of the variety of standard practice, the choice among these styles for a given compound represents one of the most common and bothersome of all style issues. A current desk dictionary will list many compounds, but those whose meanings are self-explanatory from the meanings of their component words will usually not appear. Most writers try to pattern any temporary compounds after similar permanent compounds such as are entered in dictionaries.

compound subject Two or more nouns or pronouns usually joined by *and* that function as the subject of a clause or sentence <*doctors and lawyers* reported the highest incomes for that period> <*Peter, Karen, and I* left together>. See also **agreement; collective noun**.

concord See **agreement**.

conjunction A word or phrase that joins together words, phrases, clauses, or sentences.

Coordinating conjunctions (such as *and, because, but, or, nor, since, so*) join elements of equal weight, to show similarity <they came early *and* stayed late>, to exclude or contrast <he is a brilliant *but* arrogant man>, to offer alternatives <she can wait here *or* return later>, to propose reasons or grounds <the timetable is useless, *because* it is out-of-date>, or to specify a result <his diction is excellent, *so* every word is clear>.

Correlative conjunctions (such as *either . . . or, neither . . . nor*) are used in pairs and link alternatives or equal elements <*either* you go *or* you stay> <the proposal benefits *neither* residents *nor* visitors> <she showed *not only* perceptive understanding *but also* mature judgment>.

Subordinating conjunctions (such as *unless, whether*) join subordinate clauses to main clauses and are used to express cause <*because* she learns quickly, she is an eager student>, condition <don't call *unless* you're coming>, manner <it looks *as though* it's clearing>, purpose <he gets up early *so that* he can exercise before work>, time <she kept a diary *when* she was a teenager>, place <I don't know *where* he went>, or possibility <they were undecided *whether* to go or stay>.

conjunctive adverb A transitional adverb (such as *also, however, therefore*) that expresses the relationship between two independent clauses, sentences, or paragraphs.

Conjunctive adverbs are used to express addition <he enjoyed the movie; *however,* he had to leave before the end>, emphasis <he is brilliant; *indeed,* he is a genius>, contrast <that was unfortunate; *nevertheless,* they should have known the danger>, elaboration <on one point only did everyone agree: *namely,* too much money had been spent already>, conclusion <the case could take years to work its way through the courts; *as a result,* many plaintiffs will accept settlements>, or priority <*first* cream the shortening and sugar, *then* add the eggs and beat well>.

contact clause A dependent clause attached to its antecedent without a relative pronoun such as *that, which,* or *who* <the key [that] *you lost*> <he is not the person [who] *we thought he was*>.

The predicate noun clause not introduced by the conjunction *that* <we believe [that] *the alliance is strong*> is as long and as well established in English as the contact clause. It is probably more common in casual and general prose than in formal prose. It is also more common after some verbs (such as *believe, hope, say, think*) than others (such as *assert, calculate, hold, intend*).

contraction A shortened form of a word or words in which an apostrophe usually replaces the omitted letter or letters (such as *dep't, don't, could've, o'clock, we'll*).

Contractions involving verbs used to be avoided more than they are today. In fact, many contemporary writing handbooks recommend using contractions to help you avoid sounding stilted.

count noun A noun that identifies things that can be counted <two *tickets*> <a *motive*> <many *people*>; compare **mass noun**.

dangling modifier A modifying phrase that lacks a normally expected grammatical relation to the rest of the sentence (as in "*Caught in the act,* his excuses were unconvincing").

The common construction called the *participial phrase* usually begins with a participle; in "*Chancing to meet them there,* I invited them to sit with us," the subject, "I," is left implicit in the preceding phrase, which modifies it. But a writer may inadvertently let a participial phrase modify a subject or some other noun in the sentence it was not intended to modify; the result is what grammarians call a *dangling participle*. Thus in "*Hoping to find him alone,* the presence of a stranger was irksome," it is the "presence" itself that may seem to be hoping.

Dangling participles can be found in the writing of many famous writers, and they are usually hardly noticeable except to someone looking for them. The important thing to avoid is creating an unintended humorous effect (as in "*Opening up the cupboard,* a cockroach ran for the corner").

dangling participle See **dangling modifier**.

demonstrative adjective One of four adjectives—*this, that, these,* and *those*—that points to what it modifies in order to distinguish it from others. The number (singular or plural) of the adjective should agree with the noun it modifies <*this* type of person> <*that* shelf of books> <*these* sorts of jobs> <*those* varieties of apples>.

demonstrative pronoun One of the words *this, that, these,* and *those* classified as pronouns when they function as nouns <*this* is my desk; *that* is yours> <*these* are the best popovers in town> <*those* are strong words>.

dialect A variety of language distinguished by features of vocabulary, grammar, and pronunciation that is confined to a region or group. See also **nonstandard**; **standard English**.

direct object A word, phrase, or clause denoting the goal or result of the action of the verb <he closed the *valve*> <they'll do *whatever it takes*> <"*Do it now,*" he said>; compare **indirect object**.

direct question A question quoted exactly as spoken, written, or imagined <the only question is, *Will it work?*>; compare **indirect question**.

direct quotation Text quoted exactly as spoken or written <I heard her say, "*I'll be there at two o'clock*">; compare **indirect quotation**.

divided usage Widespread use of two or more forms for a single entity (such as *dived* and *dove* for the past tense of *dive*).

double comparison Use of the forms *more, most, less,* or *least* with an adjective already inflected for the comparative or superlative degree (such as *more wider, most widest*).

This construction results from using *more* and *most* as intensifiers <a *most* enjoyable meal>. In modern usage, double comparison has all but vanished from standard writing. See also **comparison; intensifier**.

Double comparison can also occur by inflection. Though forms such as *firstest, mostest,* and *bestest* are most typical of the speech of young children, the form *worser* (which has a long literary background) still persists in adult speech. You will want to avoid it in writing.

double genitive A construction in which possession is marked both by the preposition *of* and a noun or pronoun in the possessive case.

In expressions like "that song of Ella Fitzgerald's" or "a good friend of ours," the possessive relationship is indicated by both *of* and the genitive inflection (*Fitzgerald's, ours*), even though only one or the other would seem to be strictly necessary. However, this construction, also known as the *double possessive,* is an idiomatic one of long standing and is standard in all kinds of writing. See also **genitive**.

double modal The use of two modal auxiliaries in succession, resulting in such expressions as *might can, might could,* and *might should*.

Today double modals tend to be found in Southern dialect and are unfamiliar to speakers from other parts of the country.

double negative A clause or sentence containing two negatives and having a negative meaning.

In modern usage, the double negative (as in "they did*n't* have *no* children" or "it would*n't* do *no* good") is widely perceived as a rustic or uneducated form, and is generally avoided in both writing and speech, other than the most informal.

A standard form of double negative is the rhetorical device known as *litotes*, which produces a weak affirmative meaning <a *not un*reasonable request>. It is used for understatement, but should not be overused.

double passive A construction that uses two verb forms in the passive voice, one being an infinitive (as in "the work of redesigning the office space *was requested to be done* by outside contractors").

The double passive is awkward and potentially ambiguous (did outside contractors ask for the work to be done, or were they asked to do the work?) and should be avoided.

double possessive See **double genitive**.

double superlative See **double comparison**.

false titles Appositive preceding a person's name with no preceding article or following comma, which thus resembles a title, though it is rarely capitalized <organized by *consumer advocate* Ralph Nader> <works of *1960s underground cartoonist* Robert Crumb>. The use of such titles is sometimes criticized, but it is standard in journalism.

faulty parallelism See **parallelism**.

flat adverb An adverb that has the same form as its related adjective, such as *sure* <you *sure* fooled me>, *bright* <the moon is shining *bright*>, and *flat* <she turned me down *flat*>.

Although such forms were once common, later grammarians saw them as faulty because they lacked the *-ly* ending. Today flat adverbs are few in number and some are widely regarded as incorrect.

formal agreement See **notional agreement**.

gender In English, a characteristic of certain nouns and pronouns that indicates sex (masculine, feminine, neuter) <*he, him, his, she, her, it, its; actor, actress; brother, sister; emperor, empress; heir, heiress; fiancé, fiancée; testator, testatrix*>.

genitive A form, or case, of a noun or pronoun that typically shows possession or source <the girl*'s* sweater> <nobody*'s* fool> <an uncle *of mine*> <some idea *of theirs*> <the company*'s* failure> <a year*'s* salary> <the nation*'s* capital> <a stone*'s* throw>.

The form is usually produced by adding -*'s* or a phrase beginning with *of*. While the possessive is the genitive's most common function, it has certain other functions as well; these include the *subjective* <Frost*'s* poetry>, *objective* <her son*'s* graduation>, *descriptive* <women*'s* colleges>, and *appositive* <the state *of Massachusetts*> <the office *of president*> genitives. See also **double genitive; possessive**.

gerund A verb form having the characteristics of both verb and noun and ending in -*ing* (also called a *verbal noun*) <the ice made *skiing* impossible>.

A gerund can be preceded by a possessive noun or pronoun <her husband*'s snoring*> <their *filling* the position>. See also **possessive; possessive with gerund**.

hypercorrection The use of a nonstandard linguistic form or construction on the basis of a false analogy to a standard form or construction (as in "*whom* should I say is calling?"; "this is between you and *I*"; "no one but *he* would notice"; "open *widely*").

idiom A common expression that is peculiar to itself grammatically <*it wasn't me*> or that cannot be understood from the meanings of its separate words <I told them to *step on it*> <the newspaper *had a field day*>.

imperative The form, or mood, of a verb that expresses a command or makes a request <*come* here> <please *don't*>; compare **indicative**; **subjunctive**.

implicit comparative One of a small group of adjectives (primarily *major, minor, inferior, superior*) whose meaning resembles a true comparative but which cannot be used with comparative forms (such as *more, most; less, least*) <a *major* contributor> <an *inferior* wine>.

However, two other implicit comparatives *junior* and *senior* can be used with comparative forms <a *more senior* diplomat> <the *least junior* of the new partners>. See also **comparison**.

indefinite pronoun A pronoun that designates an unidentified person or thing <*somebody* ate my dessert> <she saw *no one* she knew>.

Many indefinite pronouns should agree in number with their verbs. See **agreement**. See also **notional agreement; pronoun**.

indicative The form, or mood, of a verb that states a fact or asks a question <the train *stopped*> <they*'ll be* along> <everyone *is* ravenous> <*has* the rain *begun?*> <who *knows?*>; compare **imperative**; **subjunctive**.

indirect object A grammatical object representing the secondary goal of the action of its verb <she gave *the dog* a bone>; compare **direct object**.

indirect question A statement of the substance of a question without using the speaker's exact words or word order <the officer asked *what the trouble was*> <they wondered *whether it would work*>; compare **direct question**.

indirect quotation A statement of the substance of a quotation without using the speaker's exact words <I heard her say *she'd be there at two o'clock*>; compare **direct quotation**.

infinitive A verb form having the characteristics of both verb and noun and usually used with *to* <we had *to stop*> <*to err* is human> <no one saw him *leave*>. See also **split infinitive**.

infinitive phrase A phrase that includes an infinitive and its modifiers and complements <we expect them *to arrive by five o'clock*> <he shouted *to be heard above the din*> <*to have earned a Ph.D. in four years* was impressive>.

inflection The change in form that words undergo to mark case, gender, number, tense, person, mood, voice, or comparison <*he, his, him*> <*waiter, waitress*> <*rat, rats*> <blame, *blames, blamed, blaming*> <who, *whom*> <she *is* careful, if she *were* careful, *be* careful> <like, *likes, is liked*> <wild, *wilder, wildest*>. See also **case**; **comparison**; **gender**; **mood**; **number**; **person**; **tense**; **voice**.

initialism See **acronym**.

intensifier A linguistic element used to give emphasis or additional strength to another word or statement <a *very* hot day> <it's a *complete* lie> <what *on earth* is he doing?> <she *herself* did it>. See also **double comparison**.

interjection An exclamatory or interrupting word or phrase <*ouch!*> <*oh no,* not that again>.

interrogative pronoun One of the pronouns *what, which, who, whom,* and *whose,* as well as combinations of these words with the suffix *-ever,* used to introduce direct and indirect questions <*who* is she?> <he asked me *who* she was> <*which* did they choose?> <I wondered *which* they chose>.

    Who is frequently substituted for *whom* to introduce a question even when it is the object of a preposition <*who* are you going to listen to?> <*who* do you work for?>.

intransitive verb A verb not having a direct object <he *ran* away> <our cat *purrs* when I stroke her>; compare **transitive verb**.

linking verb A verb that links a subject with its predicate (such as *is, feel, look, become, seem*) <she *is* the new manager> <the future *looked* prosperous> <he *has become* disenchanted>.

  Linking verbs such as the so-called "sense" verbs *feel, look, taste,* and *smell* often cause confusion, since writers sometimes mistakenly follow these words with adverbs <this scent *smells nicely*> instead of adjectives <this scent *smells nice*>.

main clause See **clause**.

mass noun A noun that denotes a thing or concept without subdivisions <some *money*> <great *courage*> <the study of *politics*>; compare **count noun**.

modifier A word or phrase that qualifies, limits, or restricts the meaning of another word or phrase. See **adjective**; **adverb**.

mood The form of a verb that shows whether the action or state it denotes is conceived as a fact or otherwise (e.g., a command, possibility, or wish). See **indicative**; **imperative**; **subjunctive**.

nominal A word or group of words that functions as a noun, which may be an adjective <the *good* die young>, a gerund <*seeing* is *believing*>, or an infinitive <*to see* is *to believe*>.

nominative A form, or case, of a noun or pronoun indicating its use as the subject of a verb <three *dogs* trotted by the open door> <later *we* ate dinner>; compare **objective**; **possessive**.

nonrestrictive clause A subordinate or dependent clause, set off by commas, that is not essential to the definiteness of the word it modifies and could be omitted without changing the meaning of the main clause (also called *nonessential clause*) <the author, *who turned out to be charming,* autographed my book>; compare **restrictive clause**. See also **appositive**.

nonstandard Not conforming to the usage generally characteristic of educated native speakers of a language; compare **standard English**. See also **dialect**.

notional agreement Agreement between a subject and a verb or between a pronoun and its antecedent that is determined by meaning rather than form; also called *notional concord*.

Notional agreement contrasts with *formal* or *grammatical agreement* (or *concord*), in which overt grammatical markers determine singular or plural agreement. Formally plural nouns such as *news, means,* and *politics* have long taken singular verbs; so when a plural noun considered a single entity takes a singular verb, notional agreement is at work and no one objects <the *United States is sending* its ambassador>. When a singular noun is used as a collective noun and takes a plural verb or a plural pronoun, we also have notional agreement <the *committee are* meeting on Tuesday> <the *group* wants to publicize *their* views>. Indefinite pronouns are heavily influenced by notional agreement and tend to take singular verbs but plural pronouns <*everyone is* required to show *their* identification>. See also **agreement; collective noun**.

notional concord See **notional agreement**.

noun A member of a class of words that can serve as the subject of a verb, can be singular or plural, can be replaced by a pronoun, and can refer to an entity, quality, state, action, or concept <*boy, Churchill, America, river, commotion, poetry, anguish, constitutionalism*>.

Nouns are used as subjects <the *artist* painted still lifes>, direct objects <critics praised the *artist*>, objects of prepositions <a painting signed by the *artist*>, indirect objects <the council gave the *artist* an award>, retained objects <an artist was given the

award>, predicate nouns <Petra Smith is this year's *award winner*>, objective complements <they announced Petra Smith as this year's *award winner*>, and appositives <Petra Smith, this year's *award winner*>. See also **collective noun; count noun; mass noun; nominal; proper noun**.

noun phrase A phrase formed by a noun and its modifiers <*portly pensioners* sat sunning themselves> <they proclaimed *all the best features of the new financial offering*>.

number A characteristic of a noun, pronoun, or verb that signifies whether it is singular or plural. See **singular; plural**.

object A noun, noun phrase or clause, or pronoun that directly or indirectly receives the action of a verb or follows a preposition <she rocked *the baby*> <he saw *where they were going*> <I gave *him the news*> <over *the rainbow*> <after *a series of depressing roadhouse gigs*>. See **direct object; indirect object**.

objective A form, or case, of a pronoun indicating its use as the object of a verb or preposition <we spoke to *them* yesterday> <he's a man *whom* everyone should know>; compare **nominative; possessive**.

ordinal number A number designating the place occupied by an item in an ordered sequence <*first, 1st, second, 2nd*>; compare **cardinal number**.

parallelism Repeated syntactical similarities introduced in sentence construction, such as adjacent phrases and clauses that are equivalent, similar, or opposed in meaning and of identical construction <ecological problems of concern *to scientists, to businesspeople, and to all citizens*> <he was respected not only *for his intelligence* but also *for his integrity*> <*to err is human, to forgive, divine*>.

Parallelism is mainly used for rhetorical and clarifying effects, and its absence can sometimes create problems for the reader. *Faulty parallelism* is the name given to the use of different constructions within a sentence where you would ordinarily expect to find the same or similar constructions. Very often such faulty parallelism involves the conjunctions *and* and *or* or such other coordinators as *either* and *neither*. Consider the sentence "To allow kids to roam the streets at night and failing to give them constructive alternatives have been harmful." An infinitive phrase (*To allow kids to roam* . . .) and a participial phrase (*failing to give them* . . .) are treated as parallel when they are not. The meaning would be taken in more readily if both phrases were similar; replacing the infinitive with a participle achieves this parallelism (*Allowing kids to roam* . . . and *failing to give them* . . .). When such errors are obvious, they can be puzzling. Often, however, the problem is subtle and hardly noticeable, as in the sentence "Either I must send a fax or make a phone call." Here *or* is expected to precede the same parallel term as *either;* by repositioning *either,* you solve the problem <I must *either* send a fax *or* make a phone call>. Such examples of faulty parallelism are fairly common, but your writing will be more elegant if you avoid them.

parenthetical element An explanatory or modifying word, phrase, or sentence inserted in a passage, set off by parentheses, commas, or dashes <a ruling by the FCC (*Federal Communications Commission*)> <all of us, *to tell the truth,* were amazed> <the examiner chose—*goodness knows why*—to ignore it>.

participial phrase A participle with its complements and modifiers, functioning as an adjective <*hearing the bell ring,* he went to the door>.

participle A verb form having the characteristics of both verb <the noise has *stopped*> and adjective <a *bro-*

ken lawn mower>. The *present participle* ends in *-ing* <*fascinating*>; the *past participle* usually ends in *-ed* <*seasoned*>; the *perfect participle* combines *having* with the past participle <*having escaped*>. See also **auxiliary verb**; **dangling modifier**; **possessive**.

particle A short word (such as *by, to, in, up*) that expresses some general aspect of meaning or some connective or limiting relation <pay *up*> <heave *to*>.

parts of speech The classes into which words are grouped according to their function in a sentence. See **adjective**; **adverb**; **conjunction**; **interjection**; **noun**; **preposition**; **pronoun**; **verb**.

passive voice A verb form indicating that the subject of a sentence is being acted upon.

Though often considered a weaker form of expression than the active voice, the passive nevertheless has important uses—for example, when the receiver of the action is more important than the doer <*he is respected* by other scholars>, when the doer is unknown <*the lock had been picked* expertly> or is understood <*Jones was elected* on the third ballot>, or when discretion or tact require that the doer remain anonymous <mistakes *were made*>; compare **active voice**.

person A characteristic of a verb or pronoun that indicates whether a person is speaking (*first person*) <*I am, we are*>, is spoken to (*second person*) <*you are*>, or is spoken about (*third person*) <*he, she, it is; they are*>. See also **number**.

personal pronoun A pronoun that refers to beings and objects and reflects person, number, and often gender.

A personal pronoun's function within a sentence determines its case. The *nominative case* (*I, we, you, he, she, it, they*) is used for pronouns that act as subjects of sentences or as predicate nouns <*he* and *I* will attend> <our new candidate will be *you*>.

The *possessive* case (*my, mine, our, ours, your, yours, his, her, hers, its, their, theirs*) is used for pronouns that express possession or a similar relationship <*our* own offices> <*its* beak>.

The *objective* case (*me, us, you, him, her, it, them*) is used for pronouns that are direct objects, indirect objects, retained objects, or objects of prepositions <he told *me* about the new contract> <she gave *him* the manuscripts> <he was given *them* yesterday> <this is between *you* and *her*>. See also **indefinite pronoun**; **pronoun**.

phrase A group of two or more words that does not contain both a subject and a verb and that functions as a noun, adjective, adverb, preposition, conjunction, or verb <*the old sinner*> <*stretching for miles*> <*without a limp*> <*in lieu of*> <*as far as*> <*break off*>.

There are seven basic types of phrases. An *absolute phrase* consists of a noun followed by a modifier (such as a participial phrase) and acts independently within a sentence without modifying a particular element of the sentence <he stalked out, *his eyes staring straight ahead*>.

A *gerund phrase* includes a gerund and its modifiers, and it functions as a noun <*eating two doughnuts* is Mike's idea of breakfast>.

An *infinitive phrase* includes an infinitive and may function as a noun, adjective, or adverb <*to do that* would be stupid> <this was an occasion *to remember*> <they struggled *to get free*>.

A *participial phrase* includes a participle and functions as an adjective <*hearing the bell ring,* he went to the door>.

A *verb phrase* consists of a verb and any other terms that either modify it or complete its meaning <he *comes once a month*> <she *will have arrived too late*>. See also **noun phrase**; **participial phrase**.

plural A word form used to denote more than one <the *Browns*> <the *children*> <these *kinds*> <seven *deer*> <they *are* rich> <*we* do care>.

possessive A form, or case, of a noun or pronoun typically indicating ownership <the *president's* message> <*their* opinions> <*its* meter>; compare **nominative**; **objective**. See also **double genitive**; **genitive**; **possessive with gerund**.

possessive with gerund Use of a possessive form before a gerund.

In "the reason for everyone['s] wanting to join," either the possessive or the common form of *everyone* can be used. Writing handbooks recommend always using the possessive form, but the possessive is mandatory only when the *-ing* word is clearly a noun <*my being* here must embarrass you>. The possessive is quite common with proper nouns <the problem of *John's forgetting* the keys> but rare with plurals <learned of the *bills* [*bills'*] *being* paid>. In most other instances, either the possessive or common form can be used.

predicate The part of a sentence or clause that expresses what is said of the subject <Hargrove *threw a spitball*> <the teachers from the surrounding towns *are invited to the dinner*> <Jennifer *picked up her books and left to catch the bus*>.

predicate adjective An adjective that follows a linking verb (such as *be, become, feel, taste, smell, seem*) and modifies the subject <she is *happy* with the outcome> <the milk tastes *sour*> <he seemed *puzzled* by the answer>.

prefix An affix attached to the beginning of a word to change its meaning <*a*historical> <*pre*sorted> <*anti*-imperialist> <*post*hypnotic> <*over*extended>; compare **suffix**.

preposition A word or phrase that combines with a noun, pronoun, adverb, or prepositional phrase for use as a modifier or a predication <a book *on* the table> <you're *in* big trouble> <*outside* himself> <*because of* that> <came *from* behind> <peeking *from* behind the fence>.

Despite a widespread belief that a sentence cannot end with a preposition, there is no such grammatical rule. In fact, many sentences require the preposition at the end <what can she be thinking *of*?> <he got the answer he was looking *for*> <there are inconveniences that we must put up *with*> <they haven't been heard *from* yet> and many others are perfectly idiomatic in placing it there <you must know which shelf everything is *on*>.

prepositional phrase A group of words consisting of a preposition and its complement <*out of debt* is where we'd like to be!> <here is the desk *with the extra file drawer*> <he drove on *in a cold fury*>.

pronoun Any of a small set of words that are used as substitutes for nouns, phrases, or clauses and refer to someone or something named or understood in the context.

Pronouns can be divided into seven major categories, each with its own function. See **demonstrative pronoun**; **indefinite pronoun**; **interrogative pronoun**; **personal pronoun**; **reciprocal pronoun**; **reflexive pronoun**; **relative pronoun**. See also **agreement**.

proper adjective An adjective that is derived from a proper noun and is usually capitalized <*Roman* sculpture> <*Jeffersonian* democracy> <*Middle Eastern* situation> <*french* fries>.

proper noun A noun that names a particular being or thing and is usually capitalized <*Susan, Haydn, New York, December, General Motors, Mormon, Library of Congress, Middle Ages, Spanish Civil War, Reaganomics*>.

reciprocal pronoun One of the pronouns *each other* and *one another* used in the object position to indicate a mutual action or cross-relationship <chased *each other* around the yard> <fighting with *one another*>.

Reciprocal pronouns may also be used in the possessive <they depend on *each other's* ideas> <borrowed *one another's* sweaters>.

redundancy Repetition of information in a message.

Redundancy is an implicit part of the English language; it reinforces the message. In "Two birds were sitting on a branch," the idea of plurality is expressed three times: by the modifier *two,* by the *-s* on *bird,* and by the plural verb *were.* Many words can be accompanied by small words that give them extra emphasis <*final result*> <*past history*> <*climb up*> <*refer back*>. These are often attacked as needlessly wordy, but in most instances they are harmless, and sometimes they actually promote communication. The use and employment of many more words, phrases, and expressions than are strictly needed, necessary, wanted, or required should be avoided.

reflexive pronoun A pronoun that refers to the subject of the sentence, clause, or verbal phrase in which it stands, and is formed by compounding the personal pronouns *him, her, it, my, our, them,* and *your* with *-self* or *-selves* <she dressed *herself*> <the cook told us to help *ourselves* to seconds> <I *myself* am not concerned>.

relative pronoun One of the pronouns (*that, which, who, whom,* and *whose*) that introduces a subordinate clause which qualifies an antecedent <a man *whom* we can trust> <her book, *which* sold well> <the light *that* failed>.

The relative pronoun *who* typically refers to persons and some animals <a man *who* sought success> <a person *whom* we can trust> <Seattle Slew, *who* won horse racing's Triple Crown>; *which* refers to things and animals <a book *which* sold well> <a dog *which* barked loudly>; and *that* refers to persons, animals, and things <a man *that* sought success> <a dog *that* barked loudly> <a book *that* sold well>.

Whom is commonly used as the object of a preposition in a clause that it introduces <she is someone *for whom* I would gladly work>. However, *who* is commonly used to introduce a question even when it is the object of a preposition <*who* are you going to listen to?> <*who* do you work for?>.

restrictive clause A subordinate clause not set off by commas that is essential to the definiteness of the word it modifies and cannot be omitted without changing the meaning of the main clause (also called *essential clause*) <textbooks *that are not current* should be returned>. See also **appositive**; **nonrestrictive clause**.

sentence A group of words usually containing a subject and a verb, and in writing ending with a period, question mark, or exclamation point. A *simple sentence* consists of one main or independent clause <*she read the announcement in yesterday's paper*>. A *compound sentence* consists of two or more main clauses <*he left at nine o'clock, and they planned to meet at noon*>. A *complex sentence* consists of a main clause and one or more subordinate clauses <*it began to snow before they reached the summit*>. A *compound-complex sentence* consists of two or more main clauses and one or more subordinate clauses <*Susan left for Masters Hall after the presentation; there she joined the new-product workshop, which was already in progress*>. See also **clause**; **subordinate clause**.

A *declarative sentence* makes a statement <*the cow jumped over the moon*>. An *exclamatory sentence* expresses strong feeling <*that's ridiculous!*>. An *interrogative sentence* asks a question <*who said that?*>. An *imperative sentence* expresses a command or request <*get in here now*>.

A *cumulative sentence* is structured so that its main point appears first and is followed by other phrases or clauses expanding on or supporting it. A *periodic sentence* is structured so that its main idea or thrust is suspended until the end, thereby drawing the reader's attention to an emphatic conclusion. A *topic sentence* is a key sentence to which the other sentences in a paragraph are related; it may be placed either at the beginning (as a *lead-in* topic sentence) or the end of a paragraph (as a *terminal* topic sentence).

sentence adverb An adverb that modifies an entire sentence, rather than a specific word or phrase within the sentence <*fortunately* they had already placed their order>.

sentence fragment A group of words punctuated like a sentence, but without a subject or a predicate or both <*So many men, so many opinions.*> <*Yeah, when you think about it.*>. See also **sentence**; **clause**.

singular A word form denoting one person, thing, or instance <*man*> <*tattoo*> <*eventuality*> <*she* left> <it *is* here>.

split infinitive An infinitive preceded by *to* and an adverb or adverbial phrase <*to ultimately avoid* trouble>.
   Grammarians used to disapprove of the split infinitive, but most now admit that it is not a defect. It is useful when a writer wants to emphasize the adverb <were determined *to thoroughly enjoy* themselves>. See also **infinitive**.

standard English English that is substantially uniform, well-established in the speech and writing of educated people, and widely recognized as acceptable; compare **nonstandard**. See also **dialect**.

subject A word or group of words denoting the entity about which something is said <*he* stopped> <*it*'s clouding up> <*all sixty members* voted> <*orthodoxy on every doctrinal issue* now reigned> <*what they want* is more opportunity> <*going to work* was what she hated most> <*to sing at the Met* had long been a dream of his>.

subject-verb agreement See **agreement**.

subjunctive The form, or mood, of a verb that expresses a condition contrary to fact or follows clauses of necessity, demand, or wishing <if he *were* here, he could answer that> <it's imperative that it *be* broadcast> <they asked that the meeting *proceed*> <I wish they *would come* soon>; compare **imperative**; **indicative**.

subordinate clause A clause that functions as a noun, adjective, or adverb and is attached to a main clause <theirs is a cause *that will prevail*>. See also **clause**; **sentence**.

suffix An affix attached to the end of a word to modify its meaning <editor*s*> <county*wide*> <Hollywood-*ish*> <umbrella-*like*>; compare **prefix**.

superlative See **comparison**.

tense The characteristic of a verb that expresses time present <*see*>, past <*saw*>, or future <*will see*>.
  Aspect involves the use of auxiliary verbs to indicate time relations other than the simple present, past, or future tenses. The *progressive* tenses express action either in progress <*is seeing*>, in the past <*was seeing*>, or in the future <*will be seeing*>. The *perfect* tenses may express action that began in the past and continues in the present <*has seen*>, that was completed before another past action <*had seen*>, or that will be completed before some future action <*will have seen*>.

transitive verb A verb that acts upon a direct object <she *contributed* money> <he *runs* the store> <*express* your opinion>; compare **intransitive verb**.

verb A word or phrase that is the grammatical center of the predicate and is used to express action, occurrence, or state of being <*leap, carry out, feel, be*>. See also **auxiliary verb**; **linking verb**; **mood**; **voice**.

verbal One of a group of words derived from verbs. See **gerund**; **infinitive**; **participle**.

voice The property of a verb that indicates whether the subject acts or is acted upon. See **active voice**; **passive voice**.

Index